THE
WORLD
OF
CANADIAN
WRITING

George Woodcock

THE
WORLD
OF
CANADIAN
WRITING

Critiques & Recollections

Vancouver
Douglas & McIntyre

University of Washington Press
Seattle

Published in Canada by
Douglas & McIntyre Ltd.
1615 Venables Street
Vancouver, British Columbia

ISBN 0-88894-248-6

Published in the United States of America by
the University of Washington Press, Seattle, Washington
by arrangement with Douglas & McIntyre Ltd.

ISBN 0-295-95721-2

Canadian Cataloguing in Publication Data

Woodcock, George, 1912-
    The world of Canadian writing

    Includes index

    1. Canadian literature — 20th century —
History and criticism — Addresses, essays,
lectures. I. Title.
PS8077.W66   C810'.9'005   C80-091123-7
PR9189.6.W66

Typesetting by The Typeworks, Mayne Island
Jacket design by Nancy Legue
Printed and bound in Canada by John Deyell Company

Contents

Acknowledgements

The essays included in this volume appeared first in the following publications.

"The Dotted Points of Light," in *Saturday Night,* May 1974.

"On Editing *Canadian Literature,*" in *Books in Canada,* January 1978.

"Possessing the Land: Notes on Canadian Fiction," in *The Canadian Imagination: Dimensions of a Literary Culture.* Edited by David Staines. Cambridge: Harvard University Press, 1977.

"The Human Elements: Margaret Laurence's Fiction," in *The Human Elements: Critical Essays.* Edited by David Helwig. Ottawa: Oberon Press, 1978.

"Many Solitudes: The Travel Writings of Margaret Laurence," in *Journal of Canadian Studies* 13 (Fall 1978).

"Taming the Tiger of Power: Notes on Certain Fictions by Hugh Hood," in *Essays on Canadian Writing,* no. 13/14 (Winter-Spring 1978–79).

"Memory, Imagination, Artifice: The Late Short Fictions of Mavis Gallant," in *Canadian Fiction Magazine,* no. 28 (1978).

"Private Fantasies: Collective Myths. John Glassco's Decadent Fiction," in *Tamarack Review,* no. 65 (March 1975).

"On Ethel Wilson," in *Canadian Fiction Magazine,* no. 15 (Autumn 1974).

*"On Matt Cohen," in *International Fiction Review,* Winter 1979.

*"On Margaret Atwood," in *The Canadian Novel in the Twentieth Century: Essays from "Canadian Literature."* Edited by George Woodcock. Toronto: McClelland & Stewart Ltd., 1975.

"Remembering Roderick Haig-Brown," in *Raincoast Chronicles,* no. 7 (1977).

"Callaghan's Toronto: The Persona of a City," in *Journal of Canadian Studies* 7 (August 1972).

"This Fall in Toronto: A Late Callaghan Novel," in *Books in Canada,* October 1977.

"The Own Place of the Mind: An Essay in Lowrian Topography," in *The Art of Malcolm Lowry*. Edited by Anne Smith. London: Vision Press, 1978.

*"The Novel That Never Ends: David Watmough's Reminiscent Fictions," in *Pacific Northwest Review of Books*, Winter 1977.

"Diana's Priest in the Bush Garden," in *Boundary 2* 3, no. 1 (Fall 1974).

"McLuhan's Utopia," in *The Nation*, 1 November 1971.

"Poetry of Time and Place," in *Pacific Northwest Review of Books*, May 1978.

"Beyond the Divide (Notes on Recent Poetry in British Columbia)," in *Georgia Straight*, 9–16, 16–23 October 1975.

"On the Poetry of Al Purdy," Introduction to *Selected Poems*, by Al Purdy. Toronto: McClelland & Stewart Ltd., 1972.

"On A.M. Klein," in *Jewish Dialog*, Passover 1973.

"Private and Public Images: The Poetry of Pat Lowther," in *Catalyst*, May 1976.

"The Wanderer: Reflections on the Poetry and Fiction of Earle Birney," in *Essays on Canadian Writing*, 1980.

NOTE All these essays have been carefully revised for this edition, and minor changes have been made. In the case of those marked with an asterisk, major additions have been made to bring them up to date.

Introduction

THIS BOOK IS NOT meant as a survey or a history of recent Canadian literature. It is, rather, a mosaic picture of the world of Canadian writing from the idiosyncratic and perhaps eccentric viewpoint of one who has lived and worked at its centre over the past quarter of a century, certainly the most exciting period in the literary culture of Canada. After leaving in childhood, I returned from Britain to Canada in 1949; ten years later I founded *Canadian Literature,* the first magazine entirely devoted to Canadian writers and writing, and I continued in that role for eighteen years until I handed over the editorship of the journal in 1977. Not only did I edit a critical journal, I found my interest in Canadian writing increasing as I began to know the leading figures of this period personally and through their writings. Over the years I contributed to many magazines and books — published in Britain and the United States as well as in Canada — essays, articles and long reviews on the dominant trends and the more creative personalities of the Canadian literary world.

What I witnessed during that period was not merely the appearance of a great number of interesting and often important writers. I also participated in the creation for the first time in Canada of a genuine world of writing resembling those of London and Paris and New York, in which periodicals and publishing houses provided the kind of infrastructure that in older cultures had encouraged the emergence of a rich diversity of writing in all the genres, in criticism and biography and history as well as in fiction and poetry and drama. That such a diversity has emerged in Canada I believe the contents of this volume will testify.

The essays I include are selected from those I have written during the past decade or so. An earlier volume on Canadian writers, *Odysseus Ever Returning*, appeared in 1970, and a number of the leading Canadian writers whom the reader will vainly seek in the present collection, such as Hugh MacLennan, Irving Layton, A.J.M. Smith, Brian Moore and Wyndham Lewis, are dealt with there; I felt there was no need to say more of them when I had a sufficient field for the present collection among writers I had not discussed in *Odysseus Ever Returning*.

In *The World of Canadian Writing*, which I regard as a personal testament as well as a view of an era, I have included essays written with various ends in mind. The two opening essays are frankly reminiscent, recreating what it has been like to take an active role somewhere near the centre of the changing contemporary world of Canadian literature. And it will be evident that some of the writers discussed, like Roderick Haig-Brown and Al Purdy, Ethel Wilson and David Watmough, Margaret Laurence and Earle Birney, have been personal friends about whom I inevitably write in a different tone from that which I have used in the more formally critical pieces on, say, Hugh Hood and Matt Cohen and Mavis Gallant, all of whom I respect but do not know well.

There is another way in which the idea of presenting my essays as a vista of the world of Canadian writing has liberated me; it has allowed me to include not only larger pieces which explore a writer's achievement in some depth and detail, but also briefer and more immediate pieces composed originally as long reviews or in response to some event that moved me, like the piece I wrote on Pat Lowther after her death. It has also allowed me to ignore the boundaries of genre. The core of this volume is undoubtedly the body of long essays on Canadian fiction writers which I have produced in quite recent years, but I would have presented a distorted view not only of my own interests but also of my perceptions of writing in this country if I had not also included pieces on poetic trends and personalities and on leading critics, as well as the opening passages of pure recollection. The range of the volume and the relative informality of its construction are thus deliberate; without them the breadth and also the idiosyncratic nature of my view of Candian writers and their world could not have been truly represented.

Inevitably, the volume is selective as well as broad in scope, and I am sure that many readers, even if they collate it with the earlier *Odysseus Ever Returning,* will find that some writers they value are missing; Robertson Davies, for example, will almost certainly be mentioned. The missing writers are not necessarily unvalued by me, but I find that a degree of empathy or, more rarely, an obvious opposition of viewpoint is necessary before I can discuss a writer in what seems to me a meaningful way. There must be feeling, positive or negative, and the limits of my choice are perhaps also the limits of my sensibility. Certainly this book would cease to be the personal testament I believe it now is if I had chosen to include writers merely because I felt they were important. I include them because in some way they speak directly to me.

New Year's Day, 1980

The Dotted Points of
Light: Recollections
in 1974

WHEN I CAME back to Canada in 1949 it was still the age of the
railway, the radio and the Ryerson Chapbooks. It was also the
year and the month that Canada became complete; having
laboured across a stormy North Atlantic we edged past snow-
dusted headlands into the harbour of St. John's ten days after
Newfoundland entered Confederation.

It was a heart-sinking introduction to Canada: St. John's at the
end of winter, Newfoundland at the end of its austere separateness. The main street of the city was broken and potholed; the
side streets were mud tracks with the walls of the wooden houses
stained waist high with the splash of what little traffic passed
through them. Sealing must just have ended, for down on the
waterfront we found great barrels filled with flayed flippers that
looked like human hands, and there seemed — at least there seems
in distant memory — an abundance of little drunken men in cloth
caps being plucked out of gutters by immense policemen with
greatcoats that seemed as if they were made of horse blankets. In
the shop windows lay yellow cabbages that had been stored in
cellars over winter, and meagre piles of American tinned goods;
for up to 1949 the main North American trading of Newfoundland
was still south to Boston rather than east to Canada. My wife Inge
and I had fled an England where austerity had become a way of
life, extended long after the necessities of war by the puritanical
fanaticism of Sir Stafford Cripps. But St. John's was worse than
London, worse even than Liverpool.

I had an obsessive feeling that I must buy something, anything,
as a kind of keepsake to celebrate my coming home to the country
where I was born, but all I could find that seemed remotely pur-

chasable was a collected volume of Jane Austen, which I still have. I went back to the ship and wrote a depressed account of the Tenth Province which can be found by anyone curious enough in the back files of the *New Statesman*.

So it was in reading *Sense and Sensibility* and *Pride and Prejudice* that I whiled away the interminabilities of our journey through the reluctantly thawing land from Halifax to Victoria. After the fast trains of England and France, railway travel in Canada seemed almost tortoiselike in its leisureliness, the whistling, bell-clanging train meandering its way through the empty forests, beside the twisting lake shores, over the endless prairies, everything seeming too immense to be true, the Rockies brutal and hostile in their massiveness after the Alps.

And yet, in a way that no Canadian traveller in the early 1970s would experience (though we may be approaching the end of the age when the highway disrupted our national patterns of living), travelling by railway at the end of the 1940s gave one a real sense of the temper of Canadian life. There were in those days the long meal stops, when the unprosperous — as we certainly were — would scramble off the train to get the best place in the station restaurant in remotenesses like Rivière du Loup or Blue River or Revelstoke; there was time even to do a quick reconnaissance of prairie cities still oriented towards the station, as I did in Winnipeg, plunging out in curiosity into the city where I was born, shuddering back defeated by the freezing wind. The great stations of such cities were still centres of activity and life where one could observe all the types of the region, instead of the echoing emptinesses they have temporarily become. Everywhere, in the smaller communities where the train stopped for even a few minutes, the local people would celebrate the daily event by standing on the platform to watch the strolling passengers who had stepped off the train.

Comparing that first journey across Canada with later trips after the Trans-Canada Highway was completed, I realize what a negative benefit that much-vaunted achievement has turned out to be. Far from uniting the country, it merely provided a way of getting between the growing urban centres with the minimum contact with the intervening countryside. It glued the traveller's eyes to the road ahead rather than allowing them to rove unanxiously over the terrain, as railway travel had done. And the highway destroyed those nodes of local life which the railway towns provided, each with its radiating star of roads. But there is no need for me to proceed further in this vein, since Heather Robertson has done the job so splendidly in *Grass Roots*.

In any case, since most of my twenty-five years here have been spent on the West Coast, it is naturally in terms of British Columbia that I most see the transformation of Canada during the past quarter of a century. And certainly, when I stand in downtown Vancouver on a spring day in 1974, it takes an effort to envisage the city at which we arrived on that late April day in 1949. We had come through the mountains from the bleakness of the prairies where the first crocuses were just beginning to push their heads through the brown, sodden ground, and we looked out early in the morning to see the mists lifting over the Fraser River and the vegetation lush and green. In spite of the slashing freeways and the splotches of suburbia, one can still see that kind of view from a train window in the Fraser Valley, and with ingenuity I could take anyone on a tour of disconnected fragments of Vancouver that would give a good idea of the city I first saw. But it is hard to reconstruct now the total feeling of a city where there were perhaps three high-rise buildings instead of a forest of them covering the whole West End and quickly occupying the centre; where the West End itself consisted almost entirely of the wooden houses that Ethel Wilson wrote about in her novels; and where along Georgia Street the best and most elaborate of those houses still stood, mansions almost, with their deep verandahs and their strange Gothic turrets. In the middle of it all, on the site that the black tower of the Pacific Centre now occupies, stood the shell of the old Vancouver Hotel, a red brick cadaver, its doorways haunted by human derelicts and full of wind-blown litter. Perhaps, however, that shell of a building had a prophetic function, for its destruction marked the beginning of the end of the early Vancouver it symbolized, the growing invasion of the bulldozers, till all that really remains west of Granville Street of the Vancouver I first saw is Stanley Park.

Vancouver was not the end of our journey; we went on to Victoria on one of the old CPR ferryboats, and even of that brief journey I remember incidents that were not to happen again. Coming in 1949, we were ahead of the first flood of postwar immigrants, and indeed such rare birds to the taxi driver who took us down to the wharf that he refused to accept a tip. In Victoria we stayed in an apartment in an old converted house, and were astonished that both the front door to the house and that to the apartment were kept permanently unlocked. No one would have done that in London then, and no one would now do it in Victoria, even though it has probably changed less than most other Canadian cities of its size.

I have already written in other places about those first years we spent in Canada, living in Sooke, a village of loggers and fishermen on the southwestern tip of Vancouver Island. Personally, I suppose, we were anticipating the future, attempting the return to the land as a form of social-moral discipline which the hippie communes were to essay in the 1960s, twenty years afterwards. But though there was much that was personal and out-of-the-times in our island experiences, the times inevitably shaped those experiences. The pound suddenly fell in value from $4 to $2.80, which meant that what little royalties I could make from England became virtually worthless, and then I found what a hard place Canada at the end of the 1940s could be for anyone who wished to live by writing. But — again largely because it was before the big immigrations began in the 1950s — a great deal of the "Englishmen need not apply" attitude lingered even on the West Coast when it came to giving out manual work, and I talked like an Englishman even if I was not one. So Inge and I were forced to take what work we could from farmers almost as poor as we were, and the wages we got would astonish any citizen of Barrett's British Columbia — or of Bennett's for that matter. One dollar, seventy-five cents, even fifty cents an hour — and yet, also remember that the materials for the very adequate cabin we built with our own hands cost us less than $2,000, and when I see in my local fishmonger's window salmon priced (for God's sake, here where we catch it!) at $3.20 a pound, I remember that it cost then forty-five cents a pound, and very often in our village not even that since the fishermen were often happy to give it away.

Nowadays, when we drive on the easy highways that the Social Credit regime built through the Interior of British Columbia, I have to look back at my own book, *Ravens and Prophets*, which I wrote in 1951 on the basis of journeys made in 1950, to remember how great a venture it was in the mid-century to visit the Indian villages of the Skeena and places like the gold town of Barkerville, which are now regular calling places for tourists. Reading *Ravens and Prophets* today I realize that if it comes to be reprinted it will find its place in one of those nostalgic historical Canadiana series, so great have the changes been even in less than a quarter of a century. Then, one probed up through the Fraser Canyon by a narrow, perilous road that crept around precipitous rock faces where now wide tunnels pierce the mountainsides, and at certain points the road was actually a slippery deck of planks projecting from the cliffside and crazily supported on wooden brackets. Beyond the canyon the Cariboo Highway was so incredibly bad that by the time we returned to Vancouver no fewer than four of our tires had blown out. The towns and villages of the Interior were still very much what they had been when the mining rushes petered out, though obviously more decayed and decrepit. Along the way stood the old log roadhouses where the miners had put up; we would stay in the primitive hunters' cabins attached to these places, or sometimes in old hotels with long mahogany bars deserted since the liquor laws forbade standing drinking, and with floors half frayed away by the hobnailed workboots of generations of miners and loggers; Saturday night was still a time for ritual debauch.

I suppose the change in such parts that seems most striking to me now is the shift in attitude towards the past which has accompanied the almost total transformation, by highway and motel, by shopping plaza and supermarket, of the actual life that past represents. In 1950, when we first reached Barkerville, the place was derelict except for a few inhabited houses and cabins, and a young woman we met in the streets declared that the old buildings should be pulled down straight away as fire hazards, a statement that today would count as blasphemy in historically reconstructed Barkerville. Some of the buildings actually were pulled down after we first saw them, and all the roadhouses vanished from the Cariboo Highway during the 1950s; a few years later, and the historicist wave that built up over most of the country round about 1960 would have saved them. There is something sadly comic about modern Canadian historicism; it is really a classic case of seeing the plumage but not the dying bird, for we wait until a way of life is ended and then celebrate it nostagically, as we are now beginning to celebrate the virtues of the traditional small farm after we have allowed it to become marginal and to be virtually destroyed by the kind of factory farming which has combined with the highways to ruin our rural life. Soon, no doubt, we shall be preserving old motels and writing nostalgic books about them, though here I suspect there will be an ironic twist to the pattern, and we shall travel to visit those historic caravanserais of the automobile age by the very railways whose past age of glory we are now celebrating in *The National Dream*.

What I missed most in Canada when I came here in 1949, and what made me unhappy for several years, and undecided whether or not to return to the austerities of Britain, was the kind of intellectual and artistic community that I was used to and which now exists so abundantly here. I suppose I was at a turning point in my development as a writer, emerging—or I would never have left London—from the stage where one needs close association with writers, but not yet ready for the condition of tempered isolation in which I work now and for which I find Vancouver so congenial a setting. Of course, there was a community with which I came into contact, but so tenuous in character that I was often reminded of Auden's lines:

> Yet, dotted everywhere,
> Ironic points of light
> Flash out wherever the Just
> Exchange their messages . . . .

Dotted points of light seemed indeed to characterize the Canadian literary world in those days, and particularly if one lived in the far west. There was no University of Victoria yet, though Alan Crawley was editing *Contemporary Verse* from that city, and at the other end of Canada I made contact with John Sutherland who, it now seems incredible to remember, was editing from Montreal one of the other two literary magazines in the country, *Northern Review*; the third, the *Fiddlehead,* was appearing in Fredericton. There were a few people—Earle Birney and Roy Daniells—at the University of British Columbia, which even when I started to teach there in 1955 was still a bizarre jungle of old army huts. I gave a lecture there in 1950 on British poets of the time, and travelling lecturers were still so rare that the university actually printed it, and this brought a letter from Ned Pratt. Bob Weaver was already working at CBC, and I encountered Ethel Wilson and Dorothy Livesay and Phyllis Webb in Vancouver. Hugh MacLennan wrote from Montreal after I had done a piece on him in the *Northern Review*. And that, for years, was the sum of the literary world with which I established contact. It was late in the 1950s that one started to feel conscious of things beginning to stir, as they stirred culturally every way in Canada, and this was due to a number of circumstances which it will take historians a long time to sort out.

At the time one was inclined to think it was due largely to the influx of British and continental immigrants during the 1950s and 1960s, and undoubtedly this had its influence, though probably more limited than we first thought. In many ways it expanded the horizons of mental experience. I remember how in 1949 I obviously had something new and special to offer when I began giving CBC talks on contemporary European writers and on the classic Russian novelists; ten years later people capable of doing that would have been two a penny. The performing arts were undoubtedly strengthened by the influx of Europeans. But in the actual creative arts it is interesting to observe that very few of the names we now consider important among those who surfaced over the past quarter of a century in Canada are of people who came in their maturity; our best painters, poets, novelists, dramatists, architects — the great majority of them are Canadian born or came in childhood. The immigrants helped to provide a sensitive public, the feeling of the need for a sympathetic ambience for the arts; that was perhaps their most significant contribution. But just as much as to the immigration, I believe we owe the active artistic life that goes on now in so many Canadian centres to the kind of mutation in cultural consciousness that occurs in every nation when by obscure movements of the collective senses it realizes its own maturity. (I have often thought that parapsychology has an unacknowledged place among the tools of cultural history, for there are strange simultaneities in the history of the arts which are hard to explain by ordinary psychological schemes.)

Certainly, by 1974 the dotted points of light have been replaced by a literary community in Canada in which, despite all the lingering frustrations of existing as a writer, it is satisfying to live. Since about 1955, when I began to have the first premonitory feelings that this community was coming into being, I have had no real urges to leave Canada, which is not to say that I am happy about everything that has happened here over the past quarter of a century. I think Canadian urban development has been a disaster, even though a few great buildings have arisen; I am appalled by our virtual abandonment of the attempt to preserve a viable rural society; I am not as ecstatic as some about the proliferation of pretentious but bad pseudoethnic restaurants when I know I still have to go to France to get good food at reasonable prices; I despair of intelligence ever emerging among our politicians when I watch the manoeuvres over oil or incredulously listen to Premier Barrett of British Columbia arguing for instituting Nixonian time changes on the grounds that otherwise there will be a disruption in the enjoyment by people in his province of *American* television! Clearly some aspects of Canadian life are worse than in 1949, and some are no better, yet if one is in any way connected with or concerned with the arts the situation is so much more satisfying (as well as so much more economically viable) and so liable to throw up new people and new things to surprise and delight the mind, that the idea of ever going away has become (for me at least) unthinkable. And behind it all, the great forms of the land remain, unchanged and slowly impressing themselves on one's consciousness, so that to recognize them on returning is to enter an inner as well as outer landscape.

[1974]

On Editing *Canadian Literature:* Recollections in 1977

THIS SUMMER I ceased to be editor of *Canadian Literature,* handed over the files, the goodwill, the obsession, the glory, such as it was. Eighteen years — or, rather, nineteen from the first days of planning in 1958; one third of a life!

For my last issue of *Canadian Literature,* I wrote a review article on recent fiction in which I discussed Jack Hodgins's novel, *The Invention of the World.* Written about the vanishing frontier life of Vancouver Island, with its loggers and doxies, its English remittance men, its strange sects led by fraudulent prophets, the book reminded me of the west coast of Vancouver Island as I had known it when I returned to Canada in 1949. I indulged myself by prefacing the real review with some of my recollections, ending with the remark:

I intended, for years, to write the not-so-plain Tales of the Sooke Hills, but while I lived there the rigours of manual work left me no energy even to keep a proper diary, and in the years immediately after leaving the village other interests and travels supervened; gradually the memories lost their sharpness, until no more remains than will fill a short passage of an autobiography. But I always believed that this strange combination of people, washed up on that far shore of Canada by the tide of westering which made it the last of our frontiers, needed its chronicler, even if I had failed my memories. . . .

On the day I handed over *Canadian Literature,* a letter arrived from Al Purdy, commenting on my review and challenging me with his regret that "those memories got vague and blurred. It's probably the only part of your life you haven't written about." As I read his letter, in the mood of mental liberation that followed my abandonment of the task of editing, I began to wonder if the memories were really lost. A day or two later, by a touch of what Jung called synchronicity, the curator of manuscripts at the University of Victoria sent me copies of some letters he'd found in their Herbert Read collection. I'd written them to Read in 1949–50, about these very Vancouver Island experiences. And suddenly, with Proustian brightness as I read the letters, memories began to sparkle like fireflies on the edge of a dark wood and I thought it was time to start writing my autobiography after all and give those early years in Canada their proper vividness.

Such a mood of creative liberation would not have been possible if I had been in a state of regret over giving up *Canadian Literature*. In fact, I gave it up gladly, though I would not like that statement to be interpreted in any negative way. I did not feel bored with editing; it's a task I enjoy as I enjoy writing reviews, without feeling that in itself it's the most important thing in life. But about a year ago, it seemed to me that *Canadian Literature*, besides its everyday task of presenting a running commentary on Canadian writing and literary scholarship during the past eighteen years, had also done what I hoped for when I started it: created a nucleus around which a real tradition of criticism could grow up in Canada. That tradition existed in no perceptible form in 1959; it exists today, and I believe *Canadian Literature* played a major part in fostering it. Having achieved that much, did I want to carry on, or did I want to migrate to the fresher if not greener pastures of freelance writing and devote my time to the books I want to get finished while there is time? Obviously, the latter.

Having made this decision, I was tempted at first to treat *Canadian Literature* as a personal creation, and bring it to an end, as Eliot did the *Criterion* and Cyril Connolly *Horizon,* rather than hand it on. But I saw there were differences between the situations. In one sense I had personally created *Canadian Literature,* and to this degree created the critical movement it represents, though the peculiar statements by some writers that I created the *idea* of a Canadian literature are patently absurd; D'Arcy McGee was talking of it 110 years ago! Yet in 1959, and for years after, *Canadian Literature* was the only magazine devoted entirely to Canadian writers and writing; now there are at least seven such journals, and that alone says something about the need *Canadian Literature* encountered and in its own way satisfied. It always seemed to me that *Canadian Literature* was as much the creation of its period as it was my creation; I was there at the right time with the editorial experience and the appropriate attitude of slightly distanced objectivity.

Such being the case, obviously *Canadian Literature* was never my magazine in the same way as *Horizon* was Connolly's or — an example nearer the Canadian bone — *Contemporary Verse* was Alan Crawley's. In any case, both Connolly and Crawley killed their magazines because they felt the supply of good material was drying up. I had no reason to think that; I had two years of essays stockpiled for my successor to start with, and was rejecting a great deal of material I was sorry to let go. So to kill the journal would be pointless, provided a good new editor could be found.

He was, in Bill New, whom I respect as a critic, value as a friend, and know as a man with independent views, so that I expect soon to see *Canadian Literature* a magazine transformed. Phoenixes, I have always felt, should come out of the fire of change with different plumages.

So I find myself liberated to poetry, to reminiscence, to the massive book on the French novel I started twenty years ago, to the even more massive book on interrelationships of cultures in the ancient world with which I hope to follow it. But reminiscence, the shaping of an autobiography, is most in my mind at present, and as my memory flashes back to those years of my return to Canada, and of my indecision as to whether I would remain, which lasted from 1949 to 1951, I realize how astonishing it is that I should have founded a journal like *Canadian Literature* and should have moved into whatever modest position I may hold in the world of writing in this country. For my initial qualifications were scanty.

In France, before I returned here, I had read translations of Mazo de la Roche (but no books by Québec writers, who were not much thought of in Paris); in London I had read Grey Owl and the Penguin *Sunshine Sketches of a Little Town,* and wondered at Leacock's reputation. Roberts was for me the writer about animals I had read as a child, and my father had brought back Ralph Connor's novels and Frederick Niven's early books when the family returned to Canada from England in 1913. (My first ideas of British Columbia were shaped by Niven's *Lost Cabin Mine.*) One of my friends in London was Paul Potts, who used to sell broadsheets of his verse in Hyde Park and was mildly notorious as the

Canadian Hick Poet, but Robert Weaver is the only person I know in Canada who had ever heard of him and he has no place in *Colombo's Canadian References.* I knew A.J.M. Smith's poems because we were both contributors to Geoffrey Grigson's *New Verse,* and one day in 1948 Muriel Spark, who was then editing the *Poetry Review* in London, gave me Birney's *Strait of Anian* to review. And that was about the scope of my knowledge of Canadian writing in 1949.

Though thin, I suppose it was not an entirely unrepresentative selection of Canadian writing up to the late 1940s. But except for Smith and bits of Birney and Niven, I was not impressed. And when my wife and I did arrive on Vancouver Island, led there by the nostalgic eulogies of a Canadian seaman who wandered into the anarchist bookshop in Red Lion Street, it was a matter of proving ourselves in the wilderness that most interested us. Looking at those letters I then wrote to Herbert Read, I find them as innocent of any awareness of Canadian writers as Susanna Moodie's memoirs, but full of interest in the last Canadian frontier and its strange but unliterary human fauna.

Yet obviously the writer was anxiously looking over the would-be pioneer's shoulder, and just as Susanna, once she had endured enough roughing it in the bush, was glad to know that the *Literary Garland* existed in Montreal and that there were writers as near as Loyalist Belleville, so after a few months I started to establish my own literary contacts. I wrote to Earle Birney, then at UBC, and he came over — a brown-bearded, caustic-tongued man then in his forties — to see us in our trailer at Sooke; not long afterwards Marya Fiamengo appeared, and they were my first writer friends in Canada. Birney arranged for me to give a lecture in Vancouver on English poets. It took place on a day of blizzard and only a few people turned up, but one of them was Roy Daniells, and another long friendship began. On the night of the lecture Birney gave a party, and one of the guests, shaking the snow from his coat as he walked in, told me that the CBC news had just reported George Orwell's death. With a curious vividness, at that moment I knew that my past as an English writer was ended; my future would be in Canada.

The months that followed — 1950 going into 1951 — were a time of abandoning my pretensions to becoming a Canadian frontiersman, and finding my way into whatever literary world existed in

Canada. At first I was puzzled by much that I encountered. Coming from Europe, where we had gone through modernism and come out bedraggled at the far end, I was inclined to lay great stress on form, and the respect paid to such writers as Pratt and MacLennan, Callaghan and Grove, at first astounded me. I saw in Pratt a hudibrastic archaicist, an academic versifier using poetic measures long laid aside in England except by a few eccentrics like Roy Campbell. I found MacLennan much of the time heavily didactic, and strangely like Ethel M. Dell when he dealt with sex. For all his ability to produce direct, clear prose and his courage in taking the stance of a moralist, Callaghan struck me as insipid in his treatment of human emotions and relationships. As for Grove, while I delighted in the poised landscapism of *Over Prairie Trails*, I found his novels agonizingly ponderous, as if they were left in mid-travail, and thought — and still think — that he never developed an ear for any kind of English dialogue, including Anglo-Canadian.

Of course, there were exceptions. *Under the Volcano* delighted me, but I did not then think of Lowry, any more than I thought of myself on first returning, as a Canadian writer. I read eagerly every novel by Ethel Wilson as it came off the press, found her the most urbanely ambivalent of all the Canadian novelists of that time, and was happy when she and her husband Wallace became my friends. I thought Sinclair Ross's *As for Me and My House* one of the best Canadian novels, though I have liked nothing by Ross that has appeared since that book. As I had written my own early poems in England during the 1930s and 1940s, I was naturally first attracted by the poets who came nearest to the English tradition — poets such as Smith and Scott, P.K. Page and Dorothy Livesay, and I suppose my closest poetic affinities are still with them.

From those earliest days, visiting Vancouver from the Island, and from 1953 living there, I remember with most uneasiness the writers' circles that were then symptomatic of the state of Canadian letters. Their tone was not the arrogant hopefulness of the affinity groups of young writers needing the resistance of each other's ideas that I had known in London and Paris. It was rather the peevish desperation of writers who were often old enough and mature enough to be publishing their work and seeing it intelligently criticized in print, but who saw no chance of either of these things happening. By 1953 *Contemporary Verse* was dead, *Northern*

Review was moribund, and the popular magazines were going slow on fiction; in publishing it was still the cautious era, and in poetry that meant mostly what Ryerson Press published. It was hard to get verse into print, and even harder with short stories, though Bob Weaver kept the genre alive almost single-handedly through CBC radio. And the facilities for responsible criticism of what did appear were almost nonexistent. The writers' groups of which I am talking grew out of this situation. Painful occasions I remember them, for all the frustration of merit unrecognized would break forth, and criticism—though invited—was resented, for the very good reason that these occasions were really substitutes for publication; what the participants most desperately needed was not critics, but readers. Canadian literature, circa 1950–53! The critics were there, but the necessary infrastructure of a literary world—good magazines and dedicated publishers—hardly existed.

All that is long past in a Canada where any reasonably competent writer can achieve publication without much difficulty. But it preoccupied me greatly at the time. Yet gradually I found the edges wearing off my initial reactions to Canadian writing. John Sutherland induced me to write for *Northern Review* a long essay on MacLennan in the course of which I began to see the thematic reasons why he was the leading figure of the Canadian 1950s. I began to find myself accepting with reservations (though I did not know it at the time) Frye's opinion of the inappropriateness of trying to evaluate writing in an emergent literature according to the gradations of a critical hierarchy. Poetry, I saw, was needed before great poetry could exist. One's expectations changed from the ideal to the historically appropriate and, indeed, the historically possible.

One thing I knew even then was that the time was coming when in Canada a critical tradition must emerge, as it had done in older literatures, to complement and sustain what are often called the "creative" genres, that is, poetry, fiction, drama (though I have always agreed with Wilde that the best criticism is creative also). Echoing A.J.M. Smith, who as early as 1928 had published his celebrated "Wanted Canadian Criticism," in which he called for a philosophic criticism to "examine the fundamental position of the artist," I wrote for the *Dalhousie Review* in 1953 "A View of Canadian Criticism," in which I outlined my theory of the historic necessity, and indeed inevitability, of criticism as part of a developing literary tradition, and suggested that the time had come for a critical journal devoted to Canadian writers and their works.

Six years later I began to publish that magazine. I had spent a year teaching English in the United States, which I soon realized could never be my country, and a year in France studying Gide and Proust. Each time I had come back to Canada with a growing sense that here was my long-time and final home, and had found the literary movement of the 1950s a little more advanced: James Reaney and Phyllis Webb, Eli Mandel and Margaret Avison and Mordecai Richler appearing, Sheila Watson changing the course of our fiction with the *The Double Hook,* Layton moving into maturity and the public eye.

When I got back from France — or from Provence to be more exact in terms of cultural traditions — I took up teaching again at UBC, and a group of people there who had been thinking of a journal of Canadian studies approached me with the suggestion that I edit the very magazine I had been talking about, a magazine entirely devoted to the study of Canadian writers and their work. It seemed even to me that they were taking a risk. I wasn't an academic expert on Canadian literature. There were writers and whole periods with which I was unfamiliar. It was continental European drama and fiction that I had come back to teach. But I was a critic of some experience. I had edited a literary magazine — *NOW* — in England from 1940 to 1947, and those who invited me obviously thought professional experience of this kind, plus my relative lack of personal attachments at that time among Canadian writers, was more important than a knowledge of every phase of Canadian writing. Perhaps they were right; I like to think so. One doesn't expect the conductor of an orchestra to play the flute or the cor anglais, but to control the ensemble of instruments, and so it is with editing. As for me, I welcomed the opportunity to learn as I went along, and have been doing so ever since.

What is there to say about *Canadian Literature*? The issues are there for anyone to look back on. There are anthologies, published by Oxford and in the New Canadian Library, of some of the best essays. *Canadian Literature* has become a necessary tool in the ever-proliferating CanLit courses in universities and colleges, but I am not sure that I appreciate that rather artificial academic ferment, and I prefer to see the long shelf of eighteen years' issues of my magazine as a sensitive chronicle, a kind of ongoing history for anyone who cares to study it, of the extraordinary changes that have taken place in writing and in the ambience in which writers work since *Canadian Literature* first appeared in 1959.

And what changes! An explosion in poetry, with ten times as many books appearing each year as appeared annually in the 1950s! An extraordinary qualitative change in fiction—and a moving into formal experimentation that I did not expect from the novels I found being written here in 1959! A moving of drama out of the shadows of radio onto the stage, and the emergence of a whole school of vital new playwrights! History and biography and criticism flourishing, with scores of new titles every season! Literally dozens of new magazines and new presses appearing and—surprisingly often—surviving! *Canadian Literature* has been only one small detonating factor in what Northrop Frye has described as "the colossal verbal explosion that has taken place in Canada since 1960." I think the magazine's success owes most of all to the fact that it appeared just when it was needed; to mangle Voltaire, "If *Canadian Literature* hadn't existed, it would have been necessary to invent it." Another magazine, another editor, would have appeared to meet the need.

One reason why I feel so certain of this is the ease with which I found contributors. Skeptics prophesied that there would be neither enough material to write about nor enough critics to write; in a year *Canadian Literature* would collapse. But Frye's "verbal explosion" released an ever-growing flood of books to be criticized, and soon I had to abandon my early practice of reviewing every new Canadian novel and book of verse. And after spending two years badgering people to write articles, I found new critics emerging at a steady rate, and some of them exceptionally good ones, such as D.G. Jones, who first published parts of *Butterfly on Rock* in *Canadian Literature*, and Margaret Atwood, who wrote criticism for me before she wrote *Survival*.

These names—Jones and Atwood—say something important about the new criticism that has emerged in Canada in recent years. It is a criticism largely written by practising poets and novelists. In editing *Canadian Literature* I was always encouraging such people to write for me: I got Ethel Wilson to recount her memories; Hugh MacLennan and Mordecai Richler and Earle Birney to talk about their own writing; Al Purdy and George

Bowering and A.J.M. Smith and Margaret Atwood to write about the work of other poets. I found one interesting fact from all this: few fiction writers make good or even willing critics, though they are happy discussing the problems of their own writing. But the precisions of poetry and the precisions of criticism seem to correlate marvellously, and many of the best essays and reviews I published were by poets. Which, of course, is nothing new, when one thinks of Dryden and Eliot, Coleridge and Baudelaire. There is a strain of pure intellectuality in a great deal of poetry that combines with intuition in very much the same way as these elements combine in good criticism.

In saying this, I have no intent of belittling the contributions scholarly critics have made. Canadian criticism would have been a good deal thinner in content and insight if it had not been for the work of such people as Malcolm Ross and Milton Wilson, Desmond Pacey and Doug Spettigue and Germaine Warkentin, all of whom contributed to *Canadian Literature*. One important critic alone — but the best — chose not to be included. Except on one special occasion, Northorp Frye has always — with impeccable courtesy — avoided writing for *Canadian Literature*. A criticism without words? Perhaps — but unproven. A lamented absence? Indeed!

[1977]

Possessing the Land:
Notes on Canadian Fiction

IN HIS CONCLUSION to the 1976 edition of the collectively written *Literary History of Canada,* which brings the record up to 1972, Northrop Frye remarks on "the colossal verbal explosion that has taken place in Canada since 1960." And indeed, quantitatively there has been an extraordinary upswing in literary production, fostered by many circumstances, including cheaper printing processes, public subsidies to publishing, and a kind of creative upsurge, in some way connected with the rising up of national pride, without which these mechanical forms of assistance would have been useless. In most areas of writing the growth has been both qualitative and quantitative. A fresh sureness of voice and touch has appeared in poetry, where a surprisingly high proportion of the hundreds of new books — often by new poets — that have appeared each year have been distinctive in both tone and accomplishment. With a new sense of the past as myth as well as fact, the historians and biographers during the past decade and a half have been mapping out all the neglected reaches of the record of Canada as a cluster of regions and peoples rather than as a nation in the older European sense. Drama has moved out of the restricting field of radio, and plays that are both actable on stage and publishable as books have appeared with astonishing frequency over the past decade. Finally, criticism has achieved the kind of maturity and subtlety which is one of the signs of a literature's coming of age. When I founded the quarterly *Canadian Literature* in 1959, good critics were not easy to find; now they are numerous and creative.

In fiction alone has the situation been different. There are not more books, but those that are published in the 1970s are surprisingly better in quality than all except a few novels of past decades, and their variety of approach has increased phenomenally. One of the most striking facts I encountered when I looked back over the decades in preparing this essay was that the average number of novels published yearly by Canadians has not changed in any marked way over the past forty years, in spite of the steady growth in population. According to Gordon Roper, writing in the first (1965) edition of the *Literary History of Canada,* some fourteen hundred volumes of fiction were published by Canadians between 1880 and 1920, an average of thirty-five a year. Between 1920 and 1940, according to Desmond Pacey, writing in the same *History,* the annual average of Canadian works of fiction remained almost exactly the same, with seven hundred books appearing over twenty years. Between 1940 and 1960, according to figures presented by Hugo McPherson, there appears to have been an actual drop in publication figures, since he counts up only 570 works of fiction appearing over two decades, but I believe he did not count books published by Canadians abroad, so that the annual figure can probably be taken as very near to the thirty-five that had prevailed so consistently between 1880 and 1940. I have not made a count for all the years between 1960 and 1976, but spot checks of two years during this period revealed figures of thirty-five and forty respectively, bringing us curiously close to that average of thirty-five volumes per year which prevailed between 1880 and 1940.

Yet despite the fact that no greater numbers of novels are being published by Canadians now than in 1890 or 1930 or 1950, and although far smaller areas on bookstore shelves are now occupied by works of fiction, there is no evidence that in Canada the novel is a dying or even a sickly genre; on the contrary, the novel and the short story both occupy positions of prestige in the 1970s, among both critics and scholars, which no kind of Canadian fiction occupied in earlier decades.

The great change which has happened, while the number of books of fiction published in Canada remains so constant over almost a century, is that the quality of craftsmanship has improved and the degree of original creation has increased steadily, decade by decade, since the 1920s. As Northrop Frye remarked of the period between 1880 and 1920, "not all the fiction is romance, but nearly all of it is formula-writing." Of Canadian fiction in the

1970s, it can be said that, while romance in a somewhat different form does indeed exist, only a small proportion of the books that are published can be regarded as formula writing, which survives mainly in the curious subculture represented by nurse romances, inferior crime novels, and soft porn.

When I was invited to write this essay, it was tentatively suggested that I consider the relevance of realism to the Canadian literary tradition. I replied that any essay I might write would have a rather different approach, since realism as ordinarily defined (in terms of either Godwin's "things as they are" or Zola's naturalism or the Marxists' social realism) had not played a very significant role in Canadian fiction. Where an important novelist — such as Frederick Philip Grove or Morley Callaghan or Hugh MacLennan or Mordecai Richler — has used techniques generally regarded as "realist," the realism has almost always turned out to be one of the secondary elements in what is primarily a moral drama (Grove), a homiletic parable (Callaghan), an imaginative gloss on history (MacLennan), or a satire (Richler) which uses fantasy as much as realism to gain its ends.

A few Canadian writers could indeed be called realists in the same way as we apply that label to American novelists like Frank Norris and Theodore Dreiser. Robert Stead, the early twentieth-century novelist of the prairies and author of *The Homesteaders* (1916) and *Grain* (1926), was perhaps the most important early representative of the tradition. A genuine realist of a later generation, Hugh Garner, retains some standing even today in the Canadian literary world, and is respected for his short stories and novels of Toronto working-class life, such as *Cabbagetown* (1950). During the 1930s a few isolated novels of some merit might have been classed as vaguely "social realist," such as Irene Baird's still impressive chronicle of class struggle, *Waste Heritage* (1939), perhaps the best of its kind to be written in Canada.

But the main development of Canadian fiction in fact bypasses the matter of realism, European or North American, largely because Canadians, faced with the wilderness on one side and a dangerously powerful neighbour on the other, had little doubt as to the actual nature of their predicament; what they needed was the combination of mythology and ideology that would enable them to emerge from mere escapism and present a countervision more real than actuality. Hence the weakness of realism as a tradition in literature or, for that matter, in the visual arts, where a national consciousness was first expressed through the highly coloured and emphatically outlined formalism of the Group of Seven and Emily Carr.

What one does see, observing the transition that began in the later 1920s, is the change in the novel from formulaic and commercially motivated romance to a genuine Canadian twentieth-century romanticism, which must use fantasy and dreams as paths to reality, which must accept myth as the structure that subsumes history, which in its ultimate degree of the fantastic must recognize and unite with its opposite, satire, the logically absurd extension of realism.

Little Canadian fiction that was published before 1900 now seems worth rereading either for pleasure or for the kind of subliminally directed information that, at its most sensitive, literature can project over the centuries. The basic purpose of the early literature of any colonial culture, like the basic purpose of transplanted peasant folk arts, is not to define the future but to consecrate the past. Faced by the wilderness, man seeks to assert the familiar, not to evoke the unknown, and so colonial literature generally attempts to re-enact against the backdrop of a new land the achievements of an abandoned way of life. Nothing could be more devastating as a symbol of this attitude than the fact that the English Oliver Goldsmith, who wrote "The Deserted Village," should be followed by a Canadian Oliver Goldsmith, seeking to repair the damage to the good life with that immeasurably more banal poem, *The Rising Village* (1825).

Eighteenth-century Frances Brooke, writing the first of all novels of Canada, *The History of Emily Montague* (1769), established in her account of a garrison-limited society a pattern of defensive writing that continued for more than a century, until in the years after Confederation the American threat grew less urgent and the northern wilderness more penetrable. The novel is perhaps the genre that most requires a sense of involvement with the actual, the touch of verisimilitude necessary to authenticate the transfiguration of fantasy. And the nineteenth century in Canadian literature was not unjustly defined by the early critic John Bourinot, who in 1893 remarked favourably on the achievements of Canadians in history, poetry, and the essay, but added that "there is one respect in which Canadians have never won any marked success, and that is the novel or romance."

The most vigorous early Canadian fiction was in fact written by satirists in the Maritime provinces who had no thought of writing novels, such as Thomas McCulloch in *Letters of Mephibosheth Stepsure* (1860) and Thomas Haliburton in *The Clockmaker* (1836). Both McCulloch and Haliburton wrote episodically, each defining his series as sermons in fiction, and their purpose of presenting the ills of society rather than developing the inner and individual worlds of that society's inhabitants prevented them from ever creating the kind of self-consistent world of the imagination which is the true fictional achievement.

McCulloch and Haliburton established a long Canadian lineage of ironists and satirists, and they encouraged among Canadians a fatal illusion that they are a humorous people, but in terms of the novel it was an impasse into which they led. Even the much revered Stephen Leacock, perhaps the best-known Canadian writer in the early decades of the present century, endowed with an extraordinary ironic sensibility and a great fund of sharp and true wisdom, failed in the essential fictional task because all his aims were, in the end, didactic rather than creative. He wrote admirable and not always gentle comments in fictional form on the world of actuality, which so often distressed him with its crassness and hypocrisy, but he never united those comments into the kind of alternative world of the imagination which the true novelist erects to confront—or evade—the world of actuality.

For most of the early Canadian novelists, writing was a way of earning or supplementing a living, with—added as a special bonus—the hope of entertaining or edifying one's readers. An impressive proportion of early Canadian fiction writers were clergymen of evangelical bent, only one of whom had the kind of talent that transfigured the Reverend Charles William Gordon into the novelist Ralph Connor and in the process developed one of the three or four fictional voices that still speak out of the Canadian nineteenth century with a degree of conviction. Connor was in no authentic sense a realist, since his concerns were overwhelmingly didactic; he wished to portray the essential drama—which under his hand often turned into melodrama—of the spiritual life, and he wished to show how that life could be rendered in the unpromising circumstances of Upper Canadian settlements of Highland immigrants like Glengarry and in the vast spaces and the rough elemental society of the new West which developed in the wake of the fur traders. It would be hard to find anywhere in the literature of the British Empire a more vigorous exposition of the doctrine of muscular Christianity than in such novels by Ralph Connor as *Black Rock: A Tale of the Selkirks* (1898), *The Sky Pilot: A Tale of the Foothills* (1899), and *The Man from Glengarry* (1901). Yet Connor used some of the devices of realism skillfully in developing his heroic religious fantasies, and in some degree his books do portray what life was like in both the pioneer East and the pioneer West of Canada during the latter half of the nineteenth century.

In his own way, Connor was in fact a fairly effective exponent of the North American local-colour movement, with its aim of giving authenticity, through a vivid and detailed depiction of the setting and the characteristic local way of life, to a sentimental plot and a group of conventionally typed characters. Occasionally a book of this kind was so well done that it survived its time by the sheer appeal of the idyllic atmosphere it created; an example is Lucy Maud Montgomery's *Anne of Green Gables* (1908), with its haunting evocation of rustic Prince Edward Island, or, in a later decade, Mazo de la Roche's *Jalna* cycle of sixteen novels in which the improbable epic of an Upper Canadian squirearchical family is presented in a setting so plausibly circumstantial that for many years it was regarded, if not in Canada, certainly in Britain and even more in France, as an authentic portrayal of Canadian life.

Books like *Anne of Green Gables* and the *Jalna* cycle show how far the manipulation of authentic detail to give local colour to a for- mulaic kind of romance might be stretched in a direction opposite to that of true realism, and even in the very few remaining Canadian novels written before 1914 that stand out with some dis- tinction, one sees the devices of verisimilitude being used for pur- poses that are essentially nonrealistic in their intent. In my own estimation two such books emerge in especial vividness as excep- tions to the general mediocrity of Canadian fiction in that early age.

One is the solitary masterpiece of James De Mille, an academic who for the most part wasted a genuine talent on writing humorous potboilers and boys' adventure stories for the American market. *A Strange Manuscript Found in a Copper Cylinder* is the only book by De Mille that continues to be read; it never found a pub- lisher during his life and was not brought out until 1888, eight years after his death. *A Strange Manuscript* has some distinction as the first utopian romance written by a Canadian, and almost the last. It is a vivid and haunting tale of bizarre adventures that take the narrator into a strange world within the earth, entered by a vortex near the South Pole — a world through which De Mille, by some skillful inversions of habits and customs, presents an effective satire on the hypocritical Victorian world where he was forced to live and work. *A Strange Manuscript* has some distinct similarities to Samuel Butler's *Erewhon,* to Bulwer Lytton's *Coming Race,* and to some of the romances of Jules Verne, and Canadian scholars — myself among them — have argued at length on what De Mille borrowed from whom or whether he borrowed at all. But even if it is partly derivative, *A Strange Manuscript* is a well-written and boldly speculative book, in quite another category from most of the banal adventure narratives which Canadian writers were publishing copiously at the time.

An even sharper mind than De Mille's is evident in Sara Jeannette Duncan's best book, *The Imperialist* (1904). Sara Jeannette Duncan was one of the many Canadians, like Mordecai Richler, Norman Levine and Margaret Laurence in our own age, who matured their talents in long years abroad, in Duncan's case in England and especially in India, which became the setting of many of her novels. Like Henry James, who much influenced her, she was greatly concerned with the accentuation of both virtues and failings that takes place when people transplant themselves into alien settings, like Canadians in Britain and the British in India, yet her qualities as a writer are most admirably shown in the only one of her novels that is set in Canada. *The Imperialist* is a many-levelled novel of sophistication and wit such as no other Canadian wrote before 1914 and few have written since, a study of political motivations but also of small-town Canadian manners, observed with an eye for the comedy as well as the pathos of ambition and written with great skill and detachment.

A similar, though less successful, effort to "understand and make the reader see" is to be found in the work of the early twentieth-century writer Frederick Niven, Chilean born and oriented in his writing towards western Canada as well as towards the Scotland of his childhood. Niven, again, was a writer who used some of the techniques of realism for other purposes, since basically he was a fictional historian — rather than a historical novelist — dedicated to presenting   history as adventure. The romance of western settlement activated Niven's imagination, and he continued to write historical fiction long after it had gone out of vogue; his most ambitious novels — the trilogy concerning developments on the prairies and in the Rockies from the early to the late nineteenth century, *The Flying Years* (1935), *Mine Inheritance* (1940) and *The Transplanted* (1944) — never received the attention that was due their extraordinarily authentic re-creation of time and place. Niven was weak in developing those conventional elements of the novel, character and plot; he tended to produce episodic pageants rather than sustained narratives. But he does anticipate in interesting ways the neoromantic concern for the land and for the history it projects that has been so evident in the work of emerging Canadian poets and novelists in recent years.

It is a long step from the urban and urbane concerns of Sara Jeannette Duncan, but not so far from the action-in-a-landscape approach of Niven, to the handful of turn-of-the-century writers who produced for the first time a characteristic Canadian group expression in prose that can be compared with the more solid and celebrated achievement of the much more personally knit Group of Seven in painting. These were the nature writers, the outdoorsmen, who emerge with Ernest Thompson Seton and Charles G.D. Roberts during the last years of the nineteenth century. The outdoors story and the animal story became very popular around 1900, and this was the first period in which Canadian writers began to draw the attention of the whole English-reading world. For a considerable period, such fiction was one of the main streams of Canadian writing, and, although the vogue tended to die away about the time of the Great War, a steady interest in outdoors writing has sustained later exponents, such as the ambiguous Archie Belaney who gained celebrity as Grey Owl, and the British Columbian fisherman, naturalist and novelist, Roderick Haig-Brown, who died as recently as 1976.

Of the two leading exponents of the animal story, Seton was the better naturalist and tended to be the more didactic, striving — with many lapses into pathos — to portray the actual lives of animals as nearly as possible, and in this sense he was a realist. Roberts was the more philosophic and also the more melodramatic writer, tending to portray his animal heroes in extreme situations where they could be displayed as the tragic victims of destiny in an indifferent universe. His views are impregnated with the fashionable evolutionism of his time, but it is Huxley's pessimistic interpretation of Darwinism rather than Kropotkin's optimistic one that shadows his stories.

In seeking the common themes of Canadian writing and the myths that underlie them, contemporary Canadian critics have been inclined to make much of these turn-of-the-century creators of animal stories, and from their special viewpoint of cultural nationalism they are right, since here for the first time are writers working in Canada whom it is difficult to relegate to the fringes of more dominant literary traditions such as the English and the American. One may perhaps consider Duncan a lesser Edith Wharton, dismiss Niven as a minor Robert Louis Stevenson, but the Canadian animal writers were doing something different from either their British or their American counterparts. British animal stories have almost always been thinly disguised fables, acted out by men in animal skins to illuminate essentially human problems. (George Orwell's *Animal Farm* is an outstanding example, but even less obviously didactic works like *The Wind in the Willows* are just as essentially anthropomorphic.) American animal stories, like Faulkner's "The Bear" or Hemingway's *Old Man and the Sea,* are almost invariably stories of antagonism and confrontation, man pitting himself against the animal who becomes the symbol of all that is hostile and unreachable in nature. But Canadian animal stories are really about animals, and they are about animals with whom we are invited to empathize. We are invited to empathize with them—critics like Margaret Atwood are likely to claim—because they are invariably portrayed as victims, and we, a people colonized in many ways, are victims, too.

It does not, however, require any such deference to literary theory to recognize that in such fiction the Canadian writer is at last beginning to respond to and utilize his environment directly and without fear; it is no longer necessary to interpose the screen of European forms and values between him and the world in which he is destined to live. It is Canada's own myths that Canadians must recognize, mediated through images which at last can begin to be recognized in their true shapes. But even the animal writers of the turn of the century present us with the reality of the specific Canadian existence at one remove. For all his skill in evoking the lives of wild animals, Roberts failed when, in *The Heart of the Ancient Wood* (1900), he attempted to establish a meaningful relationship between human beings and the wilderness. Roberts failed because he created a sentimental identification of man with untamed nature rather than an organic link.

A much more successful exercise in bringing man into a fictionally viable relationship with the wilderness is Martin Allerdale Grainger's single novel, *Woodsmen of the West* (1908), a fine small work which marks an almost unrecognized transition point in Canadian writing. It concerns the loggers of the British Columbian rain forests, and even now it is probably the best work of fiction that their way of life has ever inspired. Grainger, a man of extensive outdoors experience who later rose to a high executive position in the West Coast logging industry, approached his subject not out of a sentimental attachment to a mythical natural life or a principled desire to retreat from civilization, but from the standpoint of a man who goes into the forest to wrest a living — and, with luck, a fortune — from it. Grainger knows from experience all the mundane as well as the curious details of the logger's working life; he knows the psychological frustrations and the human conflicts that woodsmen endure, but he also knows the sense of freedom that counterbalances the memories of even the most uncomfortable of logging camps and leads the men back to what most people regard as a hard existence. If one seeks a work of true realism in Canadian fiction, *Woodsmen of the West* is probably as near to a perfect example as one is likely to come by. Yet, as is the case in all the classic examples of successful realism, the vision the novel creates survives when the world it portrays has vanished, so that Grainger's camps, belonging historically to what is now a receding past, continue in our mind a detached existence in rather the same way that the birch woods of a lost Russia survive in all their rainy glitter in the pages of Turgenev's *Sportsman's Sketches,* which is another way of saying that the pursuit of realism is self-defeating, since its achievements survive in exactly the same way as those of successful fantasy in the timeless world of the reader's imagination.

Woodsmen of the West was a striking example of a phenomenon very common in Canada — the novelist who writes only one book, or only one good book, either because he is writing out of a vividly remembered but limited body of direct experience, as Grainger did, or because he has an intense but equally limited imaginative vision which can be encompassed within a single book.

The novels derived from direct experience are really by-products of the oddities of life in a pioneer society, and often, when they are rendered with natural artistry, as in *Woodsmen of the West,* they project a purer sense of locality than the writings of more professional novelists. Another especially pleasing example of this kind of book is that haunting fictional account, derived from family traditions, of the nineteenth-century Irish immigration to Canada, *The Yellow Briar* (1933) by "Patrick Slater" (John Mitchell).

The books that stem from a sharp but unrepeatable personal vision are very often written in Canada by poets troubled by some theme they cannot find expression for in verse. An especially striking example is Leonard Cohen's *Beautiful Losers* (1966), a work of remarkable decadent fantasy which followed on the failure of Cohen's much more realistic and autobiographical first novel, *The Favourite Game* (1963). Earle Birney also wrote one very good novel of comic fantasy, *Turvey* (1949), a highly stylized Schweikian vision of the absurdities of war and the military mind, but followed it by an unsuccessful stab at social realism in his novel of Senator McCarthy's America, *Down the Long Table* (1955). And P.K. Page wrote a single and rather fine romantic novel, *The Sun and the Moon* (1944), under the nom de plume of Judith Cape.

Most of these solitary masterpieces, although they cannot be ignored by anyone who wishes to appreciate the variety of modern Canadian fiction, take their places on the verge of the genre. When poets write novels they are usually individual feats of virtuosity that somehow emerge out of their poetry writing, the kind of things that in an age more tolerant of the long poem might have been rendered in satiric or romantic verse (such as Byron wrote in his time) and which have little relation to the general trends of contemporary fiction. It is certain that none of the books I have just mentioned, not even *Beautiful Losers* for all its dazzlement of the academic critics, has had much effect on the kind of books professional novelists write. Nevertheless, one solitary novel exemplifying a highly personal vision, Sheila Watson's *Double Hook* (1959), did have a great influence on younger fiction writers, and to that I shall later be returning.

As the twentieth century continues, leaving behind it the troubled complacencies of the Edwardian age, characteristic Canadian ways of writing become more evident, especially in poetry and in fiction, although probably a majority of the novels being written in Canada in the thirties and even in the forties were in general character, if not in setting, hardly distinguishable from the romances or adventure stories being written elsewhere in the English-reading world, and even the novelists of that time whom we consider now to be the pioneers of present-day Canadian fiction often carry with them the vestiges of alien influence. We all know those passages of Morley Callaghan which, taken out of context, might very easily be mistaken for Hemingway, and even before readers were aware of Grove's hidden career as a novelist in Germany, the affinities between him and European writers like Zola and Knut Hamsun were abundantly evident. Yet the stylistic influences which reached Canada as ripples of literary revolutions in Europe and America were not very important in their ultimate effects, for it was characteristic of Canadian fiction when it began to emerge as something special and distinguishable that its practitioners tended to be formally unadventurous and even conservative and to concentrate to a degree long abandoned by novelists in culturally more settled countries on the content of their books — on *what* they had to say rather than on *how* they said it. I remember very clearly my astonishment, on coming from Europe in 1949, at the importance Canadian critics attached to writers so formally conservative, even retrogressive, as E.J. Pratt and Hugh MacLennan; it took me a long time to accept that at certain stages in literatures, when they emerge from a kind of colonialism to take on their own identity, an emphasis on content rather than on form may be necessary and is to be encouraged. To this extent the recent Canadian school of thematic critics has been justified; a criticism of pre-1950s Canadian fiction based on the analysis of form would have been a task of supererogation, although the same attitude would not apply to the fiction of the past twenty years.

In the decades after 1918 there were still only a few Canadian novelists to whom we need pay attention. During the period between the wars the most popular Canadian novelist was probably Mazo de la Roche (she was certainly the most popular abroad, largely because she was writing a kind of international lady-novelism in which the setting was Canadian in a peculiar and distorted way), although if we consider fiction in a wider sense she had a rival in Stephen Leacock, who struck the chord of Canadian ironic self-deprecation so accurately that he still enjoys a repute considerably above his true merits. But if we are concerned with something more than popularity, if we seek the writers who in retrospect appear to have given in that generation the most authentic fictional expression of Canada and the Canadian consciousness, two men stand far above their contemporaries. They are the German novelist Frederick Philip Grove, who transformed himself into one of the two most memorable fictional chroniclers of Canadian prairie life, and Morley Callaghan, the Torontonian who chronicled the travails of people attempting to live with some meaning in the developing metropoles of eastern Canada.

With Robert Stead and Martha Ostenso (whose memorable *Wild Geese* appeared in 1925), Grove represents the beginnings of what eventually became a notable movement of prairie fiction that penetrated far more deeply into the actualities of western life than Ralph Connor had ever succeeded in doing. To a considerable degree the members of this movement acted as the realistic chroniclers of the region. A succession of later writers, such as Sinclair Ross, W.O. Mitchell, Rudy Wiebe, and Robert Kroetsch, have kept the prairies in the centre of Canadian fiction, and this is appropriate, for the Great Plains have served as a uniting membrane to sustain whatever collective consciousness English-speaking Canada may in fact have. More than anywhere else, more even than in the North, man grapples on the prairies with that immensity of the environment which still haunts Canadians with the vestiges of wilderness terror, and therefore it is more on the prairies than anywhere else that Canadians can symbolically face and come to terms with whatever destiny unites them. When Canada was established, the first necessary act to ensure the survival of Confederation was the acquisition and settlement of the prairies, and one of the basic differences between francophone and anglophone Canada — one of the sources of the present conflict — is that the people of Quebec took virtually no part in the great Canadian sweep westward that built up after 1870. The prairies were the place where the English and the immigrant peoples of continental Europe struggled to establish their roots in earth and achieved the one Canadian compromise that shows some appearance of lasting.

It is their consciousness of this background that gives prairie fiction a special interest to Canadian readers and gives to the novelists who write it a sense that, in a special way not open to novelists in Ontario or the Maritimes or British Columbia, they are giving form to the great symbols that express the relationship between man and the Canadian land. Everything in the prairies tends towards extremity—the climate, the winter isolation, the distances—and in response every human reaction tends towards intensity—of boredom, of faith, of despair, of prejudice, of hatred; it is no accident that the most bitter of all Canadian battles since the conquest of 1760 was that fought at Batoche in a few tragic days of 1885.

Novelists tend to respond to this harsh environment and its immoderate emotions with a combination of realistic method and symbolist intent, moving on with later writers like Robert Kroetsch into a kind of superrealistic fantasy. And it is this combination of approaches that has almost certainly made Frederick Philip Grove, despite his extraordinarily clumsy constructions and his ponderousness in thought and language, the most significant to contemporary readers of the prairie novelists who wrote between the wars.

Grove arrived bearing with him, as part of his carefully concealed mental baggage, the heritages of the two significant European movements of his time: naturalism and symbolism. *The Master Mason's House*, which he published in Germany as Felix Paul Greve in 1906 (it has had to wait until 1976 for Canadian publication in an English translation), is a late naturalist novel with expressionist overtones. But, as the translator of Wilde and the acquaintance of André Gide and Stefan George, Grove was also linked with the late days of symbolism, and his prairie novels show the influence of both movements. These works can be read as attempts as a realistic chronicling of the hard life of the early homesteaders. But if, as Desmond Pacey, Grove's first biographer, argued in the *Literary History of Canada*, Grove's *Settlers of the Marsh* was "the first novel to introduce into Canada the naturalism which, finding its chief source in Emile Zola, spread over the whole Western world in the late decades of the nineteenth century and the early decades of the twentieth," then Grove's belated tribute to Zola (for *Settlers of the Marsh* was not published until 1925) was distorted by a melodramatic degree of pessimism which makes one wonder how far Grove did in fact consider that he was writing "naturalistically" or "realistically." Certainly, insofar as we remember Grove, it is because he made men and landscapes alike into symbols of a general human destiny, into emblems of collectively generated ideas, and so it is his least realistic book, *The Master of the Mill* (1944), that we value most. What he has constructed for us in this book is not merely the great symbol of the mill with its possessing family, but, bodied forth in human conflicts and misfortunes, the whole Heartbreak House of conflicting ideologies and interests in a Canada which he saw before his death moving into the crucial period of change from a colony to a nation, from a rural to an urban society and — symbolized in the shift of venue from the prairie farm to the eventually mechanized mill — from pioneer innocence to technological experience with all its perils.

Few pairs of Canadian writers are more easy to contrast than Grove and Callaghan, the one seeking his huge symbols in a vast rural setting of high skies and fields a quarter-section large, the other working out his moral problems in the constricted setting of the city; one large and uncouth in the texture of his writing, the other lapidary to the point that any release from simplicity of form results in a complete breakdown of his writing (as happened in such recent novels as *The Many Colored Coat*, 1960, *A Passion in Rome*, 1961, and *A Fine and Private Place*, 1975).

Although he has continued to write into the century's and his own seventies, Morley Callaghan is in terms of effective achievement a writer of the late twenties and the thirties. It was during these decades that almost all his marvellously laconic short stories (collected in *Morley Callaghan's Stories*, 1959) were written, and it was during the latter decade that his three best novels appeared: *Such is My Beloved* (1934), *They Shall Inherit the Earth* (1935) and *More Joy in Heaven* (1937). These novels reflect their times in ways often reminiscent of more deliberately political writers: Callaghan portrays mordantly the social tragedies and injustices of the Depression years, the hypocrisies of the church, the presumptions of the state. But Callaghan is not drawn into the facile political solutions of the age, and always he returns to seeing the social situation in terms of individual lives. Within these lives, moreover, the essential factor is not adverse external circumstances; it is inner moral strength. Although his felicity in the use of descriptive detail may lead the superficial reader to dismiss him as a kind of realist devoted to simplicity of language, Callaghan is in fact a moralist, and his books take on their full significance only when we see them as sparely constructed parables on the human condition, their very conciseness and flatness of tone a moral matter.

To move into the 1940s is still to find the Canadian fictional landscape populated sparsely with novelists of power and vigour and originality, yet it is in this decade that three Canadian fiction writers obviously destined for lasting importance appear: Sinclair Ross with *As for Me and My House* in 1941; Hugh MacLennan with *Barometer Rising* in the same year, followed by *Two Solitudes* in 1945; and Ethel Wilson with *Hetty Dorval* in 1947, followed by *The Innocent Traveller* in 1949.

Ordered in this way, the trip brings us to one of the peculiar problems of the critic who is also a literary historian, when he is dealing with a nation and a literature that are in the process of emerging more or less simultaneously into self-consciousness. In such cases it is entirely possible that the writer who is the lesser artist may be the more important in a social and historical sense because his concern for things outside his art allows him to interpret more boldly and fully than the scrupulous artist the preoccupations of his community at a crucial point in its history. And when one is faced with the need to relate Sinclair Ross, Hugh MacLennan and Ethel Wilson, it is obvious to anyone with an even modestly developed literary sensibility that Ross, at least in *As for Me and My House,* and Ethel Wilson in everything she wrote, are vastly more subtle and complete in their fictional artistry than MacLennan.

Yet anyone with an ear for history — literary or other — must acknowledge the overwhelming importance of MacLennan in Canadian writing during the 1940s, and the 1950s as well. More than any other novelist he isolated and gave memorable expression to the significant political and moral issues of Canada in his time; more than any other writer he elucidated the collective problems that each man feels impinging on his personal existence in a country still in the process of self-creation. A consciousness of emergence into nationhood is the theme of *Barometer Rising,* the two nations within a single federation the theme of *Two Solitudes,* the perils of American dominance that of *The Precipice* (1948), and the constricting nature of the Calvinist heritage that of *Each Man's Son* (1951), while in the more complex structures of his last two novels, *The Watch That Ends the Night* (1959) and *Return of the Sphinx* (1967), many of these earlier themes are brought together in an approach that seeks to demonstrate how history lays its claims on our lives and may destroy them if we have not listened to the lessons of the past.

There is no writer other than MacLennan whom one could plausibly consider the Canadian Balzac, seeking to construct his country's special *Comédie Humaine* and trusting that if the themes are honest the forms will take care of themselves. At times he is splendid in every respect; *Each Man's Son,* which many critics ignore, is one of the best Canadian novels, precisely because the thematic impulse is subordinated to the Odyssean structure that delineates MacLennan's personal mythology. But all too often in MacLennan's books the themes take impetuous control, and we have such extraordinary failures of fictional proportion as the endings of his first two novels, *Barometer Rising* and *Two Solitudes,* both ruined to make a didactic point better reserved for an essay, or the whole structure of *The Precipice,* misbuilt in the effort to work out moral and social problems in logical terms. What makes one remember with a special warmth MacLennan's two latest novels is that neither *The Watch* nor *Return of the Sphinx* offers a facilely rational solution to the universal alienation each presents as the human predicament. In these last novels MacLennan has learned that fiction, like all the arts, may offer questions, but rarely gives answers. If the sphinx does return, it is merely to present more enigmas.

MacLennan, it seems, had to go through two decades of creative travail to acquire a knowledge Ross and Wilson possessed from the beginning. Sinclair Ross, in spite of a long literary career during which what one has always assumed to be terminal silences have been broken by long-maturing new works, is essentially a one-book man. Nothing he has written since *As for Me and My House* appeared in 1941 has attracted more than fleeting attention, and critical attempts to inflate his lesser books have always flagged before the embarrassing realization that it is *As for Me and My House* alone among his works that rends one's heart with a sense of pathetic frustration few other Canadian novels have projected. The book is isolated even among Ross's works, no doubt because it is one of the few novels whose basic theme derives from an honest perception of the perpetual nightmare of all Canadian artists at the time *As for Me and My House* was being written — the failure of imagination and of creativity. In the Canada of that distant time these gifts lacked any meaningful focus, for in 1941 where could the artist in Canada look for validation?

And that is where Canadian writers have to be perpetually grateful to Hugh MacLennan, for in his time he understood that the literary imagination had to be given a focus, and in his own honest way he gave that focus by daring to express in fictional form what many people of that day feared to discuss in any more direct way. Through his flawed but vigorous novels he helped to liberate writers thematically and to turn their attention back to problems of form and sensibility rather than to problems of national destiny, although these have never been allowed to fall entirely out of sight, since this has been, after all, as nationalist a generation as that of Yeats and Synge in Ireland. In the novels of Dave Godfrey and Marian Engel, in the verse of Al Purdy and Milton Acorn and many of the younger poets, in the historical writings of Donald Creighton, and in works of thematic criticism such as Margaret Atwood's *Survival,* the sense that Canadians are fighting as crucial a battle for their cultural independence as they fought for their political independence in 1812 is strongly manifest. The inclination that MacLennan once represented almost in solitude has found expression not only in the work of individual writers but also in the publishing houses set up in the 1960s to counter the tendency for foreign firms to take over native houses, and in the strong inclination of Canadian periodicals of all kinds to take the stance that cultural colonization, particularly from the United States, remains a threat to be countered. Much of the sense of urgency that characterizes recent Canadian writing is linked to this resurgence of national feeling with its curious mingling of apprehension and pride.

Ethel Wilson always seemed much nearer to the younger writers who appeared during the 1950s than Callaghan or MacLennan ever did, although she was the oldest of these three writers. But she began to write far later in life, and although eventually she became one of my most valued friends, I never quite understood the process by which this handsome, charming Vancouver bourgeoise emerged in her closing fifties as a writer of extraordinary subtlety and sophistication. Had there been a long period of secret practice, of ruthless self-critical rejection, or had

she been the fortunate subject of some sudden pentecost that
turned her overnight into the consummate stylist and literary
psychologist whom readers encountered with such astonishment
when *Hetty Dorval* was published? It was never revealed, but her
readers admired, and continued to admire for the brief period of
her creative life (much less than two decades in all), the combination of assurance and adventurousness, the strange equilibrium between illusion and reality, the oracular sense of the power
and irrationality of love that appeared in such novels as *Swamp
Angel* (1954) and *Love and Salt Water* (1956) or in the sparkling, dry
and ironic stories collected in her last book, *Mrs. Golightly and Other
Stories* (1961).

There was something of the catalytic imagination about Ethel
Wilson, emerging for so few years, so late in life, to project an original, urbane vision across the landscape of a young literature,
and there is no doubt that her influence on younger writers such
as Margaret Laurence and Margaret Atwood came from more
than mere friendship. The mention of Laurence and Atwood
leads us, of course, into the highly active present of Canadian fiction.

How can one begin to discuss the many interesting novelists
who have been active over the past twenty or twenty-five years in
Canada? Should one start, for example, with the brilliant immigrants who came for a while, wrote remarkable books here which
told us new things about ourselves and our world, such as Brian
Moore's *Luck of Ginger Coffey* (1960) and Malcolm Lowry's *October
Ferry to Gabriola* (1970), influenced native writers (particularly in
the case of Lowry) to the point of obsession, and then departed?
What can one say of such figures in the context of the present
essay except that they seemed to accentuate an obsession with
human solitude already dominant in the Canadian literary consciousness and to encourage younger writers to explore it to the
bizarre limits of fantasy, which became in the later 1950s an in-
escapable element in Canadian fiction?

Or should one start in the complementary direction and consider how many Canadian writers have developed themselves as
expatriates, and out of a combination of physical experience and
cultural absorption have contrived to enrich their own writing and
the Canadian fictional tradition as well, edging it further, by
the introduction of exotica, in the direction of fantasy? There is

Mavis Gallant, for example, who went to Paris and never came back; there is Mordecai Richler, who went to London and did come back, although what he will write as a returned expatriate still remains to be demonstrated. But other writers also went away and returned enriched to write their best work in Canada: Audrey Thomas and Dave Godfrey and, above all, Margaret Laurence, all of whom spent immensely impressionable periods in Africa and wrote such novels about their experiences as Thomas's *Mrs. Blood* (1970), Godfrey's *New Ancestors* (1970) and Laurence's *This Side Jordan* (1960). In the case of Laurence, Africa provided the insights which unlocked her ability to perceive and to write about her own heritage, her own country, and there emerged that splendid series of time-obsessed myths of the Canadian prairie town, from *The Stone Angel* (1964) down to *The Diviners* (1974), which Margaret Laurence has told us — in what one hopes will be an unfulfilled warning — may be her last novel.

Perhaps the most striking phenomenon of recent years in Canadian writing has been the tendency to loosen verisimilitude in the direction of fantasy and to abandon the chronological pattern with effect following cause and consequence following action which characterized most of the novels written before the later 1950s, especially the novels on which writers like Callaghan and MacLennan based their careers. Here one of the most important books for itself and in terms of influence is Sheila Watson's single novel *The Double Hook* (1959) in which the rural tale of a decaying society is mingled with the native mythology of the vanished Indians to create a strange and superb fantasy of moral strife and spiritual terror. Mordecai Richler, whose *Apprenticeship of Duddy Kravitz* (1959) was a picaresque novel in the classic manner, moving on the inspired edges of credibility but essentially conventional in its sequential form, went on with books such as *The Incomparable Atuk* (1963) and *Cocksure* (1968) into the use of grotesque fantasy for the purposes of satire, although he has never in these later works repeated the triumph of *Duddy Kravitz* and is certainly perceived by now to be of much less central importance as a Canadian writer than he seemed to many critics a decade ago.

In moving away from conventional structures and from the lingering demands of naturalistic theory, Canadian writers have also tended to abandon the didactic preoccupations of the generation of Callaghan and MacLennan. They no longer feel the need to state political or moral positions which now tend to find expression in other literary genres.

I do not suggest that there has been a diminution in the patriotic (as distinct from the stridently nationalist) frame of mind. But it is clear that, like the poets, the novelists have become concerned less with making thinly disguised policy statements than with the more basic functions of returning over time, of examining the foundations of history, of exorcising ancient guilts and celebrating ancient heroisms, of giving spirit to the land. Novels such as Rudy Wiebe's *Temptations of Big Bear* (1973), Matt Cohen's *The Disinherited* (1974) and Robert Kroetsch's *Studhorse Man* (1969) do not merely confirm for us the quality of writers whose first and promising novels had appeared in the later 1960s; they introduce a new sense of history merging into myth, of theme coming out of a perception of the land, of geography as a source of art. In the process they break time down into the nonlinear patterns of authentic memory; they also break down actuality and re-create it in terms of the kind of nonliteral rationality that belongs to dreams.

These novels embody the difference between realism and a reality that is not merely material, between literal credibility and imaginative authenticity. There is, for example, a great deal of credibility about Hugh MacLennan's characters and their behaviour; when they are not represented in sexual relationships (a notorious MacLennan weak point) they sound very much like the people one meets ordinarily in real life. But it seems extremely improbable that in real life people would literally do what they are represented as doing in, say, Margaret Atwood's *Surfacing* or Marian Engel's *Bear,* although both of these books strike one as entirely authentic once one has taken the initial step of suspending disbelief in the author's particular world of the imagination.

There are not indeed as many new novelists in Canada during the 1970s as there are new poets. To write a publishable novel, after all, still demands more industry and discipline than to write a publishable piece of verse. But the situation has changed to the extent that it is no longer possible to take one or two central figures and say that essentially this is their decade, as past decades seemed those of Grove and Callaghan, or of MacLennan and Ross. Today, amazingly many good fiction writers are working in

Canada, and the variety of approaches and talents is more impressive than any dimly perceptible common attitude.

As I have hinted already, the indications are many that during the past twenty years the literature of Canada has gone through a process of maturing into a self-consistent entity, analogous to that which literature in the United States went through earlier in the century. That writers are liberated to follow highly individual courses, no longer dominated by the thematic demands which critics were detecting even early in the present decade, is one of the signs and also one of the effects of that maturity.

[1977]

The Human Elements:
Margaret Laurence's Fiction

THERE ARE TIMES when an unconsidered remark can set one on paths of speculation that a cautiously critical approach would warn one to avoid. Recently I was involved with a friend and fellow writer in one of those interminable and inconclusive discussions of writing in Canada which always, despite Northrop Frye's warnings of the perils of evaluation, tend to become mired in arguments about comparative quality. Having let myself be led into this profitless morass, I had argued—I thought very convincingly—that more good poetry is being written in Canada today than in Britain (certainly) or in the United States (probably). Then my friend turned to the discussion of fiction. Did we—could we—have a Canadian equivalent to Tolstoy? My answer, impulsive and without any previous thought, was immediate: Yes, Margaret Laurence! My friend treated it—and so did I after a moment's thought—as one of those rash and immoderate statements one makes when cornered in a discussion. Afterwards, as I thought about what Tolstoy means to me and compared it with what Margaret Laurence means to me, I was tempted to elevate my answer from the status of a rash impulse to that of a flash of insight.

Consider the proposition, not in the terms of literary gigantism in which we are traditionally inclined to approach writers like Tolstoy, Homer, Shakespeare and Balzac, but rather (leaving posterity the futile task of comparing statures) in such terms as a writer's relevance to his time and place, the versatility of his perception, the breadth of his understanding, the imaginative power with which he personifies and gives symbolic form to the collective life he interprets and in which he takes part.

There are some writers whose visions, true as they may be, are so intensely personal, or so restricted in terms of locality or class, that whatever national flavour they may exhibit seems an undesired accident of language, place and time of birth. Others seize on such accidents to inspire and strengthen their work, and these are the writers who one can say (since greatness has become so abused a word) have a largeness of scope and vision and even of verbal texture that expands their work, without destroying any of its personal intensity, into an expression of what the German romantics called the *Zeitgeist,* the spirit of the times. And of more than the times, for what is extraordinary about such writers is their grasp of space as well as of time, so that they recreate and preserve for us in their writing a view of the land, and of the way people grow out of it. No historian conveys to us — for example — the physical texture as well as the spirit of archaic Greece so vigorously, even after two and a half millenia, as Homer does in *The Odyssey.* The same applies to most cultures; each of them has its truth-telling bard, though the genres the bards use may differ. For the true feeling of late mediaeval England, where the sense of man as an individual emerges vigorously out of a tribal past, we go to the poet Chaucer; no writer provides a truer reflection of Spain in his century (or any other century) than Miguel de Cervantes, despite the churrigueresque frame in which he enclosed the luminous mirror of Don Quixote's dreams and adventures; Thomas Mayhew, with his descriptions of the lives of the early nineteenth-century London poor, was a superb early sociologist, yet we now read his book mostly as a historic curiosity, and it is through the fictionalizing genius of Dickens that the world Mayhew described really comes alive for us.

In this company of writers who fulfil one of the great functions of art — the preservation of lost times and worlds in such a way that outsiders can imaginatively apprehend them — Tolstoy and Margaret Laurence both belong, and there is a particular closeness between them in the fact that each is seeking to deal with a land of exceptional vastness, and also to reconcile a sense of history in a time of rapid change (for revolution or not, Tolstoy's world was in rapid transformation as the steppes were opened to cultivation and the Trans-Siberian moved eastward to complement the westward thrust of the CPR) with a passionate sense of the importance of personal experiences and particular destinies.

The special quality in such writers lies not so much in the grand physical and temporal scope of their vision (for Spengler and Arnold Toynbee have had a similarly grand scope to their vision of history without being imaginative artists by any definition) as in the fact that their characters are as impressive as their settings, and their best revelations are achieved not — as Tolstoy ineffectually attempted to do in the expendable theoretical section of *War and Peace* — by the explicit statement of historical themes, but rather by the vivid, concrete yet symbolic presentation of crucial points of insight in individual lives, such as Levin's drinking of water from a rusty tin cup in the splendid mowing scene of *Anna Karenina,* or the moment in Margaret Laurence's *Stone Angel* when the despised minister, Mr. Troy, sings the first verse of the doxology to Hagar Shipley during her last days in hospital and, on hearing the line, "Come ye before him and rejoice," she suddenly realizes, "I must always, always, have wanted that — simply to rejoice. How is it I never could?" and then reaches the crucial and almost life-giving insight that "Pride was my wilderness, and the demon that led me there was fear." It was an intensely personal recognition for Hagar Shipley; at the same time one can generalize it into a description of the state of mind of a whole generation of English-speaking Canadians.

Tolstoy in his special way projected the vision of a whole generation of Russians. It was a time of exceptional literary flowering, and there were other writers who in terms of sheer artistry could certainly compete with him. Turgenev, for example, who better than any other evoked the mental turmoils of nineteenth-century educated Russian youth, the essential humanity of Russian serfs, the sight and smell of Russian woodlands on a hunter's morning; Dostoevsky, master of existential agony and of the psychopathology of a land which history seems to have condemned to recurrent tyrannies; Chekhov, unparalleled recorder of the nuances of perception and disillusionment in an intelligentsia that already, years before the cataclysm of 1917, feels itself doomed: all are splendid, as are the autobiographical chroniclers like Herzen and Aksakov and Kropotkin, but all, in comparison with Tolstoy, are incomplete, because none possesses his panoramic sense of a great steppe-land haunted by history; none, for all their skills in exploring individual psyches, was so well able to present man as a member of a living community; none understood with such agony the ambiguous role of the artist in a world of moral crisis; none was so ready to sacrifice his own art once he felt its relevance was exhausted or its function superseded.

I think we can say similar things in comparing other contemporary Canadian writers with Margaret Laurence, and this I am sure is why her image has dominated our last decade in the same way as, according to W.H. New, the fifties in Canada were dominated by the image of Hugh MacLennan, with his rather bald and elementary insistence on such basic Canadian themes as the recognition of national imperatives and the perils of the everlasting duality he christened "the two solitudes."

There are some ways in which MacLennan, too, resembles Tolstoy, mainly in his less successful didactic aspect. And Laurence is not entirely without didacticism (indeed, I have never read a major novelist who quite dispensed with it). But though she recognizes as strongly as MacLennan the national imperative and the forces that militate against its survival, she is much less inclined to subordinate the aesthetic to the homiletic in her writing. The nation and its perils are there, to be described, to be seen, to be felt, but not to be argued about, at least in fiction.

Margaret Laurence positively resembles Tolstoy in possessing the panoramic sense of space and history, developed to a degree no Canadian fiction writer can rival. She understands the importance of our newly recognized myths that bind us collectively, and to order and direct her sense of community she created her own imaginary and exemplary town of Manawaka, so near to and so far from her native Manitoba town of Neepawa that she can say, "in raging against our injustices, our stupidities, I do so *as family,* as I did, and still do, in writing about those aspects of my town which I hated and which are always in some ways aspects of myself." She has always felt a salutary doubt about the completeness of the writer's role as a seer, and she expresses it in the final pages of *The Diviners,* where novelist Morag's old friend Royland tells her that he has lost the power of finding water.

At least Royland knew he had been a true diviner. There were the wells, proof positive. Water. Real wet water. There to be felt and tasted. Morag's magic tricks were of a different order. She would never know whether they actually worked or not, or to what extent. That wasn't given to her to know. In a sense, it did not matter. The necessary doing of the thing—that mattered.

And, like Tolstoy, she seems to have the will to declare a vein of creation exhausted, for she has publicly declared that *The Diviners* is her last work of fiction, and in the years since its publication in 1974 she has shown no signs of revoking her resolution.

Such resolutions, proclaimed by a writer in her early fifties, seem made to be broken, and one can do no more than hope that Margaret Laurence's creativity will again clamour for fictional expression. At the same time, as I shall show in the latter part of this essay, there is a completeness about the Manawaka novels as they stand, not only in terms of a common setting and interlocking characters who share the same origin, but also thematically in the dominant archetypal structure.

Margaret Laurence's writing, almost entirely prose, falls into two categories, the fiction and the discursive nonfiction which is partly autobiographical and partly critical. The fiction, in turn, falls into two groups, that concerning Africa — *This Side Jordan* (1960) and the stories collected in *The Tomorrow-Tamer* (1963) — and the Manawaka books, consisting of the four novels, *The Stone Angel* (1964), *A Jest of God* (1966), *The Fire-Dwellers* (1969) and *The Diviners* (1974), as well as the cycle of stories, *A Bird in the House* (1970), really a kind of episodic novel in which time flows through the narrator's childhood, while the setting is constant and there is a recurring cast of main characters.

Except for the final novel, *The Diviners,* whose time present is set in the kind of rural Ontario background where Margaret Laurence is actually writing the book, all of her fiction is set in places, distant at the time of writing, which she experiences in memory and imagination. Africa is the setting of fiction written in Vancouver. The Manitoba where Laurence spent her childhood is the terrain of novels and stories written in Vancouver, in England and in rural Ontario. Physical and temporal distance becomes, in the Canadian novels at least, essential to the very structure of the works, which are patterned not only on the recovery of time through memory but also on the kind of consciousness of horizontal space that is peculiar to countries of vast distances and dramatically varying landscapes, like Canada and Russia.

Significantly, there is one area of Margaret Laurence's past about which she has written no fiction. This is the two years she spent in Somaliland, the years described in that superb travel book — perhaps the best ever written by a Canadian — *The Prophet's*

Camel Bell (1963). I am not proposing to discuss in any detail Margaret Laurence's nonfiction, which is subject enough for a separate essay, but there are two aspects of her writing about Somaliland which are eminently relevant to a discussion of her fiction. Both *The Prophet's Camel Bell* and her earlier book — in fact her first book — on Somali oral literature, entitled *A Tree for Poverty* (1954), deal among other things with the necessary distance from which she had to observe and then to enter, with a surprising degree of empathy, a culture that was to her intensely strange in its manner of dealing with a precarious existence in one of the world's most barren terrains. She experienced that existence imaginatively through observing — often in the harsh directness of drought and famine conditions — the lives of the Somalis, and also through the special entry into their minds that was provided by the tales and poems which she so painstakingly learnt to translate during her years there as the wife of a dam-building engineer. From this complexity of contacts she gained at least two things useful to a writer.

First, there was the ability to enter from a steadily narrowing distance into a world she wished to explore imaginatively, and this she did repeatedly in later years even when she was dealing with a society — that of the Manitoba small towns — which had once been her own. The other lesson is perhaps best explained in a statement of her own about Somali oral literature.

The most deep and far-reaching realism is combined with an acceptance of life that is neither cynical nor despairing. The Somali sees what elements make up his life, and does not seek to deny them, harsh as they may be.

In a way this statement — which one might certainly apply to the Canadian novels Margaret Laurence was to write in later years — is amplified in *The Prophet's Camel Bell,* which is not merely about the experience of being "a stranger in a strange land," but also about the parallel experience of self-discovery that can be set off by the shock of immersion in a totally strange culture.

As Margaret Laurence says on the first page of *The Prophet's Camel Bell,* "the strangest glimpses you may have of any creature in the distant lands will be those you catch of yourself." And, indeed, for those who are concerned to understand the mind that later wrote the Manawaka novels, not the least important aspect of *The Prophet's Camel Bell* is the process of the narrator recognizing and shedding one by one the pretences in and through which she has lived until she begins to see more clearly than ever before not only the reality of the land and life around her, but also the reality of her own self. And self-knowledge, accompanied as it inevitably is by a measure of self-distancing examination of one's past existense, is as priceless a gift to the novelist as it is to the philosopher. If Somaliland did not provide Margaret Laurence with material that she found appropriate for developing into a novel, it awakened in an extraordinary way the kinds of perception she needed to become a novelist, the awareness of one's own self as well as one's experience as sources the imagination can tap.

That West Africa rather than Somaliland should have provided the content of Margaret Laurence's earlier fiction can doubtless be explained in two ways. First, the people of the Gold Coast, as it was then called, were more accessible than the Somalis in terms of everyday personal intercourse, partly because in the cities at least they had absorbed a great deal of the colonizing culture, partly because many of them spoke English or at least pidgin, and partly because their resentment against the imperialists, though doubtless as intense as that of the Somalis, was not so frequently expressed in terms of open hatred. For these reasons, relations between the whites and the subject peoples were at the same time freer and more ambiguous on the Gold Coast than in Somaliland. The Somalis were so certain of the rectitude and sufficiency of their Moslem culture that liberation for them meant merely reestablishing their own Islamic world, free of infidels and infidel influences. The West Africans, on the other hand, found their way towards freedom at least in part through accepting alien political concepts; those most adept at combining new political techniques with old loyalties would eventually rise to the surface as the political leaders of liberated Africa.

The understanding of such truths meant a further stage in Margaret Laurence's journey through self-knowledge and knowledge of the world, to the possession of her imaginative kingdom. It is significant that she wrote her fiction on West Africa, as she wrote *The Prophet's Camel Bell,* not on the spot, but after she had left the continent of Africa in the fair certainty of never returning. She herself has told how she found that the diaries she had kept in Somaliland provided only the notes for the narrative that emerged eventually as *The Prophet's Camel Bell*, and we can assume the same to be true of *This Side Jordan* and the stories that make up *The Tomorrow-Tamer*. In these books she was writing of the Gold Coast hovering on the edge of the independence that would transform it into the modern state of Ghana. She wrote partly out of experience and partly out of imagination, and it is important to observe, in view of the widespread notion that the Manawaka novels are successful because they are autobiographical, that the most imaginative passages of the African writings — those most detached from their creator's own life — are the more convincing.

On the one side in *This Side Jordan,* the side of experience, is the group of whites who represent a British export firm on the Gold Coast. Somaliland taught Margaret Laurence the danger of distinguishing between white imperialists and other whites in a colonial situation, and her representatives of empire are now shown with a mingling of irony and compassion. These are not grand imperial conquerors; they are, like most of the British who went out to the colonies, men who were or have become unfitted for life at home, so that they live a double exile, like so many of Margaret Laurence's characters, even in her Canadian novels. They range from the tragic figures like Bedford Cunningham, a perfect gentleman whose time has passed and left him stranded in a morass of alcoholic failure, through Johnny Kestoe, the feral product of a London Irish slum who is willing to betray any of his associates for the sake of promotion, to Kestoe's incongruous wife Miranda, a well-meaning romantic whose attempt to create a bridge of understanding to the African world involves the black schoolmaster, Nathaniel Amegbe, in humiliation and dishonour.

The world of the Cunninghams and the Kestoes is the one to which Margaret Laurence belonged in Africa, the one she knew from day-to-day participation. If Miranda Kestoe is clearly not a self-portrait, she shares the enthusiasms of her creator's first years in West Africa, for, as she remarks in a recollective essay in *Heart of a Stranger,* Laurence then "wore my militant liberalism like a heart on my sleeve" and was anxious to impress educated Africans "not only with my sympathy with African independence but also my keen appreciation of various branches of African culture. . . ." Before she left the continent, Laurence had grown out of these naive manifestations of interest in African culture. The empathetic understanding that followed enabled her to enter imaginatively into the lives of her African characters, poised as they are between three worlds — the pagan past, the colonial and missionized present and the independent future. She dramatically rendered those tensions in the inner conflicts and shifting emotions of Nathaniel Amegbe, son of one of the great pagan drummers, but also a practising Christian and a believer in the struggle for freedom, shocked by the despair of his English-educated journalist friend, Victor Edesui, who prophesies with bitter accuracy the generations of oppression by their own people that political liberation will bring to Africans. This aspect of *This Side Jordan* reveals a splendid power of intuitive insight into minds shaped by another culture, and it lives with brilliant authenticity in the mind. But in delineating the white world that parallels the changing native world of the Gold Coast, Margaret Laurence is trapped in the excessively literal recollection from which she tries unsuccessfully to escape by grotesque devices like the series of macabre coincidences (a mother who bleeds to death in his presence from self-abortion, an African bush girl who bleeds when he lies with her, Miranda's redeeming blood when he witnesses her childbirth) that seem vainly directed towards turning Johnny Kestoe from the rather ordinary cad he is into a figure of melodramatic interest.

The stories in *The Tomorrow-Tamer,* which appear to have been written after *This Side Jordan,* are Margaret Laurence's best early work, more unified in form and texture than *This Side Jordan,* and written with a vivid sense of physical detail that memorably recreates the African setting. As she does later on, in the stories that comprise *A Bird in the House,* Laurence seems to be using these short fictions as experimental devices to work out techniques she will later elaborate into larger forms, for many of the pieces, like "The Rain Child" and "The Drummer of All the World," are really life stories, small novellas, in which a character mingles recollection with self-analysis in the attempt to discover the meaning of his life and — of course — of his world. For no Laurence character is a solipsistic island; Violet Nedden, the missionary teacher in "The Rain Child," reveals herself through her concern for the children who are misfits both in her school and in the African community around it (the actual "rain child" is an African girl marred by British education who finds her own people's way of life as incomprehensible as she finds their language), and the tragedy of the narrator in "The Drummer of All the World" is that Africa, his real home where he was born and brought up—a missionary's child among native children—has changed so much that there is no longer a place for him, and the very friends of his boyhood reject him as an alien. *The Tomorrow-Tamer* is, indeed, largely a book about aliens and alienation. Some of the whites, like the characters I have just discussed, have come in their varying ways to think of Africa as their own land, and when they return to the country called home they face an exile that will end only in death. Others mingle hope with resignation; they have to because Africa is the end of their roads. In "The Perfumed Sea," perhaps the most beautiful and the most convincingly triumphant story of all, the hairdresser Mr. Archipelago declares gaily, "I am flotsam"; he and his woman partner Doree, with their mysteriously innocuous pasts, had wandered far over the earth before they encountered each other in a small West African coast town where the wives of the imperialists provide their living. Independence comes, the white women go, but Mr. Archipelago and Doree are of neither the imperial nor the native world; they are even curiously detached from each other, though they share the same business and the same sea-sprayed house (their main common pleasure is the guessing of exotic perfumes at nightly sniffing sessions). Yet there is a loyalty which their predicament calls forth; they adapt, as they have always adapted in the past, winning a black in place of a white clientele, and so these two pieces of human flotsam evade submersion; survival is their victory. Thus, by concentrating on the theme of the "stranger in a strange land" which first occurred to her in the bewilderment of her early days in Somaliland, Margaret Laurence breaks away from the cliché situation of racial confrontation, and by evading the excessively documentary portrayal of the white world abroad that marred *This Side Jordan,* she anticipates some of the major thematic and structural concerns of her later Canadian novels, involved as they are with the complexities of a multicultural society.

Particularly important in such a context is the curious kind of reconciliation at a subterranean level that takes place in the stories of *The Tomorrow-Tamer* between the apparently opposing worlds of imperialists and Africans. The most powerful stories about Africans in this volume, those which resonate most persistently in the mind and in memory, are also of alienation and of types of exile. In "The Voices of Adamo" a bush boy whose kin has been wiped out by an epidemic finds a new village and a new tribe in a regimental military band where he serves as a drummer, and when he finds after five years that through a misunderstanding he is being led to accept at the time of independence a discharge which will take him away from the band and his beloved drum, he kills the white bandmaster. A black officer, Major Appiah, visits Adamo in his cell, and the bush boy's only fear is that he will lose the regiment that has become his family and his village. "I will stay?" he asks.

Major Appiah had come to tell Adamo when the trial would be held, perhaps even to prepare the man for the inevitability of the verdict. But he said none of these things, for he saw now that they could make no difference at all. Adamo would discover soon enough what ritual would be required for restitution. Perhaps even that made little difference. It was not death that Adamo feared.

"Yes," Major Appiah said, and as he spoke he became aware of a crippling sense of weariness, as though an accumulation of centuries had been foisted upon himself, to deal with somehow. "You can stay, Adamo. You can stay as long as you live!"

He turned away abruptly, and his boots drummed on the concrete corridor. He could bear anything, he felt, except the look of relief in Adamo's eyes.

Adamo's survival is possible only through the group; he is in everything a tribal man, and alienation from the tribe is for him death. But even in the African world, there are those who do not belong to the tribe, whom some flaw like genius or dwarfdom has placed outside tribal normality. In *The Tomorrow-Tamer,* this condition is exemplified in one of Laurence's most haunting stories, "Godman's Master." Moses Adu, a westernized African travelling in the bush, unwillingly rescues a midget who has been kept in a stuffy box by a village juju man to serve as an oracle. He takes Godman, the midget, into the city, and there he finds his life dominated by this strange small being who defines their roles with so much assurance.

"You are my priest," Godman said. "What else?"

Moses could not speak. Godman's priest, the soul-master, he who owned a man. Had Godman only moved from the simple bondage of the amber-eyed Faru to another bondage? And as for Moses himself—what became of a deliverer who had led with such assurance out of the old and obvious night, only to falter into a subtler darkness, where new-carved idols bore the known face, his own? Horrified, Moses wondered how much he had come to depend on Godman's praise.

Eventually, plagued by conscience yet anxious for liberation from this dwarfish incubus, Moses expels Godman, and only sees him months afterwards when he has become a robed fortuneteller in an African freak show. They meet, and the talk is of fulfilling one's role in existence.

Godman shrugged.
"I have known the worst and the worst and the worst," he said, "and yet I live. I fear and fear, and yet I live."
"No man," Moses said gently, "can do otherwise."

The same could be said by and of a great many of Margaret Laurence's later characters in novels and stories set in Canada, and this, I think, underlines the importance of the stories in *The Tomorrow-Tamer* as representing an advance in Laurence's awareness of the human condition. In a changing world the colonists and the colonized alike feel the pangs of exile and alienation.

Yet once we have recognized the generalities of the human condition, it is in the particular instances that we can best express them, and above all in the particular contexts we most intimately know. This, I suggest, is why after writing the remarkable group of stories on Africa collected in *The Tomorrow-Tamer*, Margaret Laurence abandoned the continent as a setting for her fiction, turning back to her own country and—since Canada is a confederation of regions rather than a nation in the ordinarily accepted sense—to her own *patria chica* of the Manitoba small towns, from which her protagonists emerge to challenge and eventually to endure the world. They fear and fear, like Godman, and yet they live.

It seems appropriate now to go on to *A Bird in the House,* rather than to the Canadian novels that preceded it in terms of publication, not only because it also is a volume of stories, though of a much more intimately united kind than in *The Tomorrow-Tamer,* but also because its stories were written during the same period as the first three novels about Manawaka people, *The Stone Angel, A Jest of God* and *The Fire-Dwellers.* Furthermore, as Margaret Laurence tells us, *A Bird in the House* is "the only semi-autobiographical fiction I have ever written."

To admit even to semiautobiography is quite extraordinary in an age when novelists are inclined to react with some ferocity to the suggestion that they are really writing about themselves. In the broad sense, of course, they write about no one but themselves; as Flaubert said on the legendary occasion, "La Bovary? C'est moi!" But there are differences between the process of shucking off various personae to isolate the germs of one's more important characters which — being relatively uninventive beings — most novelists do in most of their novels, and the much more direct process of reshaping one's own crucial life experiences, usually undergone in adolescence, until they acquire the plausibility of good fiction, as D.H. Lawrence did in *Sons and Lovers* and Joyce in *Portrait of the Artist.* It needs, I think, a high degree of cultural certainty to write this type of openly autobiographical fiction, and this may explain why in Canada, where colonial inhibitions weighed heavily upon writers until very recently, it has rarely been done successfully, just as there have been few really satisfactory Canadian autobiographies. In this context Margaret Laurence's own remarks in *Heart of a Stranger* about *A Bird in the House* are very interesting, because they illuminate not only the extent to which autobiographical elements can dominate writing against the writer's will and largely without her being aware of it, but also suggest where the real-life town of Neepawa, in which Laurence was born and brought up, merges into what she had fervently maintained to be a fictional microcosm, Manawaka.

In the essay entitled "A Place to Stand On," discussing the differences between those real and imagined towns, Laurence says of the people who founded prairie towns, "They were, in the end, great survivors, and for that I love and value them." She then goes on:

The final exploration of this aspect of my background came when I wrote — over the past six or seven years — *A Bird in the House,* a number of short stories set in Manawaka and based upon my childhood and my childhood family, the only semi-autobiographical fiction I have ever written. I did not realize until I finished the final story in the series how much all these stories are dominated by the figure of my maternal grandfather, who came of Irish Protestant stock. Perhaps it was through writing these stories that I finally came to see my grandfather not only as the repressive authoritarian figure from my childhood, but also as a boy who had to leave school in Ontario when he was about twelve, after his father's death, and who as a young man went to Manitoba by sternwheeler and walked the miles from Winnipeg to Portage la Prairie, where he settled for some years before moving to Neepawa. He was a very hard man in many ways, but he had had a very hard life. I don't think I knew any of this, really knew it, until I had finished these stories. I don't think I ever knew, either, until that moment how much I owed to him. One sentence, near the end of the final story, may show what I mean. "I had feared and fought the old man, yet he proclaimed himself in my veins."

And this account of recognition is followed by a statement that must be given weight — but not too much weight — in considering Margaret Laurence's major novels.

My writing, then, has been my own attempt to come to terms with the past. I see this process as the gradual one of freeing oneself from the stultifying aspect of the past, while at the same time beginning to see its true value — which, in the case of my own people (by which I mean the total community, not just my particular family), was a determination to survive against whatever odds.

More than any other of Margaret Laurence's Canadian books, *A Bird in the House* can be seen as fulfilling this role of exorcising "the stultifying aspect of the past," and this makes one wonder how far the writing of these stories, during the period when the first three Manawaka novels were written, in fact served as a kind of valve by which the feelings of personal identification and agony that surged up while writing about a prairie setting were deflected from the major works in progress.

Yet these stories and the novels that are contemporary with them are really very closely linked. *A Bird in the House*, after all, is about childhood and adolescence in Manawaka, and this is an experience which the central figures of all the novels share with Vanessa McLeod, as they share the departure from the town that she makes by the end of the book. Places like Manawaka are made to escape from and then to remember the rest of one's life. But while the others mostly remember (for only Rachel Cameron in *A Jest of God* lives out the novel's present in Manawaka) through the screen of an intensely lived present (Hagar's dying days, Stacey's marital agony, Morag's writer's travails), Vanessa recollects, in almost total and unimpeded clarity, how the child's eye saw and the child's mind interpreted that vanished past. We are given a clear and primal vision of Manawaka undistorted by later passions; a vision of the family — or rather the conjoined families of the Irish O'Connors and the Scottish McLeods—as the micro-cosm in which all the passions life will later magnify are seen in miniature, in the frustrations and conflicts Vanessa perceives with a knowing child's foresight will become her lot in womanhood. On the rare occasions when the narrator's present does intrude it is to give a symbolic emphasis to something a child has seen clearly but without full understanding, as in the story dealing with the death of Vanessa's grandmother and her grandfather's inarticulate grief. It is entitled "The Mask of the Bear," and it ends:

Many years later, when Manawaka was far away from me, in miles and in time, I saw one day in a museum the Bear Mask of the Haida Indians. It was a weird mask. The features were ugly and yet powerful. The mouth was turned down in an expression of sullen rage. The eyes were empty caverns, revealing nothing. Yet as I looked, they seemed to draw my eyes toward them, until I imagined I could see somewhere within that darkness a look that I knew, a lurking bewilderment. I remembered then that in the days before it became a museum piece, the mask had concealed a man.

Margaret Laurence's four Manawaka novels are concerned with the masks of women (and let us remember that the original meaning of *persona* was a mask used by a player) and the be-wildered real selves who peer through them at the world. In every case there is a concealed self, sustained by a flow of memory and inner monologue; there is a mask that is kept perpetually in place when one moves in the world; and the world is a place where beings masked by prejudice and fear confront each other and oc-casionally drop their masks and come together in freedom and love. Just as *A Bird in the House* has settings and characters in com-mon with the novels, so it has this double pattern of love and con-flict, exemplified in the heart of Vanessa's own life by the conflict between the Scottish and the Orange traditions and in the village by the conflict between the vastly contrasting lifestyles of the puritan pioneers like Grandfather Connor and the métis family of the Tonnerres, descendants of one of Gabriel Dumont's rebel followers in 1885, who live in a peripheral shack hamlet as a perpe-tual reproach to Manawaka's conscience until at last, in *The Diviners,* the conflict is resolved in the person of Pique, daughter of Scottish Morag Gunn and Jules Tonnerre, and the symbol of freedom through reconciliation.

But, despite the constant shading off between *A Bird in the House* and the four novels, the latter stand on their own, and are far more closely linked than they first appear. There is of course the common physical ambience of Manawaka, with its single main street and its prominent cemetery and "nuisance grounds" (garbage dump). There is the fact that individuals and clans, like the Camerons and the McLeods and the Kazlicks and the Tonnerres and the Pearls move in and out of the novels from beginning to end. There is the fact that every central figure is a woman, which establishes a line of biological and cultural consistency through all the emotional and attitudinal differences between four such variant personalities as Hagar Shipley, Rachel Cameron, Stacey McAindra and Morag Gunn. There is also the underlying sense that, in a much less overt and didactic way than MacLennan in the preceding generation, Margaret Laurence is presenting a paradigm of the Canadian condition, with the relationships of its characters exemplifying the divisions and distrusts and imperfect understandings and frustrated longings that make up the collective psyche of Canada; Anglo-Celts and later immigrants opposed and meeting only for mutual injury in *A Jest of God*, alien and native strains finding their painful way together in *The Diviners*, the puritan cult of duty and the call of desire meeting to make the hell of *The Fire-Dwellers,* and in *The Stone Angel* the rigidities of invading mercantilism opposed to the vanishing liberties of the frontier in the marriage of Hagar Currie and Bram Shipley. All the characteristics and complexities of our national existence, at least so far as it has been lived west of the Laurentian Shield, can be found in these four novels by those who search diligently enough, and this comprehensiveness would be alone sufficient to justify regarding Margaret Laurence as the kind of national novelist I have suggested she is.

When we come to look at what unites the books — even though they are not a formal tetralogy — on a deeper and more mythical level, we encounter a pattern which may not be deliberate, but which nevertheless seems clean and definite. There are four novels, and though the group is discontinuous in the sense of having no uniting plot line, and is never closed off by any decisive event, Margaret Laurence has declared very firmly that *The Diviners* is the last novel she will be writing. Such a statement made before her fiftieth year by a writer of great creative and mental vigour can hardly be accepted as final in terms of Margaret Laurence's lifework, but it can be taken as meaning that a phase of writing has ended, and that *The Diviners* does in fact complete a task Margaret Laurence had in mind when she began to draw Manawaka out of her imagination and to give its people life in the pages of her books. It completes a pattern.

The pattern that I see uniting the four books and defining them as a group is an ancient one. It is embraced in antique and mediaeval medicine and derives from the 2500-year-old theory of Empedocles that the universe is composed of four elements: earth, air, fire and water. Out of this conception emerged the theory, more familiar in literary history, of the four humours that dominate human physiology and temperament. The humour corresponding to earth is the choleric; to air, the phlegmatic; to fire, the sanguine; and to water, the melancholic. Scientifically both theories may be primitive and disproved; in terms of myth they are as potent as the zodiac, and the links between the humours and the elements run through poetry and drama and fiction from classical antiquity down to the present. When we look at Margaret Laurence's four Canadian novels in the light of such archaic concepts of the nature of matter and of man, the correspondences between her works and the ancient patterning are far too close to be dismissed.

If the very title of *The Fire-Dwellers* were not itself loaded with intent, the novel's two epigraphs should be sufficient to establish the dominance of the element of fire. The first is a verse of Carl Sandburg, in which he speaks of himself as "I who have fiddled in a world of fire,/I who have done so many stunts not worth doing," and the second is the old rhyme, "Ladybird, ladybird,/Fly away home;/Your house is on fire,/Your children are gone." When we read the extraordinary monologue of middle-aged Stacey McAindra (born Stacey Cameron, the Manawaka undertaker's daughter) remembering her prairie past, trying to live in her precariously middleclass Vancouver present, keeping the peace with and between four children and longing for sexual adventures before it is too late, it is not only the fire of a world threatened with holocaust that we — like Stacey — are aware of, but also the inferno of unsatisfied urges in Stacey herself, the fires of a sanguine and insatiable temperament.

For Stacey's sister, Rachel Cameron, spinster schoolteacher who has never escaped from Manawaka, her mother's impositions or her own fears, the epigraph of her novel *A Jest of God* is equally meaningful, for it begins with the lines: "The wind blows high, the wind blows high,/The snow comes falling from the sky...." Wind is air and air is undoubtedly Rachel's element: air the insubstantial, the wavering, that which flees from fire yet feeds it, as in the crucial incident when she is unwillingly touched by the flames at a Pentecostal meeting and realizes to her horror that she has been speaking with tongues before strangers. Rachel, according to her humour, is essentially phlegmatic in behaviour, for apathy as well as timidity prevents her from making decisions until they are forced upon her. Earth is as hostile to her as fire; When Nick Kazlick lays her on the ground and takes her middle-aged virginity, the result is not the pregnancy she half hopes for and half fears, but a benign tumour that is earth's mockery manifested as flesh. When her wind shifts and she leaves for her new life in Vancouver (a change of air as it were), it is air that seems to convey her, for the image she conceives of the bus carrying her and her mother away at last from Manawaka is not that of a creature running on the earth, but of one that "flies along, smooth and confident as a great owl through the darkness." Air is her element and in the end her liberation.

The stone angel, whose likeness Margaret Laurence first saw in a cemetery in Genoa on her way to Somaliland (and recorded in *The Prophet's Camel Bell*) is, of course, hewn out of the earth and blind as creatures that live in earth, and as such is an appropriate symbol for Hagar Shipley, the choleric earth mother who inhabits *The Stone Angel*. That novel—of all Margaret Laurence's works—shows the most sensual awareness of the earth's surface, of its creatures (animal or vegetable), of its colours and textures and smells. Hagar is an intensely visual but even more an intensely tactile person, concerned with what is evident to the sense of feeling, whether it is sex remembered vividly and in detail into her nineties, or the texture of a dress she wears in old age. Even her own body she often apprehends in terms of earthly mass, as one feels sculptors apprehend the forms within the mineral masses with which they work. Earth in the sense of land is also important to her, and it is as much to live on his farm as to be ploughed sexually by him that she marries the socially impossible Bram Shipley; she resents the fact that Bram wastes his land on grazing horses, instead of tilling it and making it productive. Even

...e approaches death and her life tends to be more and more
...inated by the immaterial world of memory, the memories themselves tend to be defined and initiated by the material objects from the past that surround her and which she treasures.

To this passion for the earth and its emanations in sensation and memory, Hagar adds the choler of her appropriate humour. In anger she confronts her equally choleric father and insists on marrying Bram. In anger she finally leaves Bram, in anger she drives her son John from the house and thus indirectly causes his death, in anger she flees to her illusory seaside refuge in the deserted canning factory when her other son Marvin proposes to put her in an old people's home. Every one of the people she encounters is seen through the dark screen of her choler, and it is only in the end that the black bile seems to leave her and she is able to regret the absence of rejoicing in her life and to accept the blessings of another element; though even when she takes the water as her life ebbs, she still reacts, as she had always done, with choler. The nurse offers her water:

"Here. Here you are. Can you?"

"Of course. What do you think I am? What do you take me for? Here, give it to me. Oh, for mercy's sake let me hold it myself!"

I only defeat myself by not accepting her. I know this—I know it very well. But I can't help it—it's my nature. I'll drink from this glass, or spill it, just as I choose. I'll not countenance anyone else's holding it for me. And yet—if she were in my place, I'd think her daft, and push her hands away, certain I could hold it for her better.

I wrest from her the glass, full of water to be had for the taking. I hold it in my own hands. There. There.

And then—

We are what we are, Margaret Laurence seems to be suggesting in *The Stone Angel*, and the nature we have been given will shape our lives and remain with us to the end. Hagar is always Hagar, with all that name signifies in terms of bondage, whether she changes her surname from Currie to Shipley, and no matter how she may change her status; at most—as a grace—she can have a vision of what she might have been if she had not been herself.

But Hagar is the most bound by her nature of all Margaret Laurence's heroines, and bound perhaps because of the special opacity of the earthborn. Stacey, like fire, is more mutable, able to shift from the blaze of self-destructive passion to the glow of love and loyalty, and Rachel finds that natures of air compounded can soar and escape as well as waver before more solid natures.

Water provides the governing symbol of *The Diviners,* and here again the pattern of the elements and humours continues. Water begins the novel — the image of the river beside which the novelist Morag Gunn lives and writes and remembers, and which appears to run both ways, as our inner life does.

The river flowed both ways. The current moved from north to south, but the wind usually came from the south, rippling the bronze-green water in the opposite direction. This apparently impossible contradiction, made apparent and possible, still fascinated Morag, even after the years of river-watching.

Note that in this effect, right at the beginning of *The Diviners,* there are two elements involved, air and water; this, as we shall see, is a novel largely concerned with the elements reconciled.

Yet water is dominant. The river is not merely a pleasant foreground for Morag's dwelling; it is also a thoroughfare by which her neighbours visit her, and among these neighbours there is one — old Royland — who acts almost the same role in the novel as the old magician archetype in Jungian mythology, and who — like Merlin but in another way — is the diviner.

Royland divines water, and for Morag the link between his occupation and hers is obvious. She also is a diviner, plunging into the depths (the very word we use is significant) of human hearts, though what she emerges with may not be so tangible as Royland's findings.

The imagery linking writing with water is of course copious. The poets draw their inspiration from the fountain of the muses on Mount Helicon and from the Castalian spring sacred to Apollo at Delphi. We think of their poetry as flowing, we talk of streams of consciousness in fiction. We associate Shakespeare with a river — the Avon — he left in youth, and see a special significance in the association of Coleridge and Wordsworth with the Lakes; we find a particular appropriateness in Shelley's death by drowning (the drowned poet has even become a dominant image in Canadian verse), while we remember with a special poignancy that Keats described himself as "one whose name was writ in water." So the association of Morag's craft with the river that flows before her door is traditionally appropriate. (But note another mingling of the elements here; it is water welling from the earth — as Royland detects water held by the earth — that inspires the poets.)

But there is more to divination than finding water so far as this novel is concerned. Divination has occurred earlier in Morag's life, long before she met Royland, when the town scavenger of Manawaka, Christie Logan, would "tell the garbage" to determine the fortunes of the community's inhabitants. And Christie Logan, who took the orphan Morag into his house after her father and mother died in her infancy, introduces Morag to her Celtic past, to her ancestor Piper Gunn who led his people onto the ships for the long voyage (water again) to their homes in Lord Selkirk's Red River Settlement, and to the Celtic self that lives within her, the Dark Celt she sees as Morag Dhu, the self whose melancholy is the humour related to the element of water. (Morag is related to the Welsh name Morgan, and Morgan-le-Fay was an enchantress skilled in divination.)

Morag herself is indeed like water, secretive but enduring in her passions, able to flow round life's obstacles, caught in the endless stream of creation and full of the pools of intuition from which inspiration can be fished by the assiduous angler. The end of *The Diviners* is undefined, incomplete, flowing on into the unknown, according to the nature of water. Morag walks beside the river, sees it seeming to flow both ways, and detects here a paradox within her own consciousness. *"Look ahead into the past, and back into the future, until the silence."* And then her questioning:

How far could anyone see into the river? Not far. Near shore, in the shallows, the water was clear, and there were the clean and broken clamshells of creatures now dead, and the wavering of the underwater weed-forests, and the flicker of small live fishes, and the undulating lines of gold as the sand ripples received the sun. Only slightly further out, the water deepened and kept its life from sight.

Yet there is another aspect of *The Diviners* to be noticed, for the truth of divining, as of writing and other arts, lies in perceiving relationships, and it is an essential aspect of the ancient doctrines of elements and humours that they cannot exist apart. A healthy world is the elements combined in balance, though destiny lays a bias on each of us by giving us special natures, and we spend our lives trying to achieve the equilibrium. Hagar is only aware of the need for equilibrium at the very end, but Stacey and Rachel progress in their own ways of understanding, and Morag, because of her calling and largely despite herself, comes nearest to an understanding of the pattern.

She is helped towards it by her relationships with three men. One is the professor of English she marries, Brooke Skelton, as much a being of air as Rachel was, fearful of the hostage he will give to earth if he and Morag have a child, and concerned in literature with the aspects that least relate to the surface of the earth, the real passions of women and men. Dan McRaith, Morag's painter lover in London, is a man of earth, tied to the Cromarty seashore whose forms and colours dominate his paintings and faithful in his fashion to the woman who has been his wife since girlhood and has borne his children. The human eyes in his paintings look through the forms of rock or fossil and the emotions they express are of distance and dispossession, of spirit by earth imprisoned.

Fire is in Jules Tonnerre, Morag's first lover and the father of her child Pique. Apart from the fact that his very name is linked to the natural fire of lightning, he is associated in memory with the fire that destroyed his demoralized sister Piquette and her children and which Morag witnesses as reporter for the Manawaka newspaper. Her daughter by Jules is given Piquette's name, perpetuating the link with fire; at the same time, like fire and water, Jules and Morag can never live together, though it is tempting to think of her inspirations as the emanations of their contact, springing like gilded mists from a river touched by the sun's fires.

If in these personal ways Morag's life suggests the reconciliations existence demands between and within human beings, in a more general way *The Diviners* presents the summation of Margaret Laurence's vision of her land and her cultures, and places her firmly in the humanistic and quasi-realistic tradition of the true novel as distinct from the other forms of fiction (parable, fable, satire, fantasy, romance) in which the creation of plausible worlds of the mind is not essential. Manawaka is a plausible world, because we recognize in it Canada — or English-speaking Canada at least — in microcosm. Margaret Laurence has contended that our mental roots do not go very far back, which is why the Manitoba small towns of her parents and grandparents are for her the essential rooting place of a Canadian consciousness. Yet she recognizes that such a consciousness can be expanded by experience, and Morag, like all Laurence's leading characters, departs for Vancouver (and lives in Ontario, which the others do not); she also makes the pilgrimage to her ancestral home of Scotland, and her reaction is much like that which Laurence expressed for herself in *Heart of a Stranger*:

I care about the ancestral past very much, but in a kind of mythical way. The ancestors, in the end, become everyone's ancestors. But the history that one can feel personally encompasses only a very few generations.

Yet the myth remains essential, the Scottish myth of exile from the Highlands for Christie and Morag, the metis myth of Riel and Dumont for Jules Tonnerre. But myths gain their greatest significance when writers give them the forms in which they influence the collective mind of a people and continue to stir collective memories. The Trojan War would have been an unremembered tribal skirmish without Homer's epics, which turned it into a myth that has inspired men for millenia. Macbeth would have been a virtually forgotten minor figure in the history of a bleak northern country if Shakespeare had not made him into a great exemplum of nervous villainy; and what Spaniards would think of their past if Cervantes had not written *Don Quixote*, or the French of theirs without Balzac, it is now impossible to say. The novels of Manawaka, I suggest, are already playing this mythical role for Canadians. Hugh MacLennan was also a mythographer, presenting us to ourselves on the heroic level; it is amazing how many of his leading characters are sketched as Homeric giants (soldiers, boxers, crusaders, politicians, all larger than life). But the need for that kind of self-image has been fulfilled. Now we need to see ourselves as we are, as those who survive in that ordinary life where the only heroism is to endure — often to endure one's own given nature — and, to the best of one's ability, to create. It is thus that Margaret Laurence has shown us to ourselves in these superb novels, which are the best of our place and generation.

[1978]

Many Solitudes: The Travel Writings of Margaret Laurence

M ARGARET L AURENCE has written only one travel narrative in the conventional sense, which is *The Prophet's Camel Bell,* and that book, produced a decade after the period of life in Somaliland which it narrates, she has described as the most difficult of all her works to write. The difficulty is not evident in the finished version, and the existence of difficulty at any time seems at first a little surprising, since the creation of a natural setting and the placing of human drama in that setting (which is the main content of *The Prophet's Camel Bell*) are prime constituents of all Laurence's writing. Her novels are all in a sense travel books, vividly descriptive in terms of environment, involving a great deal of journeying, both inner and outer, and coming at the end to those self-transforming realizations that are the destinations of all internal voyagings.

I suspect that a great deal of the difficulty incurred in the writing of *The Prophet's Camel Bell* arose from the fact that, while it is a narrative in which an inner journey and an arrival at a personal destination run parallel, as in the novels, with a great deal of external and physical wandering through a dramatic landscape, in this case the inner journey is not that of a fictional persona; it is the author's own. *The Prophet's Camel Bell* is much more than a mere narrative of exploration; it is an autobiographical document, a guidebook to a large area of the mental world in which Laurence's novels, from *This Side Jordan* to *The Diviners*, were conceived.

The Prophet's Camel Bell is not the only piece of travel writing Margaret Laurence has done. The first book she ever published, *A Tree for Poverty,* is to all appearance a brief treatise on Somali oral literature, with selected translations of poems and stories, but even here the experience of a traveller is evident, as it is in Laurence's only book of literary criticism, *Long Drums and Cannons,* concerning the work of West African novelists who emerged during the 1950s and 1960s. More directly relevant, however, are the occasional travel pieces collected in her one volume of essays, *Heart of a Stranger*; these, as the title suggests, are concerned largely with the places that have been important to Margaret Laurence in both her life and her writing. They cover the important periods of her life, from childhood in Manitoba, through the crucial experience of Africa, in later years to the Scotland she visited in search of her ancestry, and back to the Ontario where she now lives, in full consciousness that the land of her birth has more significance for her than the land of her fore-fathers, of which she has neither direct recollection nor even a vicarious memory transmitted through immediate relatives. Perhaps, indeed, one can describe the final effect of *Heart of a Stranger* as an arrangement of personal myths in their order of relevance.

It is, of course, possible to treat these various books as sources of clues to the content of Margaret Laurence's fiction. The essays in *Heart of a Stranger* lay out the physical background — that part of Manitoba where the prairie begins to roll in the direction of the northern forests — of the fictional town of Manawaka that figures in the four Canadian novels and also in the cycle of stories, *A Bird in the House,* which Laurence confesses in *Heart of a Stranger* is "semi-autobiographically" modelled on her own childhood in the actual town of Neepawa. There are people mentioned in these essays whose characteristics were obviously combined with those of others to make characters in the novels. A water diviner and an ageing boatman neighbour, two different people in real life, come together and form the nucleus of the wise old man Royland who provides a title and much of the plot for *The Diviners.* Margaret Laurence's friendship with "Mensah," the Ghanaian, which she describes in the essay entitled "The Very Best Intentions," resembles Miranda Kestoe's with Nathaniel Amebge in *This Side Jordan*, though "Mensah's" acerbic nature and his pessimism regarding the future of Ghana after freedom obviously contributed more to the character of Victor Edusei in the same novel than to Nathaniel's.

One can similarly turn to *The Prophet's Camel Bell* — that narrative of fact so strange and so startling in its impact that Margaret Laurence seems never to have had any desire to turn it into fiction—and find touches that were later melded into the fiction of other places. The marble angels which Laurence saw with such astonishment in the Staglieno cemetery at Genoa on her way to Somaliland not only appear in the short story "The Perfumed Sea," in *The Tomorrow-Tamer*, but also, of course, provide the most commanding image in *The Stone Angel*. The child prostitute encountered in the Somali desert reappears in the West African child Ayesha in "The Rain Child." The double solitude of Italians in Somaliland, isolated from both the native peoples and the British overlords, is reflected in the predicament of the Italian hairdresser, Mr. Archipelago, marooned in a West African town in *The Tomorrow-Tamer*. Diligent readings can disinter many echoes and links of this kind without in the least detracting from the essential imaginative autonomy of Margaret Laurence's novels, and clearly the importance of *The Prophet's Camel Bell* and *Heart of a Stranger* lies in another direction, in what they reveal of the state of mind out of which Margaret Laurence's novels and stories emerged.

There is no question of the experience of Somaliland having started Margaret Laurence in the career of writing, though all her publications postdate it. Indeed, it may have beneficially delayed the maturing of a talent—and at this point there is no reason to doubt the autobiographical hints given in *A Bird in the House*—which she had already begun to develop as an assiduous scribbler during her Manitoba childhood. Obviously the early experience of Somaliland, and particularly that of a moving camp in the drought-ridden desert, produced the kind of culture shock which often makes it hard for a writer to say anything immediately about a country in which she has moved as "a stranger in a strange land," and forced Margaret Laurence into a salutary reexamination of her own character which prevented her writing more about the country while she lived there than the brief descriptive paragraphs which are part of the introductory material to *A Tree for Poverty*. Her literary activity in Somaliland, restricted mainly to translating the poems and stories in *A Tree*, was perhaps excellent work under the circumstances, since it brought her into contact through their own literature and traditions with a number of Somalis and so gave an insight into the land and its people which no merely external observation could have produced, as well as providing a temporary substitute for more originative writing.

In Somaliland Margaret Laurence also kept a diary, but she found that when she returned to the experience a decade later she had to begin anew, recreating and giving something of a literary structure to the phase of life which *The Prophet's Camel Bell* re-enacts. It is significant that when, in West Africa, she experienced another strange land and strange culture, the inhibitions regarding making fiction out of it no longer existed, and the first version of *This Side Jordan* was actually written in Ghana, though even here — as Margaret Laurence remarked in "Ten Years' Sentences," an article published in *Canadian Literature* in 1969 — departure from Africa provided a new perspective and much of the novel had to be rewritten to suit the more distanced view.

The Prophet's Camel Bell is in fact a much more complex work than the travel narrative it may appear at first sight to be. In the Laurence chronology it stands after *This Side Jordan* and *The Tomorrow-Tamer,* and we have to view it with this experience of fiction-writing in mind. Much of the basic content may indeed have been provided by the original diary; the shaping is that of an experienced novelist, and if we see *The Prophet's Camel Bell* as representing an intermediate genre between the novel and the ordinary travel narrative, we can appreciate most fully what the book has to offer.

There are really three levels on which *The Prophet's Camel Bell* moves forward. A landscape is described, with the kind of vivid feeling for the surface of the earth that had already become evident in her West African fiction, and on that bizarre terrain — usually barren but at times bursting into fantastic blossomings — a people is observed which has created a way of life and an accompanying philosophy as specialized and as closely adapted to survival in an extreme environment as that of the Eskimo. Like so many Canadian writers a generation or so away from the pioneers, Margaret Laurence was interested in the theme of survival long before Margaret Atwood made it the subject of a perhaps excessively celebrated book, and in 1970, looking back over her career in the essay "A Place to Stand On" (in *Heart of a Stranger*), she made some remarks that have an obvious bearing on her reaction to the Somalis and their existence.

The theme of survival — not just physical survival, but the preservation of some human dignity and in the end some human warmth and ability to reach out and touch others — this is, I have come to think, an almost inevitable theme for a writer such as I, who came from a Scots-Irish background of stern values and hard work and puritanism, and who grew up during the drought and depression of the thirties and then the war.

At the second level, *The Prophet's Camel Bell* provides a series of rounded character vignettes, with four of the Somalis being given a chapter each, and chapters being devoted to the Italian workers Margaret Laurence and her husband associated with in the course of their dam-building project, and also to "the imperialists," including many kinds of Englishmen in Somaliland. Finally, on the third level, it is a study of the author's own mental development, and of the transformation of her reactions to a strange world during the two years she lived in Somaliland; this process of unfolding self-revelation runs through the whole book from beginning to end, and is not only its profoundest theme but also its main structural connection.

The construction of the *ballehs* (earth dams) which was entrusted to Jack Laurence took place in the Haud, the arid inland region of Somaliland that Margaret Laurence found "so seemingly remote that one almost doubted the existence of the rest of the world." It was a place of drought, broken by rare and violent periods of rain, of which there was only one during the Laurences' term of service; one was enough, for they only narrowly escaped disaster in the flash floods that tore down the dry watercourses. At the time of their arrival there, the Haud was in the grip of one of the great prolonged droughts known as *Jilal*. The Haud then

seemed to be no place for any living thing. Even the thorny bushes, digging their roots in and finding nourishment in that inhospitable soil, appear to have a precarious hold on life, as though at any moment they might relax their grip, dry up entirely and be blown away.

But the thorny bushes did not blow away, any more than the people became extinct, no matter how many human beings and camels died during the *Jilal*, and Margaret Laurence was to see a resemblance between the men of the Haud and the vegetation they moved among. "There was a toughness deep in these people, like the fibre of desert cactus, the ability to eke out life, the refusal to die easily."

The tough vegetation even provided a shelter and a symbol for the faith of the Somali herdsmen. Arriving at a tiny desert hamlet, Margaret Laurence saw an enclosure of thorn, and when she asked its purpose, she was told that this was the mosque.

I looked again at the thorn boughs that formed the place of worship. It seemed to me that more genuine faith might reside in this brushwood circle than in the jewelled and carved magnificence of the Blue Mosque at Istanbul.

She saw the Somalis in the *Jilal* as "a dying people in a dying land. The dust filled their nostrils like a constant reminder of mortality." Yet as a people they did not die.

They were not a passive people. They struggled against terrifying odds to get through to the wells. But always in their minds must have been the feeling that if Allah intended them to make it, nothing would prevail against them, and if he did not intend them to go on living no effort of theirs would be of any use. This fatalism did not weaken them. On the contrary, it prevented them from wasting themselves in fury and desperation.

Margaret Laurence finds herself as unable as Ivan Karamazov would have been to accept with Islamic calm the fate of the innocents in such a world, yet is forced to recognize the relevance of such a religious attitude to the realities from which it emerges:

So the Qoran gives suffering a meaning and refuses the finality of death. I saw the necessity of this belief, without which life for these people would have been intolerable. I would have shared such a faith, if it had been a matter of choice, but I could not. To me, it seemed that these children died pointlessly, and vanished as though they had never been, like pebbles thrown into a dark and infinite well.

With most of the Somalis who lived that hard life and professed that faith of resignation, Margaret Laurence's meetings were necessarily fleeting, and limited by the lack of a common language or anything in the way of a shared view of existence, yet often they had the epiphanic quality which only such brief encounters can acquire, and it is a measure of Margaret Laurence's artistry that she recognized their value as revelations. Episodes of this kind punctuate her book, and constantly strengthen its authenticity as an account of a strange and stark culture. One of the most striking of such vignettes describes an encounter with a woman at the height of the *Jilal*, and I quote the incident in full because it is an admirable example of her traveller's perceptiveness and of her narrative skill, deepened but never softened by the compassion that accompanies them and not merely unites us empathically with the Somali woman but also takes us into the centre of Margaret Laurence's mind as she experiences and reflects in memory on the incident.

Driving along the Awareh-Hargeiss road, we saw two burden camels laden with the crescent-shaped hut-frames and the bundled mats. They were halted by the roadside, and as we drew near, we saw one of the beasts slide to its knees, sunken in the apathy of thirst and exhaustion. Beside them, squatting in the sand, was a woman, a young woman, her black headscarf smeared with dust. She must have possessed, once, a tenderly beautiful face. Now her face was drawn and pinched. In her hands she held an empty tin cup. She did not move at all, or ask for water. Despair keeps its own silence. Her brown robe swayed in the wind. She carried a baby slung across one hip. The child's face was quiet, its head lolling in the heavy heat of the sun. We had a little water left in our spare tank, and so we stopped. She did not say a word, but she did something then which I have never been able to forget.

She held the cup for the child to drink first.

She was careful not to spill a drop. Afterwards, she brushed a hand lightly across the child's mouth, then licked her palm so that no moisture would be wasted.

To her I must have seemed meaningless, totally unrelated to herself. How could it have been otherwise? I had never had to coax the lagging camels on, when they would have preferred to stop and rest and die. But what I felt, as I looked into her face, was undeniable and it was not pity. It was something different, some sense of knowing in myself what her anguish had been and would be, as she watched her child's life seep away for lack of water to keep it alive. For her, this was the worst the *Jilal* could bring. In all of life there was nothing worse than this.

What we could do here was only slightly more than nothing. Maybe she would reach the wells. Maybe she would not. She might with good reason have looked at us with hatred as we began to speed easily away, but she did not. She was past all such emotions. She knew only that she must keep on or she would perish, and her child with her. As we drove away, we saw her rise slowly and call the burden camels. The beasts struggled up and began to follow her.

Other vignettes tell of communities, of the temporary halting places in the desert or the old and decaying towns on the coast, where only vestiges remain of the flamboyant past of Arab merchants and slave traders, of pearl divers and warring sheikhs whose exploits have been magnified in tribal legend. Such a place was Zeilah, where they stayed in a residency haunted by the ghost of an English administrator who had killed his wife and then shot himself. There was something ghostly also about the people of

Zeilah, who lived in memories of their past as traders and pearl divers, and

chanted songs whose meaning they had forgotten. The words were Galla, or Danakil, mixed with Arabic or archaic Somali, all so blended and changed that they were unrecognizable. They would chant them over and over, the mysterious words and phrases of a dead past, possibly imbued now with a magical significance.

The Somalis whom Margaret Laurence got to know reasonably well were already men between two worlds, the servants and tractor drivers who retained some links with their tribes, but who had already been affected by their contacts with the modern world. There was Hersi Half-tongue, the interpreter and teller of traditional tales who suffered a speech defect for which he compensated by a dramatic style of narration in which he acted out elaborately every role he recounted. There was Abdi, the tough old warrior whose loyalty turned to bitterness when he realized that the reward for faithful service would not be the automatic employment of all the fellow clansmen he cared to propose. Abdi was a man of immense courage and anger who "never knew — and who probably could not have borne to know — that his truest and most terrible battle, like all men's, was with himself." And there was Mohamed their servant, the first and the last Somali whom Margaret Laurence saw, and whose relationship with her and her husband was a matter of satisfying his own code of service rather than of personal devotion, as she had first imagined.

But only slowly did we come to see that Mohamed's identification of his own interests with those of his employer would have taken place whoever the employer happened to be. He acted not in response to what we were, but to what he himself was.

All these people come alive, not only in their actions, but also through Laurence's extraordinary ear for eccentricities of speech, so that she can convey a twist of Somali character in the very way a man speaks brokenly in the alien tongue of English. Her gradual recognition of the complexity of Somali motives and the ambiguities of relationships with these people was as much part of Margaret Laurence's self-transforming education as were the horrors and harshnesses of life in the Haud during the famine of the *Jilal*. She learnt how excessively simplified had been her assumptions about a nation of tribal peoples who nevertheless adhered to one of the world's great civilizing religious traditions.

Parallel with this humbling acquisition of knowledge about another people (accompanied as it was by the loss of illusions created by that most foolish of travellers' expectations — the wish to be liked), there was another process of adjustment to be made, towards the British in Somaliland. When she first reached the colony, Margaret Laurence tells us:

I believed that the overwhelming majority of Englishmen in colonies could properly be classed as imperialists, and my feeling about imperialism was very simple — I was against it.

But from the beginning, when her first English acquaintance in the colony turned out to be a foreman mechanic with no pukka English airs who spent his life patiently instructing Somali drivers in the ways of a mechanized world, she found her attitude changing. Alongside the conventional imperialists (a pathetic lot of insecure people as she later realized), she met those who spent their lives doing what they could for the people, and sometimes earning the respect and even the reverence of the Somalis, who normally hated the British as infidels. One such man was the Padre, a wispy Anglican clergyman who never made a convert among the Somalis, but who was universally accepted by them as a holy man and who wandered the desert confident that the poorest tribesman would protect him and shelter and feed him if it were necessary.

Because his faith illuminated him so, it was tempting to see him simply as a saintly man, some gentler John the Baptist. But how intricate must be the forces that make life seem possible to some men only in the wilderness.

What Margaret Laurence was encountering, as have many others in the dwindling Empire, were representatives of that strange breed, more common in the British than in other empires, who were drawn towards the colonies not for the sake of money or career or the opportunity to dominate, but because there was a need in them to live in some way as "strangers in a strange land."

I had not really believed such people existed. Yet here they were, confounding every preconceived notion of old colonials or pukka sahibs, and defying any neat labelling. Each was unique, utterly unlike anyone else, and yet they had this in common — they were all intensely concerned with this land and with the work they were doing here, and they were all drawn to Africa, or some place far from home, deeply and irresistibly.

Laurence was drawn to these people, largely because she felt that her own attitude had become very much like theirs, as she indicates in analyzing her feelings on leaving Somaliland.

It seemed to me that my feeling of regret arose from unwisely loving a land where I must always remain a stranger. But it was also possible that my real reason for loving it was simply because I was an outsider here. One can never be a stranger in one's own land — it is precisely this fact that makes it so difficult to live there.

And finally, she recognized the paradox that was latent in this situation so far as her own behaviour was concerned.

This was something of an irony for me, to have started out in righteous disapproval of the empire builders, and to have been forced at last to recognize that I, too, had been of that company. For we had all been imperialists in a sense, but the empire we unknowingly sought was that of Prester John, a mythical kingdom and a private world.

Essentially, it is the experiences of foreignness, of the special self-recognition that comes to exiles, of the difficulty of communicating over cultural barriers, that carry forward from Margaret Laurence's life in Somaliland into her later work and make *The Prophet's Camel Bell* so important as a key to understanding her writing. As late as 1976 she called her very personal book of essays *Heart of a Stranger;* the phrase dates from the beginning of her Somali sojourn when, lacking reading matter on the voyage out, she read for the first time in her life the five books of Moses — in a Gideon Bible.

Of all the books which I might have chosen to read just then, few would have been more to the point, for the Children of Israel were people of the desert, as the Somalis were, and fragments from those books were to return to me again and again. *And there was no water for the people to drink — and the people thirsted.* Or, when we were to wonder how the tribesmen could possibly live and maintain hope through the season of drought — *In the wilderness, where thou hast seen how that the Lord thy God bore thee, as a man doth bear his son, in all the way that ye went.* Or the verse that remained with me most of all, when at last and for the first time I was myself a stranger in a strange land, and was sometimes given hostile words and was also given, once, food and shelter in a time of actual need, by tribesmen who had little enough for themselves — *Thou shalt not oppress a stranger, for ye know the heart of a stranger, seeing ye were strangers in the land of Egypt.*

The last sentence lingered on, echoing through Laurence's career, summarizing a recurring sense of being a stranger, and taking on a new relevance when she found that "my experience of other countries probably taught me more about myself and even my own land than it did about anything else." Certainly the Somali experience, as it affected Laurence herself and other Europeans, underlines the preoccupation with exile, from one's own land, from one's adopted land, even from a traditional way of life, that is so prominent a theme in *This Side Jordan* and *The Tomorrow-Tamer*. Some of the remarkable stories in the latter collection, like "The Rain Child" and "The Drummer of All the World," are about the complexities of being a stranger: as they affect Europeans for whom Africa has been a home and who will return to their nominal homes as melancholy exiles, or even Africans, like Ruth in "The Rain Child," the Ghanaian girl brought up in England and incapable of fitting in at the missionary school where she is placed when her father returns to his own country. Always behind these stories about exiles or misfits or people thrust out of their traditional ways by the forces of change, there looms a deeper strangeness, which comes from the difficulty of human communication at the best of times, and it is perhaps appropriate that Margaret Laurence should have drawn out this point in her 1968 book on African writers, *Long Drums and Cannons.* Of these writers she obviously feels the greatest affinity with the Nigerian novelist Chinua Achebe, and she might be talking about her own novels—including those set in Canada as well as in Africa—when she stresses his preoccupation with communication between men, and ends her study of him in this way.

Beyond Achebe's portrayal of the old Ibo society or his portrayal of a contemporary society in the throes of transition, there is one theme, which runs through everything he has written—human communication or the lack of it. He shows the impossibly complicated difficulties of one person speaking to another, attempting to hear—really to hear—what another is saying. In his novels we see man as a creature whose means of communication are both infinitely subtle and infinitely clumsy, a prey to invariable misunderstandings. Yet Achebe's writing conveys the feeling that we must attempt to communicate, however imperfectly, if we are not to succumb to despair or madness.

Surely the difficulty and yet the necessity of communication is not only the major theme of such novels as *The Stone Angel* and *A Jest of God* and *The Fire-Dwellers,* but is even a leading preoccupation of the principal characters in each of these works. In *The Diviners*, Morag Gunn's special gift and so her special reward is the capability of understanding—of divining—more than other people about the hidden strangenesses of the human heart, including her own. So we understand what Margaret Laurence means when she says at the beginning of *The Prophet's Camel Bell* that "the strangest glimpses you may have of any creature in the distant lands will be those you catch of yourself" and—at the end of the book—"yet the voyage that began when we set out for Somaliland could never really be over, for it turned out to be so much more than a geographical journey."

As I hope I have shown, *The Prophet's Camel Bell* lies at the centre of Margaret Laurence's achievement; it has many of the characteristics of fiction (for the character sketches often read like stories and the book has a novelistic kind of structure), and it is as much an autobiography, dealing with a key phase of life, as a travel book. It was, one now realizes, a difficult book to write but one that demanded writing, for nobody returns to an experience after ten years unless there is some special inner reason to give it the permanence of recording, and in so doing, to understand its real significance.

Margaret Laurence's other travel writings, the essays which form the greater part of *Heart of a Stranger*, are largely occasional pieces, produced on commission, like the two sketches of the Valley of the Kings and the Suez Canal written during a winter month in Egypt ten years ago, and "Sayonara, Agamemnon," written for *Holiday* after a first visit to Greece. Like any tale of experiences, these narratives do tell us a certain amount about the writer and the way she sees her world, while other essays like "The Poem and the Spear"—about Mohammad, 'Abdilla Hasan (the so-called Mad Mulla of Somaliland)—and "The Epic Love of Elmii Bonderii"—about a Somali poet—must really be read as supplements to *The Prophet's Camel Bell* and *A Tree for Poverty,* deepening our view of the breadth of Margaret Laurence's sympathies, but not really telling us much that is new about her or her work; the same might perhaps be said of "Man of Our People," a generous essay on my own book on Gabriel Dumont which gives a nonfictional expression to the special feeling for the tragedy of the métis that plays so large a part in *The Diviners* and indeed enters all but one of Margaret Laurence's Manawaka books through the presence of the métis family of the Tonnerres.

The geographical pieces in *Heart of a Stranger* that in a more or less direct way bear a relationship to Laurence's fiction similar to that of *The Prophet's Camel Bell* are two essays, "A Place to Stand On" and "Where the World Began," about her origins in Manitoba; another essay, "Road from the Isles," which tells how she came to terms with her Scottish ancestry and its mythical implications; and two pieces, "Down East" and "The Shack," which relate to the parts of Ontario formerly associated with Catherine Parr Traill and where in recent years she has chosen to live.

Curiously, at first sight at least, Ontario seems to be the only place she has been able to set in fiction at the time she was experiencing it. She wrote successfully of Africa only when she had reached Vancouver, but, as she says in one of these essays, "I always knew that one day I would have to stop writing about Africa and go back to my own people, my own place of belonging." But going back is in the mind, and not a physical return, for, as Laurence also says: "Living away from home gives a new perspective on home. I began to write out of my own background only after I had lived some years away."

And one can follow the removes by which Laurence makes sure, after she has finished writing of Africa in Vancouver, that she is still distant enough to write with fictional detachment about the worlds of her past. Going to England, she writes of Vancouver in *The Stone Angel, A Jest of God, The Fire-Dwellers,* and locates the present tense of two of the novels there. Even more, in these novels and also in the stories of *A Bird in the House,* she writes of the mythical small town of Manawaka, where the past of all the Canadian novels, and the present of *A Jest of God* and *A Bird in the House*, are set. This is the country of which Margaret Laurence says, in "A Place to Stand On":

I doubt if I can ever live there again, but those poplar bluffs and the blackness of that soil and the way in which the sky is open from one side of the horizon to the other—these are things I will carry inside my skull for as long as I live, with the vividness of recall that only our first home can have for us.

At another point in the same essay, she remarks that: "Writing, for me, has to be set firmly in some soil, some place, some other and inner territory which might be described in anthropological terms as 'cultural background'." In the Canadian novels as much as in the African novels this sense of an outer territory every bit as sharply apprehended as the inner territory of the mind is vividly present; I know of no living novelists—and very few in the past—who have quite so marvellously balanced the two necessary landscapes of fiction.

I think the relationship of *The Diviners* to what Laurence has to say about the role of place in her novels is in some ways a major key to her work, certainly as it has been manifest during the past fifteen years. At the end of the essay "Ten Years' Sentences," to which I have already referred, she makes a distinction between the local character of her writing on Africa and the more universal applicability of her writing on Canadian life.

A strange aspect of my so-called Canadian writing is that I haven't been much aware of its being Canadian, and this seems a good thing to me, for it suggests that one has been writing out of a background so closely known that no explanatory tags are necessary. I was always conscious that the novel and stories set in Ghana are *about Africa*. My last three novels seem just like novels.

One has the feeling at the same time that Laurence regards her coming to literary maturity as being linked closely with her ability to express in convincing fictional and almost mythical form her perceptions of her own country, the place of birth and childhood, and this gives a profound significance to the shifting terrain of *The Diviners*. Morag Gunn's beginnings are in Manawaka and especially linked through her scavenger guardian Christie Logan with the town dump, known, as in Margaret Laurence's native Neepawa, as

"the nuisance grounds," a phrase fraught with weird connotations, as though the effluvia of our lives was beneath contempt but at the same time was subtly threatening to the determined and sometimes hysterical propriety of our lives.

In Vancouver, Morag's child Pique is born, sired by the métis Jules Tonnerre; last of a line descending from Riel's warriors, the Tonnerres' presence long troubled the consciences of Manawaka people. And in Scotland, like Margaret Laurence, Morag comes face to face with the real meaning of her ancestry, and could have said, as her creator does in "Road from the Isles": "But this, my first view of Scotland, was in some strange way also my first true understanding of where I belonged, namely, the land where I was born," i.e. the Canadian prairie. Perhaps this experience is best summarized in Laurence's final reflections in the same essay on her trip to Scotland.

I am inclined to think that one's real roots do not extend very far back in time, nor very far forward. I can imagine and care about my possible grandchildren, and even (although in a weakened way) about my great-grandchildren. Going back, no one past my great-grandparents has any personal reality for me. I care about the ancestral past very much, but in a kind of mythical way. The ancestors, in the end, become everyone's ancestors. But the history that one can feel personally encompasses only a very few generations.

As I have said, *The Diviners* goes beyond any of Margaret Laurence's other novels because it includes the region where she is actually writing the book and a simulacrum of the river she looks out on while she works. Experience and its transmutation, in other words, have drawn together in terms of time and place, and this is the kind of encounter one can understand a writer facing with awe and perhaps regarding as creatively terminal. Yet though *The Diviners* contains the artistic transfiguration of all the experience that relates to Margaret Laurence's ancestry and youth — the memories that make her the kind of writer she is — Africa is dropped out. Unlike Laurence, Morag Gunn never goes to Africa, or anywhere outside Canada except to Britain. At this point, one has the feeling that Africa played in Margaret Laurence's writing the cathartic role, teaching her the necessary distance between experience and its imaginative reconstruction; teaching her the value of the stranger's role; preventing her — as she remarks — from writing an autobiographical first novel about her prairie youth that would have been "too prejudiced and distorted by closeness"; and giving her the subject matter out of which she could write her early fiction (too fine to be classed as apprentice work) and the magnificent farewell of *The Prophet's Camel Bell*. After that she was liberated to attempt the great task of her life up to the present, the Manawaka tetralogy. Perhaps one can end a survey of the significance of her travel writing no better than with some sentences from the final pages of *Heart of a Stranger*. For me they express — with a vividness I have rarely encountered elsewhere — the importance to novelists like Margaret Laurence of an organic link between the creative sensibility and the living environment.

The land still draws me more than other lands. I have lived in Africa and in England, but splendid as both can be, they do not have the power to move me in the same way as, for example, that part of southern Ontario where I spent four months last summer in a cedar cabin beside the river. 'Scratch a Canadian, and you find a phony pioneer,' I used to say to myself in warning. But all the same it is true, I think, that we are not yet totally alienated from physical earth, and let us only pray we do not become so.

I am not very patriotic, in the usual meaning of that word. I cannot say 'My country right or wrong' in any political, social or literary context. But one thing is inalterable, for better or worse, for life.

This is where my world begins. A world which includes the ancestors — both my own and other people's ancestors who become mine. A world which formed me, and continues to do so, even while I fought it in some of its aspects, and continue to do so. A world which gave me my own lifework to do, because it was here that I learned the sight of my own particular eyes.

[1978]

Taming the Tiger of Power: Notes on Certain Fictions by Hugh Hood

"LE METIER, C'EST tout," says the filmmaker Jean-Pierre Fauré in Hugh Hood's second novel, *The Camera Always Lies* (1967), and he goes on to attempt an adequate translation of the term into words comprehensible to a White Anglo-Saxon Protestant mind.

"Professionalism. No. Devotion to craft. No. Seriousness, calling, vocation, technique, all these things. Expertise is a part of it, but not the whole, which is where Americans go wrong, thinking that technique and expertise can storm the gates of heaven. You have to have devotion too, love, consuming ambition to use the medium properly."

Doubtless in this book Fauré is not meant to act in any direct way as Hugh Hood's spokesman, but what he says reflects Hood's sense of the complex importance of occupation, vocation, work, métier — whichever of these subtly differing words one may elect to use — in the personal as well as the collective lives of human beings, as the guarantees of private sanity and public health. I am by no means the only critic to observe that Hugh Hood's special contribution to Canadian fiction stems from his "Balzacian gift," as Dennis Duffy called it in *Canadian Literature 47*, his unique ability to show us "people seen and magnified through the technical details of their jobs." And not only their jobs, one might add, but their leisure activities as well, on which, like the football players who give the title to *A Game of Touch* (Hood's third novel), they can expend as much skill and attention as on any occupation they may follow to earn a living or to fulfil a sense of vocation.

The extraordinarily exact and particular way in which their occupations and working lives are described place Hood's characters very firmly within a social continuum. Hood has an almost mediaeval sense of the necessary pattern of vocations within which men operate, at least in a healthily functioning society, and of the importance of occupation in establishing personality. In *A Game of Touch* (1970), the country boy Jake Price begins by trying to live a "free" (and freeloading) life in Bohemian Montreal, but he only starts to show maturity as a human being after the building in which he gets free lodging is burnt down; then he gives up his vague ideas of becoming an artist at other people's expense, accepts what looks like a very mundane occupation, and settles down to marry a French-Canadian girl of startling propriety. In the reverse direction, a society without a proper pattern of occupations is seen as unviable. In Hood's fourth novel, *You Can't Get There from Here* (1972), the new country of Leofrica, cobbled out of two tribal African territories, is so economically and occupationally limited that it cannot survive as a political unit in the modern world, and the men who attempt to steer its future fail not so much because they are inept as politicians, as because there is no power for them to manipulate and therefore no way for them to pursue the political calling except nominally during the brief interlude between the declaration of independence and the collapse of the new state.

It is with this relation between occupation and power, and with the various levels on which power operates in Hood's longer fictions that I am concerned in this essay, and to illuminate these themes I shall discuss the three of his books I have already mentioned — books in which the presence and absence of power are both of central importance.

In my first references to these books, I described them all loosely as novels, meaning book-length fictions. In fact, the only one that really attempts to be a novel, in the sense of a psychologically penetrative and multidimensional study of human relations, and also succeeds as such, is *A Game of Touch*. The other books have to be viewed within their own somewhat different pretensions, where their apparent weaknesses as novels will be seen to dissolve.

In *The Camera Always Lies,* for example, Dennis Duffy and other critics have pointed to the shallowness of the actress Rose Leclair, the heroine of the book. But if one views *The Camera Always Lies* not as a novel but as a romance with satiric overtones, then Rose (devastatingly dismissed by one of the characters with the adjective "virtuous") becomes an archetypal figure, a projection of audience fantasies proper to her time of whom we no longer expect novelistic verisimilitude. Similarly, one can see *You Can't Get There from Here* as a mixture of political fantasy and political satire, written with at least half a wall-eye directed at Canada instead of Leofrica. Then the initial implausibility of the narrative acquires relevance as analogous to a geological fault that, once we accept it, shifts us into the self-consistent world of satirical fantasy. For satirical fantasy, like a mirror, is a surface where we can perceive our actual world reflected but not reproduced.

The Camera Always Lies in fact parodies the mood and reproduces the structure of the romantic Hollywood film belonging to the era that came to an end roughly when Grace Kelly abandoned acting for another kind of histrionic romance life as the Princess of Monaco. Like Kelly, Rose Leclair recognizes that the American film industry has itself become an antiromance, and she moves into the area of true romance when she marries Jean-Pierre Fauré and goes off with him at the end of the novel to play in nouvelle vague films. The book falls into three parts, "Down There," "Going Down" and "Coming Up," but "Down There" is in fact a very short prelude resembling the background action to the titles in a film, two pages describing an as yet anonymous woman lying in a motel room knocked out by an overdose of drugs and reaching for the telephone in animal reaction to death, and two further pages telling us that this is Rose Leclair and saying merely how she arrived at the motel after seeing a film called *Goody Two-Shoes* with a sense of "shame, betrayal, embarrassment and defeat."

The rest of the book completes a pattern which Hood quite often follows, "Going Down" moving to climax point about two-thirds the way through, and "Coming Up," the last third of the book, following events through to the defeat of the evil forces and the predictable happy ending. (In *You Can't Get There from Here,* where evil forces rampage uncontrolled, the ending is unhappy, but equally predictable).

Within this structure an essentially romantic plot is worked out. Rose Leclair is a comedy actress who moves out of her depth by consenting to become the star in a musical (*Goody Two-Shoes*) which involves ambitious dance sequences she is unable to master. The teen-aged supporting actress, Charity Ryan, is a better dancer than Rose and more sexually dynamic; with the connivance of the evil gnome-producers, she not only steals the film but also steals Rose's husband. Aggrieved and humiliated, Rose makes her attempt at suicide, thus undergoing the traditional romantic rite de passage, the surrogate death, and emerging to be emotionally awakened by Jean-Pierre Fauré, the prince charming of the novel, and to frustrate the producers who try to blackmail her into keeping to a contract they have morally broken by diminishing her role in the film.

There are two aspects of *The Camera Always Lies* that, as it were, anchor the romance and prevent it from drifting off into the mawkishness that always threatens when Rose (a bland and stupid heroine of a kind much favoured by Canadian novelists from Hugh MacLennan onwards) is present. One is the densening of texture by the highly particularized presentation of how films are actually made, so that one is drawn deeply into the occupational world of the participants by detailed and obviously authentic presentations of film financing, of actors' agents at work, of dance directors arranging the spectacular numbers in a musical, and, in a particularly fascinating scene with the corsetière Madame Sylvie, of dress designers making up for the imperfections of a star's body.

If such details tie *The Camera Always Lies* to the earth of verisimilitude, the sense of power working away in the background gives a seriousness of feeling that no mere narration of the plot can convey. The only kind of power absent from *The Camera Always Lies* (unlike the two other books I am discussing) is political power. But enough other kinds of power operate in counterpoint to each other to provide a complex thematic substructure.

There is the power film producers and directors exert in their manipulation of stars, their creation and destruction of careers and reputations, and the power that actors in their turn exert over the imagination of the public whose fantasies they largely create and inhabit. There is the power of sexual attraction that at one point enables Charity to destroy Rose's marriage, and at another point enables Rose to defeat Horler and Lennehan by enlisting on her side the power of finance in the person of the banker Callegerini who is able to prove how the two producers plotted from the beginning to involve Charity and Rose's husband so as to make publicity for the film. There is the creative power of the imagination which emerges in the accounts Jean-Pierre gives of the art films he has made, and the power of organization that takes its place in Max Mars, the survivor from the great days of German film who has given up his early ideals to make profitable mass-audience productions.

Directing a movie was like conducting a battle from an unhandy command post, except that a general had a staff and an intelligence service and a logistics team to supply his wants, whereas most of the co-ordinating on a film had necessarily to be planned by the director, who decided what the unit would do today and what they would do tomorrow unless it rained, in which case they would do something else, or something else.

As this passage suggests, no form of power is ever complete, in the sense that it can be used with entirely predictable results, and in fact one of the implied lessons of *The Camera Always Lies* is that different kinds of power, representing different conscious or unconscious interests, work to frustrate each other, to the benefit of the individual who is lucky enough not to get caught when they happen to work in unity. It is the sense that she is powerless, unavoidably the victim of others' manipulations, that drives Rose almost to her death; it is the sense of power reawakening within her, when Jean-Pierre offers her both love and a new career, that brings her back to life.

The Camera Always Lies is of course a double-edged title evoking the essential and proper illusionism of the cinematographic art but also the fact that the particular film in which Rose is involved and the whole operation connected with its production are mendacious in every way. The plot of the film merges into a plot in the other sense of the word, against Rose's career and her marriage, but Rose herself is trapped only because she has consented to the kind of Hollywood filmmaking which creates an artificial persona for her and which never uses her true potentialities, as we are promised Jean-Pierre Fauré will do.

If in so many ways the model for *The Camera Always Lies* is the cinematic romance, the model for *A Game of Touch* is, as we need go no farther than the title to know, the game. It is, like *The Camera Always Lies*, a title with calculated ambiguities. Seeing it first, I identified "touch" with the game of my childhood, Touch, or Touch-and-Run, in which one of the players pursues the others, trying to touch one of them as they flee him; having made a touch, he then runs like the rest and the one he has touched pursues. Overtly in the novel the game of touch is the informal kind of rugby football for a few players which provides Jake Price with his introduction to the Montreal personalities whose fluid relationships fill the novel. But right at the beginning, when Jake arrives in Montreal, a naive and gabby boy escaping from small-town Ontario, and sees the group of men playing in a park, he remarks: "Touch. That's a game I'm crazy about because you get to run and run." So it is, after all, touch and run, and the game of the novel is a pattern which becomes complete when all the characters have ceased to feel the need to run, from their pasts mostly, but sometimes from themselves.

In *A Game of Touch*, once again, people are identified by what they do. The central pattern of the book involves two interlinking personal triangles, the first involving Roger Talbot, Duncan McCallum and Marie-Ange Robinson, and the second Marie-Ange, Jake and Yvonne, but the personal pattern is dependent on the pattern of power which provides a structure for the whole novel, the structure of a game in which rewards and defeats come from the right power plays, on whatever level—political, economic, professional, amatory—power may at that moment be operative. And success in the game of power, we soon understand, does not lie in rigid adherence to a planned strategy—as is shown by the failure of Duncan's elaborate patterning of his side's play in football—but from willingness to give way and to push at the right times, and to sacrifice illusory for real success, as Roger Talbot demonstrates at the climax of the book when he assures the triumph of the political policy he has developed by accepting his own political destruction by scandal as the price for it.

Here, in assessing the development of the theme of power in *A Game of Touch*, one could add, though Hood does not make use of the term, the concept of *habileté* to that of *métier* evoked in *The Camera Always Lies*. The man who is successful in the game of power is the man who is *habile*—clever and adroit and perceptive at the same time. And one of the ways in which we can judge the *habileté* of a man is—as always in Hood—to see him in terms of his occupation. So when the two men who compete most seriously for Marie-Ange's love are introduced, we are immediately told what they do and how materially successful they are.

Duncan "was in Personnel Evaluation, doing very nicely. He had his M.A. in psychology, with a speciality in testing and personal assessment." And Duncan himself says of Roger, "he's doing mighty well for himself at the U. of M., not that anybody gets rich teaching in a university, but he does consulting for both the federal and provincial governments and sometimes in industrial work, and he does some writing. He has money of his own too. . . ."

The cultural and personal ambiguity of Marie-Ange (who first made her appearance as "Bicultural Angela" in Hood's book of stories *Around the Mountain,* and whom Jake eventually recognizes as a girl several years his senior in the school in Stoverville, Ontario) is emphasized by the fact that at first Jake does not know what she does; in Hood's terms an occupationless person is suspect. Later he finds that she conducts radio interviews for the CBC, and is actually a good craftsman in her limited field, but the very freelance fluidity of her work fits in with her dilettantish flirtations with French culture (which lead her in and out of a series of multilingual beds) and with her role as the pivot of the two triangles and thus a decisive figure in shaping the outcome of the novel.

When Jake sees Marie-Ange washed of her cosmetics and her pretences at the end of the great paint-in in Duncan's apartment, he recognizes her; afterwards he chooses Yvonne and the life of a regular salaried citizen Yvonne's mores demand. And Marie-Ange herself decides between Duncan and Roger, the finalists among her bed-partners. It is Duncan she chooses, rejecting Roger, in spite of the wealth that attracts her, because he was unable to translate his influence over the intellectual youth of Montreal into visible political power. With that choice, a play for sexual power that has been going on throughout the novel is worked to its conclusion. Marie-Ange shows her power by forcing Roger to demand a choice; she confirms Duncan's power — the power of racial kinship among other things — by choosing him; by rejecting Roger, she confirms him in his special kind of power, which is that of the solitary man who lives by his own moral strength.

It takes Roger a long time to realize this — to recognize his true métier. As an academic political theorist he becomes involved as consultant turned negotiator in the power play of federal-political negotiations in Ottawa. He is a kind of Trudeau without Trudeau's political ruthlessness. He talks of the "idea of the first really modern state — a post-Marxist state — a rationally organized society where the needs of all groups are met with real flexibility — to take the ball away from the anarchists."

But when he goes to Ottawa, he discovers that power there is not seen as the ability to create a rational society; it is regarded as a force in its own right, a gift to be grasped and held. He sees "the need for power, and I don't understand it. I don't need power." For him the real issues "had something to do with people's feelings, with their wish to be let alone and run their own lives." But precisely because he has not courted the people, has not learnt their whims and prejudices, has dedicated himself to the achievement of an "international economic community," Roger finds himself vulnerable, is branded in Québec as a traitor and a *vendu*, and has to be content that his policies are successful though he is a political failure.

"It's no good having the best of intentions if you have no power base . . . . Never let your conscience be your guide, Roger," says the minister on receiving Talbot's resignation. "I see that," answers Roger. "I see that." He returns to the academic world stripped of his illusions of a politics of reason, and deprived of Marie-Ange, who symbolically reinforces his remark that "power is just disguised sensation, and mainly sexual sensation." Roger has the last sentences of the book, as the players gather for the game of touch and he is not present. "I'd be just as glad if Roger didn't come out," says Duncan. "He never stays in his patterns."

Whatever power Roger has is the power of the morally and intellectually detached man who can retain his integrity in the face of public and of personal defeat alike. But this is a very different kind of power from that of the patternmaker. Ideally, Duncan is a radical utopian, thinking in socialist patterns, but in fact he is deeply involved in the capitalist patterning of human beings. The sinister alliance of managerial power and psychological manipulation in such patterning is shown when Hood portrays Duncan at work as a personnel officer for the multinational combine significantly called Continental. Duncan, in reality, is no more than an adroit student in this particular game of power, for the great manipulator is Sam Tate, a heavily moustached man of dubious antecedents and unfathomable nature, somewhat like Wyndham Lewis's jocular-sinister hollow-men characters.

Nobody at Continental knew better than Sam Tate how the whole picture fitted together. He didn't know anything, and cared less, about finance or design or sales. What he could grasp immediately and with the insight of genius was the way in which men related to one another, the way their power struggles would evolve, how their hidden reactions to each other would affect their functioning together. He had enjoyed three sensational, eye-opening successes in the seven years he'd been at Continental. In the first year he'd been asked to evaluate a potential vice-president (finance) and had sent in a thumbs-down. His report had been ignored and the appointment made. Fourteen months later this vice-president had killed himself after a series of disastrous policy errors.

Sometimes people had overridden Sam's recommendations after that but never without thinking about them long and hard; he had gone from strength to strength and now enjoyed a position that was assailable, but not very.

On a large and blatant scale, Sam Tate and Duncan are doing what most of the other people in the novel, even pseudoinnocent Jake Price, do all the time; manipulating other people less for what can be gained than from the sheer pleasure of manipulation, which confers a sense of power. Even strait-laced Yvonne has her moment of realized power when she knows she has extricated Jake from Marie-Ange's spell. And this pattern of manipulation finds an appropriate form in the multiple points of view from which the action of *A Game of Touch* is seen. Jake, with his *faux-naif* chatter, is the narrator whose search for a haven in Montreal enables him to look into the lives of all the other characters; he alone speaks in the first person, and eleven of the twenty-four chapters are given to his *ingenu*, Emperor's-clothes view of the lives of the people he encounters and eventually, when he enters the employ of Continental, joins as an equal. The other thirteen chapters are divided among Roger, Duncan, Marie-Ange and Yvonne, and now the omniscient novelist speaks in the third person, and exposes the minds and motives of the characters as well as recording their actions and their speech. So what Jake sees is constantly opposed to what happens in the minds of the other characters, and we see how much people hide in the game of power they play with each other on so many levels. Touch-and-Run is the name of the game, and because we are meant to see it as a game, nobody is hurt in the end. Everyone comes, with some pain, to a degree of self-understanding. Like Jake, whose great trial comes when he escapes from a building in flames and gets away with a few harmless burns on his legs, they are scorched in the flames of disillusionment, Roger with Ottawa and all it represents, Jake with the life of the artist, Marie-Ange with the biculturalism of the bed, and emerge in some way tempered, sadder certainly and perhaps wiser.

In *You Can't Get There from Here* there are no reprieves for those unfitted to handle power, and if it is not quite a situation in which "The best lack all conviction, while the worst / Are full of passionate intensity," it is certainly true that the best lack political adroitness and mostly die, while the worst possess it and survive.

Leofrica, the mythical land in which this brutal and sardonic tale unfolds, is strangely isolated in both history and geography, with no common past but the political unity which alien administrators imposed on its two great tribes, the Ugeti of the highlands and the Pineals of the coastal plains, and no real context in space, since we know nothing about the unnamed country beyond the mountains from which the Albanian Zogliu eventually engineers his bid for power, or the country beyond the river from which Amélie de Caulaincourt arrives in the guise of a pitiful refugee from political persecution. Leofrica is a land whose coast is shrouded in perpetual mists and protected by shifting quicksands. It has no industrial life and its economy is based on a great production of groundnuts by the Pineals, whose oil comprises the only export, and on subsistence herding among the Ugeti, whose cattle are virtually dying from interbreeding. Politically, it is almost an innocent land, since the two tribal peoples, in spite of legendary hostilities, have in fact had very little harmful contact and only really recognize each other when power seems a reality in their land and they begin to struggle for it.

But the structures and the skills on which modern political power is based do not really exist in Leofrica. "Do you remember the tabula rasa theory of the mind?" says the multinational industrialist MacSweyn to the American Ambassador. "This place feels like that. It's like living in a balloon filled with a very thin, rather intoxicating sun. Nothing exists yet in this country."

Even when Leofrica emerges as a country, it has no financial foundation, and no national power structure. A provisional government is appointed, headed by Anthony Jedeb, the country's most celebrated scholar. "In another country Anthony Jedeb might have been a county agricultural expert. In the emerging Leofrica he was President and Prime Minister." Jedeb, who sees his police force as the only stable institution in the country, gathers a cabinet of amiable and unamiable incompetents, carefully balancing Pineals, Ugeti and useful nonindigenes, but one of his two closest and most capable advisers is an agent of the American secret service and the other of the Russian NKVD. Amélie de Caulaincourt, the Russian agent, with whom Anthony is in love, remarks of him: "He is not a fool at all, but he is a kind, good man, and this makes him politically incapable."

Anthony is in fact the one man in the country who is a real Leofrican, because he is able to rise above tribe, and to conceive not only of his people as a unity but also of the world. The speech he makes at the exhibition of Ugeti art shortly after his assumption of the illusion of power is one of the rare clear moral moments in this sardonic book. Speaking on a sudden impulse, as he eats the food of his Ugeti ancestors during the ceremonial dinner, he talks of the murderousness of the notions of group identity that dominate people in so many ways.

"My people, my tribe, my class, my clan, my caste, are not yours and cannot be yours. It is the exclusiveness of these notions that makes them so bloody. Even scientists give them this exclusiveness. The anthropologist tries to get clear the peculiarities of tribe or caste or clan. The political scientist shows how nation or people insist on separateness. Of these notions, only that of the family is peacefully neutral, for when we think of our family we take others in — not thinking of them as outsiders. We speak easily of the family of mankind, of human brotherhood, of the fatherhood of God. Indeed God is member of no clan or caste. But He is Our Father, and the creator of the family. Strange truth.

"Sitting here, eating this communal meal, I am again a member of my tribe."

This statement created a minor sensation and coincided with louder noises in the street.

"This makes me feel happy and good, but it is a false contentment, spurious goodness. I cannot now regress to tribalism."

Glances from one Ugeti cabinet minister to the next. Startled exchanges between Americans. Russian silences.

This speech develops Anthony's earlier statement, at the inauguration of the new state, that "In our country a man is first of all a herdsman of the highlands or a planter of the lowlands. That is the first fact we have to recognize in the founding of our united state. There are two peoples here." It is a statement that in true Hoodish manner emphasizes the occupational meagreness — and hence social backwardness — of Leofrica, but it also provokes the thought that on one level *You Can't Get There from Here* is an oblique satire on modern Canada, which has two peoples and is occupationally too little varied (with its excessive dependence on primary industry and its vulnerability to American pressures) for its economic good. The theme should not be overemphasized, but an alertness to it will reveal a number of wryly disguised reflections on the perils of dependence that can be applied to the Canadian condition.

When Anthony is making his speech against divisiveness, he is already a lost man and Leofrica a lost country, though he is not yet aware of it. *You Can't Get There from Here* is built up in an almost classically tragic structure, with the first part, "On the Surface," presenting the picture of a new democracy emerging, if not exactly full of promise, decidedly hopeful, and looking forward to the kind of postimperial survivorship that many small countries have sustained for decades by playing off the main power groups against each other. "Leofrican foreign policy could only have one tendency, that of getting as much money into the country as possible, from any source that offered."

The speech at the Ugeti art show takes place towards the end of the second and largest part of *You Can't Get There from Here,* entitled "Underground," during which we are made aware that Leofrica has become the scene of fervent plotting, not only on the part of the Americans and the Russians, with their agents in the government, but also of Zogliu, the Albanian minister and undercover representative of the Chinese Communists. There is a peculiar twist to these imperial ploys. Tired of a plethora of uneconomic client states, both the Russians and the Americans are seeking to saddle each other with unhappy Leofrica. The Russians send a scientific expedition into the interior, and then engineer an Ugeti massacre of their own experts to prove that this is an impossible country for mining enterprises. The Americans burn down their own groundnut oil plant so as to leave the Russians with a ruined economy to shore up. Each country exercises its power negatively, to evade rather than assume control, and so they create a vacuum into which move the only outside power interested in controlling Leofrica and the only man in Leofrica who has a genuine sense of power. Zogliu, drawing on Chinese resources, provides the means for a neo-Maoist coup, and Abdelazar, second-in-command of Jedeb's beloved constabulary, deserts with his best men to join Zogliu in the Ugeti country and create a "liberating" army in the highlands. Giving a modern twist to Napoleon's reputed statement that "An army marches on its stomach," Abdelazar and Zogliu win over the hungry Ugeti tribesmen by advancing with brigades of field kitchens.

The third part of the book, "Underwater," shows Leofrica in disintegration; the consequences of the betrayals already described take their course and end in inevitable catastrophe. The Leofrican currency receives no support in foreign markets. The finance minister and the justice minister flee with the country's foreign currency reserves. Another minister is murdered by Abdelazar and a fourth dies of heart attack through overwork. When news of the situation in Ugetiland reaches the coast, tribal conflict — unknown before in Leofrica on a mass scale — breaks out, as the Pineals hunt down and massacre the Ugeti workers in the towns and plantations. As the Russians and the Americans make their getaways, the semblance of government as well as the real underlying order vanish, yet the lust for power remains as the mobs range through the shabby capital of Newport and General Abdelazar's army is poised to attack the lowlands. Anthony flees from the presidential palace with the mob on his heels, and escapes to the river dividing Leofrica from the unnamed neighbouring country. He swims for safety and seems within reach of the farther shore when soldiers stationed there start shooting at him.

They did not want to admit him into exile. This fire grew intense and the current was carrying him towards it. In moments he was on the edge of a grid of bullet tracks. Then he was into it. Then he was hit twice in the right shoulder. That's it, he thought, Amélie's work, she has kept up her contacts. These people weren't firing arbitrarily. They were firing at him personally, and they were coming closer. The right arm was useless. He dived again, this time right to the bottom.

If there is a lesson one might extract from these three books, it can possibly be stated in terms of the relationship between power and order. Hood seems to suggest that power is a reality and order a desideratum in any kind of social existence. When a pattern of moral balances exists between people, as it does in both *The Camera Always Lies* and *A Game of Touch*, the abuse of power in personal relationships is not allowed to get out of hand, and when an accepted moral order exists in a society, political power tends more often to be turned to positive than to negative ends. But when power ceases to be related to the sense of order and is used, as the Americans and the Russians do in *You Can't Get There from Here*, to subvert what order exists and to destroy the men who, like Anthony, represent the seeds of good in a society, then it is entirely negative in its consequences. In creating a moral vacuum, power without order opens a way to the starker forms of power in which the semblance of order is used to disguise tyranny. The process is stated with exemplary cynicism by Mr. Zogliu. " 'Regularity in all things, even in revolution. It is the cardinal principle of statecraft, the principal means of making a usurper seem legitimate.' "

This, of course, is only one of a series of possible glosses on the three novels I have discussed. Another—which I find personally more attractive—is that the moral man (Roger in *A Game of Touch,* Anthony in *You Can't Get There from Here*) can survive and fulfil his proper destiny only outside the fatal circle of power. In other words, as Proudhon said, "anarchy is order," and true order is different in its nature from power. Roger thinks to "take the ball away from the anarchists," but leaves it with them when he fails through allying himself with the politicians. Of course, I am far from suggesting that Hood really thinks that in his great game of touch the ball does remain with the anarchists, yet that is one of a series of possible projections of the three fictions I have discussed. Equally credible is the other projection which sees power as a necessary evil of our human condition, the burning tiger of our destiny, and philosophy as its uncertain tamer.

[1978]

Memory, Imagination, Artifice: The Late Short Fictions of Mavis Gallant

... je suis seul, isolé, expatrié au milieu de ma famille et dans ma patrie!

Blaise Cendrars

ABSOLUTE PLAUSIBILITY, though not mimesis as such, I take to be one of the principal goals of fiction. The vision, no matter how fantastic, must convince the reader through its self-consistency. And absolute plausibility demands absolute artifice, not faith to actuality, which is why Flaubert outshines Zola and Chekhov outlives Guy de Maupassant. It is also why Mavis Gallant, though little recognized in Canada, outwrites most other Canadians. If I had to define her short fictions — novellas and short stories — setting aside obvious matters of theme and narrative construction, I would — and shall — talk about the impeccable verbal texture and the marvellous painterly surface of the scene imagined through the translucent veil of words, the kind of surface that derives from a close and highly visual sense of the interrelationship of sharply observed detail.

It would need a whole volume for the kind of study that might examine and relate the autonomous worlds of all Mavis Gallant's short fictions, of which there must be about a hundred, by no means all of them collected into volumes. In this essay I have decided to restrict myself to sixteen stories, which fall into three rather clearly defined groups in terms of terrain and theme. They are all fairly late stories, the first of them dating from the early 1960s and most from the 1970s, at least in terms of publication. Given Mavis Gallant's inclination to work intermittently on stories over long periods, the date of publication is not an entirely reliable clue to the time when writing first began, though it usually is an indication of the completion point of the work which emerges out of the long process of reordering and reduction to which every story by Gallant is subjected almost as if it were sculpture.

These sixteen stories all concern people who in some way or another are alone, isolated, expatriated, even when they remain within their families or return to their fatherlands. One of the most significant features of Mavis Gallant's fiction is that, while she has never restricted herself to writing about Canada or about Canadians, and has written more than most creators of fiction on people of other cultures whose inner lives she could enter only imaginatively, she has never, during her period as a mature writer, written from immediate observation of people living in her here-and-now. Distance in time and place seem always necessary.

Almost all the stories I shall be discussing have been written in Paris, where Gallant has lived most of the time since she left Canada in 1950. By now she has so lived herself into the Gallic environment that most of her friends speak French, and the depth of her involvement in French affairs was shown very clearly in "The Events in May: A Paris Notebook" (*The New Yorker,* 14 September, 21 September 1968), which recounted her adventures and observations during the abortive revolutionary situation of 1968 in France.

The "Notebook" dealt almost exclusively with French people and their reactions to events around them, and it showed the same sharp observation of action, speech and setting that one finds in Gallant's stories. There were parts, one felt, that only needed to be taken out of the linear diary form and reshaped by the helical patterning of memory for them to become the nuclei of excellent stories. Perhaps one day they will, but up to now Mavis Gallant has rarely written in fiction about these Parisians among whom she lives. What happens when she infrequently does so is shown in "The Cost of Living," where the two young French bohemians of the story (only one of them a Parisian) are less important than the two Australian sisters whom they exploit and whose education in "the cost of living" — to be interpreted emotionally as well as financially — provides the theme as well as the title of the story.

Similarly, though Mavis Gallant has written on occasion about Canadians in Europe, who usually find it hard to accept the life-styles they encounter (or avoid encountering), it took her twenty years after her departure from Montreal to turn to the imaginative reconstruction of the vanished city of her childhood and youth, in the five interlinked Linnet Muir stories which have appeared in *The New Yorker* but are as yet uncollected. These examples of memory transmuted, which in intention at least bring Mavis Gallant very close to the Proust she has admired so greatly, form one group among the stories I shall be discussing.

It is virtually impossible to escape memory as a potent factor in Mavis Gallant's stories, and the next group of fictions, while they do not draw on the memory of personal experience, are imaginative constructions in which remembered observations and remembered history play a great part. They concern the Germans (a people Mavis Gallant does not know from experience as well as she knows the Canadians or the French or even the English), and specifically the post-Nazi Germans. One novella and six stories are here involved. The novella and five of the stories comprise the volume entitled *The Pegnitz Junction;* one other German story, "The Latehomecomer," appeared in *The New Yorker* (8 July 1974), but so far it has not been collected.

The last group are tales of people trapped as foreigners in the meretricious vacation worlds of continental Europe. The main characters in three of the stories — all set on the Riviera — are English, remnants of a decaying imperial order, at once predators and victims: these are "An Unmarried Man's Summer" (*My Heart is Broken,* 1964), "The Tunnel" (*The End of the World and Other Stories,* 1974), and "The Four Seasons" (*The New Yorker,* 16 June 1975). The fourth, "Irina" (*The New Yorker,* 2 December 1974), is one of those rare stories in which Mavis Gallant touches on the literary life; its eponymous heroine is the widow — Russian by descent — of a famous Swiss novelist, but here too there is an English character who is not quite minor.

These four stories I shall discuss first, since they are more closely linked than the other groups with the earlier and perhaps more familiar Gallant stories about English-speaking foreigners travelling or uneasily resident in Europe which form the greater part of her earlier volumes, *The Other Paris* (1956) and *My Heart is Broken.* And they show fairly constant Gallant characteristics.

To begin, there is no real generic division so far as Gallant is concerned between short stories, novellas and novels. She rarely writes the kind of story which Chekhov and de Maupassant so often produced, in which an episode is treated as if it were a detached fragment of life, and the psychological insight or the moving symbol or even the ironic quip at existence is regarded as sufficient justication for the telling.

Mavis Gallant never uses fiction with such aphoristic intent; she is neither an episodic writer nor an intentional symbolist, though in her own way she is certainly an ironist. Her stories are rarely bounded by time or place. Where the overt action is trapped in a brief encounter at one place, memory is always there to deepen and extend whatever action we have witnessed; sometimes the memory emerges in dialogue, sometimes in the thoughts of the participants, sometimes it is offered by the narrator, and this multiplicity of viewpoints is again typical of Mavis Gallant, and creates a kind of story never bounded by what "happens" within it, always extending in time beyond the overt present, and tending, no matter what way of evoking memory is used, to produce a kind of fictional "life," however condensed it may be.

This kind of biographical sweep is one of the special features of Gallant's fiction, making a story like "An Unmarried Man's Summer" the life portrait not only of an individual but also of a whole doomed caste of Englishmen. It means that her stories are never like fish hauled out of the flow of existence and left to gasp rapidly to their ends; they are, rather, left to swim in their element, which is the imagination that rejects the beginnings and ends necessary to linear fiction. Every one of the four stories I am now discussing is in this sense suspended in mid-flow; we are made aware of the past that has brought us to this particular eddy in time, and we even have an inkling of how the future might flow on out of the eddy. Gallant's novellas, and her novels, only differ from the short stories in their greater complexity and in the fact that more of a life is worked out within the observed present of the fiction.

I think the point I have made about Mavis Gallant's lack of an inclination towards intentional symbolism is really related to this aspect of her fiction. It is not a naturalistic fiction, but it is a fiction of enhanced reality, in which life is reshaped by artifice, but not distorted; part of the artifice is in fact to give this imaginative reshaping of existence a verisimilitude more self-consistent than that of existence itself. This means that what the story actually contains and not what it may suggest is of primary importance. The final effect of the story may be symbolic, but it is not written with symbolic intent in the same way as, say, plays like Ibsen's *Wild Duck* and Chekhov's *Seagull,* in which the named and central symbol becomes so important that the very action is shaped to fit it and in the end the ultimate goal of the whole work seems to have been no more than to give the symbol a manifestation in human life.

The difference can be seen if we look directly at "In the Tunnel." In this longish story a Canadian girl named Sarah, infatuated with a half-baked professor of sociology, is shipped off by her father to Grenoble, which she immediately leaves by the Route Napoleon, heading for the Mediterranean. Here she falls in with an Englishman, a former colonial civil servant named Roy Cooper, who charms her into going to live with him in the Tunnel, which turns out to be "a long windowless room with an arched whitewashed ceiling," in the grounds of a bungalow in the hills away from the sea, belonging to a couple named Tim and Meg Reeve, who actually detest the Mediterranean and have come here as refugees from the enormities of labour governments in Britain.

Sarah falls hopelessly, masochistically, in love with Roy, who turns out to be appropriately sadistic, a typical English cad in whom the colonial years of witnessing hangings and inspecting prisons have encouraged a natural cruelty and a brutal conservatism. The Reeves are lower middle class "characters," speaking an absurd private language, feeding coarsely, despising everyone who is not English, and treating their impossible dogs (the "boys") to endless "chocky bits." They openly talk of Sarah as yet another in Roy's long succession of feminine appendages, and Sarah shows herself endlessly vulnerable. "In love she had to show her own face, and speak in a true voice, and she was visible from all directions."

Everything seems to go well until Sarah cracks her ankle and limps around with a grotesque swelling on her leg. Roy immediately turns away from her with distaste; his sadism is accompanied by an aesthete's repugnance for anything ugly or imperfect (he describes hangings as ways of ridding the world of flawed people), and Sarah's flaw, however accidentally produced, robs him even of desire, let alone the love he pretended to feel. He turns insultingly cold and, after a final monstrous incident in which they go on a picnic to visit a chapel housing a painting of the hanged Judas, and Sarah gets drunk on the liquor from a jar of plums in brandy, he refuses even to speak to her, and she trails away, swollen ankle and all, in despair. It is only at this moment, as Sarah goes on to her next failure in love, that the Reeves show themselves, under their coarse exteriors, as possessing the remnants of human kindness, covered over by layers of prejudice that clog their perceptions and allow them to reveal their good qualities only under stress and always too late.

The Tunnel is there in the solid centre of the story, the place where Sarah and Roy live, typical of the sluttier fringe of life on the Côte d'Azur. Victim and predator are trapped within this one room so that when the relationship becomes impossible, when the predator is sated, the only way out is for one — the victim — to go. Thus we first see the Tunnel as part of the actual area of living. It is the physical setting and in part the physical cause of what happens rather than — primarily — its symbol. But on another level it is a figure suggesting the tunnel of self-repetition in which each of the characters lives, the narrowness of insight and of view that limits their sense of life. Sarah at least can flee; for Roy and the Reeves the tunnels are unending, with darkness all the way. But the symbol is secondary and consequent; it is not contained within the story as the real Tunnel is.

Less obvious in its cruelty, though as devastating in revealing the futility that marks the life of a class of people for whom history has no further use, "An Unmarried Man's Summer" is the tale of Walter Henderson, a harmless homosexual living on the Riviera with his Italian valet Angelo, a repellent youth whom Walter rescued from slum life when he was still a graceful boy. Walter has not always been what we see him in the present of the story, when he is living in the villa called Les Anémones (where only irises grow), pursuing an empty routine "where nothing could be more upsetting than a punctured tire or more thrilling than a sunny day." The story coils from past into present and back to past again, telling us through flash after flash of memory about Walter's past, about the wartime heroism he has chosen to forget, about the childhood which in the summer of the story comes galloping back when his beloved sister and her born-to-failure Anglo–Irish husband, on their way home from an effort at farming in South Africa, plant themselves on him with their two undisciplined children.

There is a sharp ironic tone to "An Unmarried Man's Summer," in which Gallant is pursuing one of her favourite aims, to reveal the inconsistency between expectations — particularly romantic expectations — and reality. Summers are the dullest times in Walter's years, when his phone never rings because the rich ladies on whom he dances attendance have gone away to avoid the hordes of summer vacationers, whom he escapes by hiding in his villa with Angelo and his old cat, William of Orange. Theoretically, the arrival of his sister, to whom he was once deeply attached, should relieve the seasonal tedium. In fact, it merely disrupts Walter's routine of life-avoidance and tangles the web of illusion in which he prefers to remain suspended.

Walter's brother-in-law is coarse and boring. His sister perpetually criticizes him, trying to show up the emptiness of his parasitic existence. And parents and children alike spoil Angelo, who turns under their influence into a sulky lout far different from the appealing boy Walter had thought he would always remain; they even try to entice him away to work on the farm they propose to start in England. When they go, leaving behind them a discontented and intolerable Angelo, the summer is ended, the rich ladies come back, and Walter remakes the invasion into a series of amusing stories as he returns to the empty relationships that make his life.

He tells his stories in peaceful dining rooms, to a circle of loving, attentive faces. He is surrounded by the faces of women. Their eyes are fixed on him dotingly, but in homage to another man: a young lover killed in the 1914 war; an adored but faithless son.

People in Mavis Gallant's stories tend to live vicariously and on a surface whose perturbations show their inner storms; tend to reveal pathos rather than tragedy. What she writes is a kind of comedy of manners, dry as Austen, sharp as Peacock. Her characters have tragic flaws enough, but catastrophe always looms, either in past or future, and rarely materializes in the present of the stories. People are not seen to die, though deaths may be remembered or foreseen or happen in the distance. And, as in

Greek tragedy, a great power is often built up by the mere sense of violence offstage or of doom impending but delayed.

A good example of this aspect of Mavis Gallant's work is "The Four Seasons," a story about expatriates on the Italian Riviera, seen through the eyes of Carmela, an Italian village girl who becomes a maid to the Unwins, a feckless English couple living rather meagrely by providing a variety of services — a real estate bureau, hand printing, etc. — for the local foreign community. The story is bounded by Carmela's arrival one Easter and her departure a year afterwards, and the stages of her experience are marked by sections corresponding to the four seasons of the title — spring, summer, autumn, winter, with a final section devoted to the spring of her departure when Italy enters World War II and the English leave.

On one level it is the story of Carmela's education through her encounter with these always incomprehensible foreigners. On the other it is a picture of expatriate society seen through Carmela's eyes; the distancing her view provides enables us to watch from the outside, as we would in a theatre, the behavior of these people who reveal themselves by what they say and do, not by what they think. In this sense the story is very dramatic, its key scenes being passages of dialogue that take place mostly in rooms and in which some people who deeply influence the action are spoken of but never appear. The use of Carmela as an observer enables us to gain a close knowledge of expatriate behavior without too many scenes in which characters are directly involved. To give one example, a great deal is made by English ladies of the rash pulpit remarks of the new young clergyman in view of the difficult political situation in this year of European war, but we are never taken to church and we encounter the priest only twice, once in Mrs. Unwin's house and once in a café. Yet by the reactions of the expatriates we are able to understand not only their prejudices but also the fears they hardly dare express.

For behind all that goes on overtly, behind the chitchat in villas and the compulsive cheeseparing manoeuvres of the Unwins (who live with vague scandals in their background), stands the reality of war. Nobody is killed, and when Italy finally enters the conflict it looks as though the English colony will all escape, even if they are beggared in the process. Only the Jews are arrested, yet even their fates are in suspension, threatened but not consummated.

Near the Franco-Italian border Carmela sees the wise and amiable Dr. Chaffee being led under armed guard.

As though he had seen on her face an expression he wanted, he halted, smiled, shook his head. He was saying "No" to something. Terrified, she peeked again, and this time he lifted his hand, palm outward, in a curious greeting that was not a salute. He was pushed on. She never saw him again.

In the end it is not the Unwins who have exploited her that Carmela most vividly remembers, but this encounter whose tragic intimations she appears to sense: "What she retained, for the present, was one smile, one gesture, one man's calm blessing."

"Irina" takes us out of the moribund society of English expatriates on the Riviera to the between-world of Switzerland that is the frontier of the Germany of *The Pegnitz Junction*. Irina's own origins are not Germanic but Russian-Swiss, and there is a clue to them in the fact that two months before the story appeared in *The New Yorker* Mavis Gallant published in the *New York Times Book Review* (6 October 1974) an extensive review of *Daughter of a Revolutionary,* whose central figure is Natalie Herzen: after associating with those formidable revolutionaries, Michael Bakunin and Sergei Nechaev, Natalie lived out her long life as a Swiss lady of Russian birth and independent means. Irina's antecedents are deliberately left rather vague, to show how far, until widowed, she fell in the shadow of her husband, Richard Notte, one of those dynamically boring European literary men, rather like Romain Rolland, who were on the right side in every good cause, writing, speaking, signing manifestos, and behaving with profligate generosity to everyone but their own families, who were expected to exist in self-sacrificing austerity.

He could on occasion enjoy wine and praise and restaurants and good-looking women, but these festive outbreaks were on the rim of his real life, as remote from his children — as strange and distorted to them — as some other country's colonial wars.

The early part of "Irina" is seen through the eyes of a third person narrator; it is a look at the literary life, and significantly it is an outside look. Gallant, as she remarked to Geoffrey Hancock in an interview published in the *Canadian Fiction Magazine* (No. 28, 1978), found after she had written the story that she identified not with her fellow writer, the formidable Notte, but with Irina, his patient wife. And this implicit rejection of the great man of letters prompts one to remark, in parenthesis, how little of the conventionally literary there is in Gallant's attitude or even her work. She avoids literary circles and has no theories about writing; she does not compose self-consciously in advance, but, as she reveals in the interview I have already mentioned, writes it all down in a compulsive rush and then reduces and polishes; it is then that her power of artifice comes into play and the composition that emerges is likely to be spatial like a painting rather than linear like conventional fiction, and the visual appeal to the mind's eye is as important in it as the verbal appeal to the mind's ear. There is perhaps a vestige of Gallant's past of left-wing enthusiasms in Notte, but that past she has abandoned completely, and this may be why she attaches it to a male writer made safely dead by the time the story begins. Her mature work is in no way male and ideological; it is feminine and intuitive, and the rightness of detail and surface which are so striking come not from intellectual deliberation but from a sense of rightness as irrational but as true as absolute pitch.

"In loving and unloving families alike," the narrator remarks, "the same problem arises after a death. What to do about the widow?" Irina in fact arranges matters quietly but very much to her own satisfaction, so that it is she whom we find in control of the posthumous fate of Notte's papers, and displaying a caustic and independent good sense in assessing their importance. Yet her children still feel obliged to carry out a kind of King-Lear-in-miniature act by entertaining her by turns at Christmas. Finally the Christmas comes when every son and daughter is abroad or engaged or in trouble, and there is nowhere for Irina to go. The solution is to send Riri, her grandson, to spend the season with her, and the boy sets off with great self-sufficiency, arriving to find that his grandmother already has a visitor, an old Englishman named Mr. Aiken. The rest of the story is seen a little through Irina's eyes, but mainly through Riri's, and what the child's eye reveals is the liberation which can come with someone else's death, for Irina now follows a vague and comfortable life that is very much her own, indulging without needing them, her children's anxieties about her, thinking a little of the great Notte —her recollections of whom bore Riri—but finding in her renewed friendship with Aiken the sweet pleasure of looking down a path her life might have taken but did not. Hers is the marvellous self-sufficiency which realizes that "anything can be settled for a few days a time, but not for longer."

In the four stories I have been discussing, memory is important both as method and content, and the past, whose relationship to the present may seem as much spatial as chronological, is vitally there in our awareness. To an even greater extent this is true of the Linnet Muir stories, which are nothing less than deep immersions in memory, divings into a sunken world. A condition in which memory takes one constantly between past and present seems to Gallant a normal state of mind. And that gives a special significance to the group of stories about Germany, mostly included in *The Pegnitz Junction*, which are quite different from anything else she has written.

They are about people whose memories have become atrophied; about people who have drawn blinds over the past. In writing such anti-Proustian stories Mavis Gallant was deliberately abandoning the very approach through reminiscence, with all its possibilities of suggestive indirection, which she had used so successfully in her earlier stories. She was entering into situations where the present had to be observed and recorded directly and starkly since memory had become so shrivelled and distorted that only what was before one's eye could give a clue to the past. Memory can play a part only in the limited sense of the author's remembered observations. Such a rigorous departure from an accustomed manner is a test, and Mavis Gallant passed it well; her German stories are some of her most impressive, and I think she is right when she says to Geoffrey Hancock that the novella "The Pegnitz Junction" is "the best thing I've ever written."

In the same interview, Gallant traces these stories to her interest in "the war and Fascism" and sees their origin in a set of photographs of concentration camp victims which she was given to write a newspaper story about before she left Montreal. Once she had got over the immediate horror, the deeper questions began occurring to her. "What we absolutely had to find out was what has happened in a civilized country, why the barriers of culture, of religion, hadn't held, what had broken down and why." The questions remained with her and she went to Germany "like a spy" to find out for herself. "*The Pegnitz Junction,*" she says, "is not a book about Fascism, but it's certainly a book about where it came from."

In the last paragraph I have repeated what Mavis Gallant says elsewhere because she presents in her stories something different from what I have seen through my own experience of marrying into a German family and of having gone to the country to live at fairly close quarters with Germans at least every other year since 1950. In my view, what Mavis Gallant really discovered, and what she presents in these stories, is not where "Fascism" (I would prefer the exacter word *Nazism*) came from, since that world of Nazi origins hardly exists in the memories of Germans who are not historians, but rather the emerging world of modern Germany which the Nazi age like a black curtain has cut off from the traditional past, so that only men in their eighties talk of "the good old Kaiserzeit" and nobody talks of the Weimar age.

I shall deal especially with "The Pegnitz Junction" itself, since this novella has a unique interest on a number of levels, but first I would say that what strikes me most about the other German stories is that they are almost all about people whose pasts have been mentally and even physically obliterated: people in other words who are exiled in the most dreaded way of all, by being banished from themselves. As the narrator says in "An Alien Flower," when she talks about her daughter born since the war: "I saw then that Roma's myths might include misery and sadness, but my myths were bombed, vanished and whatever remained had to be cleaned and polished and kept bright."

The central character of "An Alien Flower" is a girl named Bibi, doomed to the suicide that eventually overtakes her, who comes to western Germany out of Silesia by way of refugee camps, having lost a past she may have forgotten deliberately, or involuntarily — we are never sure which.

She never mentioned her family or said how they had died. I could only guess that they must have vanished in the normal way of a recent period — killed at the front, or lost without trace in the east, or burned alive in air raids. Who were the Brünings? Was she ashamed of them? Were they Socialists, radicals, troublemakers, black-marketeers, prostitutes, wife-beaters, informers, Witnesses of Jehovah? . . . Whoever the Brünings were, Bibi was their survivor, and she was as pure as the rest of us in the sense that she was alone, swept clean of friends and childhood myths and of childhood itself. But someone, at some time, must have existed and must have called her Bibi. A diminutive is not a thing you invent for yourself.

The use of the word "pure" in this context is significant, since it expresses the desire to see suffering as expiation, but it has a certain grim irony when one associates it with the narrator's remark that: "Anyone who had ever known me or loved me had been killed in one period of seven weeks." The idea of purification and the idea of forgetting or losing the past are closely linked in these stories. In "The Old Friends," a police commissioner has a sentimental attachment to an actress, Helena, cherished in West Germany as a token Jewess, one who as a child inexplicably survived the death camps. "Her true dream is of purification, of the river never profaned, from which she wakes astonished — for the real error was not that she was sent away but that she is here, in a garden, alive." As for the commissioner, knowing "like any policeman . . . one meaning for every word," he cannot deny the horror of the experiences forced on his friend as a child, but he seeks desperately in his mind for a reason to think it all a mistake, something for which a single erring bureaucrat could be punished, rather than something for which his people as a whole might bear some responsibility.

He would like it to have been, somehow, not German. When she says that she was moved through transit camps on the edge of the old Germany, then he can say, 'So, most of it was on foreign soil!' He wants to hear how hated the guards were when they were Slovak, or Ukrainian. The vast complex of camps in Silesia is on land that has become Polish now, so it is as if those camps had never been German at all. Each time she says a foreign place-name he is forgiven, absolved. What does it matter to her? Reality was confounded long ago.

Then there is Ernst, the demobilized Foreign Legionary in "Ernst in Civilian Clothes," whom we encounter in the Paris flat of his friend Willi; Ernst is about to return to the Germany he left as a teenage prisoner many years before. Ernst, we are told,

knows more than Willi because he has been a soldier all his life. He knows there are no limits to folly and pain, except fatigue and the failing of imagination. He has always known more than Willi, but he can be of no help to him, because of his own life-saving powers of forgetfulness.

When Thomas Bestermann, in "The Latehomecomer," returns from France, where he has stayed too long because the records of his past (and hence his official identity) were lost, he meets a man named Willy Wehler who with a certain peasant cunning ("All Willy had to do was sniff the air") has managed to slip through the Nazi age without becoming as scarred as most survivors.

He pushed back his chair (in later years he would be able to push a table away with his stomach) and got to his feet. He had to tip his head to look up into my eyes. He said he wanted to give me advice that would be useful to me as a latehomecomer. His advice was to forget. "Forget everything," he said. "Forget, forget, forget. That was what I said to my good neighbour Herr Silber when I bought his wife's topaz brooch and earrings before he emigrated to Palestine. I said, 'Dear Herr Silber, look forward, never back, and forget, forget, forget.' "

In "An Autobiography" the narrator, a schoolmistress in Switzerland whose German professor father was shot by Russians in Hungary, had met in her poor refugee days a boy named Peter who as a child—like Helena in "The Old Friends"—miraculously escaped death by being arbitrarily taken out of one of the contingents of Jews headed for the gas chambers. Now when she is firmly settled in the womb-like refuge of Switzerland, she encounters Peter once again and realizes that he has become a mythomane, constantly changing his past to suit the company, but for that reason uneasy with someone who knew him in his actual past.

But I had travelled nearly as much as Peter, and over some of the same frontiers. He could not impress me. . . . He knew it was no good talking about the past, because we were certain to remember it differently. He daren't be nostalgic about anything, because of his inventions. He would never be certain if the memory he was feeling tender about was true.

And even during that German past which everyone in Mavis Gallant's stories wants to avoid or to remember as it never was, those fared best who had the power of shedding their earlier pasts and hence their identities. An example is Uncle Theo, an amiable Schweikish nobody in the Bavarian story, "O Lasting Peace." Uncle Theo avoided involvement in the war almost literally by losing himself. When he went for his medical examination he found that all the physical defects he could rake up were insufficient to get him rejected.

He put on his clothes, still arguing, and was told to take a file with his name on it to a room upstairs. It was on his way up that he had his revelation. Everything concerning his person was in that file. If the file disappeared, then Uncle Theo did, too. He turned and walked straight out of the front door. He did not destroy the file, in case they should come round asking; he intended to say he had not understood the instructions. No one came, and soon after this his workroom was bombed and the file became ashes. When Uncle Theo was arrested it was for quite another reason, having to do with black-market connections. He went first to prison, then, when the jail was bombed, to a camp. Here he wore on his striped jacket the black sleeve patch that meant "anti-social." It is generally thought that he wore the red patch, meaning "political." As things are now, it gives him status.

And so Uncle Theo lives on, a survivor by evasion who enjoys the repute and pension of a hero in a Germany that does not want to remember too precisely.

A striking feature of Gallant's German stories is the importance of childhood. There are those whose lives are shaped by ruined childhoods — Bibi and Helena, Thomas the latehomecomer who was bearing arms in his teens, and Ernst who was incorporated as a boy in the Werewolves. But children also seem to offer promise of a future in which there will be a memory of a real past, and it is significant that both the character Michael in "An Alien Flower" and Thomas in "The Latehomecomer" will marry girls who are mere children in the present of the stories. This is the generation that will again be able to think of "misery and sadness."

In "The Pegnitz Junction" we are on the verge of this world where renewal may be thought of. One of the important characters is the little boy Bert, four years old. And the central figure is Christine, eighteen years old and so too young to have any personal memory of the Nazi past. She comes indeed from a place where the re-creation of an older past has made it unnecessary to remember what went on more recently: "a small bombed baroque German city, where all that was worthwhile keeping had been rebuilt and which now looked as pink and golden as a pretty child and as new as morning." Yet she does not need to ignore the real past because she does not know much about it; she carries with her a volume of the writings of Dietrich Boenhoffer, one of the anti-Nazi martyrs.

It is through Christine that "The Pegnitz Junction" assumes its special quality. It is the most experimental of Gallant's works, in which she makes no attempt at that special Gallant realism where the web of memory provides the mental links that make for plausibility. Here she is trying to create, in a structure as much dramatic as fictional, a kind of psychic membrane in which recollection is replaced by telepathy.

Christine, it is obvious from the description which opens the story, is the kind of person who becomes a psychic medium or around whom poltergeist phenomena are likely to happen.

She had a striking density of expression in photographs, though she seemed unchanging and passive in life, and had caught sight of her own face looking totally empty-minded when, in fact, her thoughts and feelings were pushing her in some wild direction. She had heard a man say of her that you could leave her in a cafe for two hours and come back to find she was still smoking the same cigarette . . . .

Although Christine is engaged to a theological student, she is erotically involved with Herbert, and with him and his son, Little Bert, she makes a trip to Paris. The main part of the novella is devoted to a frustrating journey home which takes them to the Pegnitz Junction. There is an airport strike at Orly, so they return by train. When they change at the German border they find that railway movements have been diverted because of heath fires, and instead of going straight home they must travel in a great arc, changing at a station close up to the barbed wire and watchtowers of East Germany, and finally reaching Pegnitz Junction, where the train to Berlin should be awaiting them. It is not, and when the novella ends they are still at Pegnitz, waiting.

"The Pegnitz Junction" is a work of much complexity, and deserves an essay of its own. I will be content to dwell on three aspects that mark its distinctiveness among Mavis Gallant's stories. The first is the intrusion of what appears to be a much stronger element of intentional symbolism than one finds elsewhere in Mavis Gallant's writings. One cannot avoid seeing the train journey as an elaborate figure, representing the wanderings, without an as yet assured destination, of a Germany which has not recovered a sense of its role in history and, indeed, fears what that role might be if it were discovered.

Then there is the peculiar relationship between Christine and the other passengers. With Herbert it is mostly a simple matter of conversation and her inner thoughts about their relationship, and with Little Bert it is a question of exchanging fantasies. But with the other people encountered on the journey Christine falls into a state of psychic openness, so that messages are exchanged, and their flows of thought emerge to multiply the range of viewpoints.

Their immediate fellow passengers are a Norwegian professional singer with a mania for yogic breathing and an old woman who is constantly munching food from the large bags she has brought with her. The Norwegian, occupied with singing and breathing, has merely a few comments to offer, but from the mind of the old woman there emerges an extraordinary unspoken monologue. Surprisingly—in the context of these stories—it is a reminiscent one that reconstructs a past elsewhere; she lived through the dark years in America and came back to Germany to bury her husband and water his grave after the war ended. But there are remoter messages which trip the levers of Christine's telepathic sense. When the train stops at a level crossing, she suddenly enters the minds of the people waiting, and at the station on the East German border she catches a refugee's memories of the girl in his lost village. Then, at Pegnitz Junction, there is the pregnant country girl who pretends to be an American army wife, from whom Christine receives the strangest message of all: the contents of a letter about racketeering in PX stores from one GI to another that she is carrying in her bag. Not only does this technique give a dramatic quality to the novella, since it becomes so largely a pattern of voices heard in the mind's ear, but there is a cinematic element in the way the outer, visible and audible world cuts away from the inner world and back again; one is reminded of Mavis Gallant's days in a NFB cutting room.

Finally, there is the centrality of the child, Little Bert, who is present and intervening throughout the novella, occasionally making an Emperor's-clothes remark of penetrating aptness, but most of the time involved in his fantasy of the life of the sponge he calls Bruno, which he shares with Christine, but over which he seeks to maintain control, so that he rejects versions of Bruno's adventures that go beyond his ideas of plausibility. For Bruno after all—as Bert makes clear on occasion—is merely a sponge to which he has given a life. History—the irradiation of actuality by imagination—seems to be stirring in this infant mind.

The final group of stories I am discussing is the Linnet Muir cycle, set in Montreal between the 1920s and the 1940s. Mavis Gallant had already used Montreal as a setting in her novella of the 1950s, "Its Image in a Mirror" (included in *My Heart is Broken*) and in stories like "Bernadette," written at the same period. But the Linnet Muir stories, which have not all been published and will presumably form a volume on their own, are so closely interlinked that one sees them as the chronologically discontinuous chapters in a major novel avowedly devoted to *la recherche du temps perdu.*

I use the Proustian phrase deliberately, since Mavis Gallant's own account of the origin of the stories in the Hancock interview leaves little doubt that an impulse of involuntary memory set them moving and that in general they represent a release of the imagination into memory and the past, after the self-disciplines of writing about the world of *The Pegnitz Junction* where time seems irretrievably lost.

The Linnet Muir stories are no more autobiographical than Proust's great fictional quest, and no less so. Linnet Muir is about as near to Mavis Gallant as the linnet (a modest English song-bird) is to the mavis, which is the Scottish name for the magnificent European song thrush. There are things in common between writer and character, and just as many dissimilarities. Gallant, like Linnet, spent her childhood in Montreal where she was born. Her father died when she was young, and at the age of eighteen one of the first things she did on returning to Montreal — this was 1940 — was to try and find out how he died. A few people and a few incidents thus stepped from real life into the stories. But everything has been reshaped and transmuted in the imagination so that what emerges is a work of fiction on several levels. It is a portrait of Linnet Muir as a child isolated in her family, and later as a young woman between eighteen and twenty isolated in her fatherland. But it is even more, as Gallant herself has insisted, a reconstruction of a city and a way of life which have now been irrevocably engulfed in time past but which, as Gallant has said, were "unique in North America, if not the world" because the two Montreals, the French and the Anglo-Scottish, were so completely shut off from each other. And, since in this way these stories form a fiction about a collectivity rather than about individuals, one of their striking features is that the narrator, through whose consciousness everything is seen and who is the one continuing character, does not stand out more vividly in our minds than most of the other characters; all of them, down to the slightest, are portrayed with an almost pre-Raphaelite sharpness of vision.

I am not sure how many of the stories in the sequence are yet to be published; certainly we have not had the "very, very long story . . . about the war" which Mavis Gallant talks of and which is intended to terminate the series. But what we do have is already an extraordinary addition to that peculiarly Canadian type of fiction concerned with the changing relationships of cultural groups.

In order of appearance in *The New Yorker,* which I assume is roughly the order of completion, the first story, "In Youth is Pleasure," sets the theme by showing Linnet in search of the lost world of her childhood. A girl of eighteen, having suffered the contemptuous ignorance of Americans about the country above their borders, she returns to Montreal with a few dollars and immense self-confidence. Almost without thought, she seeks out the French-Canadian nurse of her childhood, and is given unquestioning hospitality. But when she moves into the other Montreal, that of her own people, and tries to find out about her father, she encounters reserve, distrust, even fear. The search for her father is significant in view of Gallant's own theory that perhaps the one distinctive Canadian theme is to be found in the role of the father, who in our literature seems always more important than the mother. Linnet remembers her mother in somewhat derogatory terms as a person who "smiled, talked, charmed anyone she didn't happen to be related to, swam in scandal like a partisan among the people." But the search for the father is, in a very real sense, the beginning of Linnet's search for truth. She never really does find out how he died; all she can assemble is a cluster of conflicting rumours and theories, so that she is never sure whether he actually died of the tuberculosis of the spine that attacked him in his early thirties or shot himself with a revolver she remembered seeing in a drawer in her childhood. In the end she shapes the past in her own mind: "I thought he had died of homesickness; sickness for England was the consumption, the gun, the everything." She realizes all at once that this is not her past. "I had looked into a drawer that did not belong to me." But what she finds in the process is that the world which saw him die with such indifference was a narrow provincial world where wealth and influence were the only virtues, the world of the Montreal tycoons.

"Between Zero and One" and "Varieties of Exile" are further stories about Linnet's experiences when she returns to Montreal, and they are dedicated to obsolescent kinds of people. In the first story Linnet works in a Montreal draughtsman's office (as Jean Price does in "Its Image in the Mirror") and all the people around her, until a woman bitter from a failed marriage joins the staff, are either men too old to fight in World War II but full of recollections of an earlier conflict, or unfit men. It is an entirely English world — an office that does not contain a single francophone, a collection of men with the prejudices of their time who neither know nor wish to know the other nation that shares Quebec with them. Canada, for them, is English; its loyalties are imperial. And they have accepted limitations for themselves as well as for their world. It is a world to which Linnet does not belong, any more than does Frank Cairns, the remittance man in "Varieties of Exile," with whom she strikes up the precarious relationship of two people out of their place and world when she encounters him on the train going from her summer lodgings into Montreal. Frank and his kind, the castoff young men of English families, were the nearest thing in Canada to the superfluous men of Russian literature, and as a species they vanished when World War II dried up the flow of cash from home and most of them went back to fight for a country that had thrown them out. Strangely enough, if the men in the office taught Linnet how narrow life can be made, Frank Cairns, who seems happy only when he is going home, helps to open her mind with his own restless questing, and when she hears of his death she is happy that "he would never need to return to the commuting train and the loneliness and be forced to relive his own past."

All these three stories display memory doubly at work. Linnet the narrator is looking back thirty years to another Linnet exploring a lost Montreal whose doom was sealed by the social changes World War II began in Canada. But the Linnet of thirty years ago in turn is remembering, seeing her own childhood again as she experiences aspects of the city of which she was unaware when she lived protected in the family which is the subject of the two stories that follow and that up to the present complete the published cycle: "Voices Lost in the Snow" and "The Doctor." They are stories of a family of the age between the wars: father and mother still young, but already separated by work ("I do not know where my father spent his working life; just elsewhere") and by relationships, for in "Voices Lost in the Snow" the father, who is already dying though nobody knows it, takes the child to see a woman, an estranged friend of her mother, with whom he still maintains contact.

In these stories, once again, we have the sharp visuality of Gallant's earlier work, and the gripping evocations of a Montreal that has long vanished beneath the blows of the wrecker's ball.

The reddish brown of the stone houses, the curve and slope of the streets, the constantly changing sky were satisfactory in a way that I now realize must have been aesthetically comfortable. This is what I saw when I read 'city' in a book; I had no means of knowing that 'city' one day would also mean drab, filthy, flat, or that city blocks could turn into dull squares without mystery.

As "The Doctor" shows, Linnet's family inhabits a shifting frontier territory where the two cultures of Montreal meet, as they rarely do elsewhere.

This overlapping in one room of French and English, of Catholic and Protestant — my parents' way of being, and so to me life itself — was as unlikely, as unnatural to the Montreal climate as a school of tropical fish. Only later would I discover that most other people simply floated in mossy little ponds labelled "French and Catholic" or "English and Protestant," never wondering what it might be like to step ashore, or wondering, perhaps, but weighing up the danger. To be out of a pond is to be in unmapped territory.

A frequent guest to her parents' house is Dr. Chauchard, who in another role is the pediatrician attending Linnet at the age of eight. The bicultural salons are dominated by a flamboyant Mrs. Erskine, who has been the wife of two unsuccessful diplomats and moves in Montreal society escorted by Chauchard (now transformed into genial Uncle Raoul) and various attendant young Québecois intellectuals. But even such encounters take place in a no-man's-land so insecure that the common language is always English, and Linnet does not know, until Dr. Chauchard dies, that he had another life in which he was a notable Québec poet, as she discovers on seeing his obituaries, one for the pious member of his family, one for the doctor, one for the writer.

That third notice was an earthquake, the collapse of the cities we build over the past to cover seams and cracks we cannot account for. He must have been writing when my parents knew him. Why they neglected to speak of it is something too shameful to dwell on; he probably never mentioned it, knowing they would believe it impossible. French books were from France; English books from England or the United States. It would not have entered their minds that the languages they heard spoken around them could be written, too.

Vignettes of a dead time; of a lost world; of a vanished city. Yet it is easy to lay too much stress on the social-historical nature of the Linnet Muir stories. (Though Gallant herself gives some support to such emphasis when she talks of the "political" nature of her stories.) They are so successful as records of an age because they are inhabited by people so carefully drawn and individually realized that the past comes alive, in its superbly evoked setting, as experience even more than as history. And that is the true rediscovery of time.

[1978]

Private Fantasies: Collective Myths. John Glassco's Decadent Fiction

IN ENGLISH-READING countries at least, the movement which, for lack of a more inclusively descriptive title, we call the Decadence suffered a long twilight that lasted from the trial of Oscar Wilde until comparatively recent years. In the thirties, whose dominant spirit was as diametrically opposed as one could imagine to that of the Decadents, volumes of the *Yellow Book* and collections by poets like Lionel Johnson and Ernest Dowson could be bought for a few pence on the Farringdon Road bookstalls; the excellent anthology of nineties poets which A.J.A. Symons then published was quickly remaindered. It was not merely that the literary manner of the Decadents was repugnant to those politically minded writers — left-wing or right-wing — who favoured a stark and vigorous statement; this was not in fact always the case, since George Orwell, for example, admired and was influenced by *The Picture of Dorian Gray* and once told me that he was somewhat "pro-Wilde." It was rather that both critics and their public uneasily saw the Decadence as a retreat into unreality and hence a denial of the Victorian and post-Victorian longing for reassurance by writers that the world was not merely real but also capable of being arranged in desirable ways. Any piece of writing that contains an element of the realistic is, positively or negatively, making a statement about the world we live in and implying a direction of transformation. The writer who creates a private world impossible of realization performs the unforgivable rebellion; he turns his back on that cult of the possible and the progressive which has consumed our age; he joyfully abandons hope.

This has not been understood fully even by those who have studied Decadent literature and the public reaction to it. In his recent book, *Violence in the Arts,* John Fraser suggests that the writings of the Marquis de Sade were innocuous because they projected private fantasies that were impossible of realization. But was it not Sade's very denial of the possible, rather than the specific detail of his fantasies, that turned against him both Robespierrian revolutionaries and Bonapartist revisionists, the men who lived — and sometimes died — to reshape the future?

The recent revival of interest in Decadent writing and art has been related closely to the steady sapping of our faith in the progressive and the possible. When Camus maintained that hope must be abandoned for man to acquire even passing happiness or tranquillity, when oriental doctrines of quietism became fashionable, when the counter-culture began to attack the cherished moral imperatives of the Protestant world (and also of post-Protestant Marxism), the Decadence could become once again something more than the province of a few scholars and frayed devotees.

This change in attitudes is reflected not only in the steady growth of interest in John Glassco's essentially pessimistic poetry but also in the fate of the three novellas which he has published in a collection called *The Fatal Woman* (1974). He tells how one of the tales,"The Black Helmet," on which he worked from 1936 to 1944, was later rejected, despite seven rewritings, by many publishers, "until 1960 when I at last laid it aside in discouragement . . . ." Indeed, the only part of *The Fatal Woman* previously published was a fragment of "The Black Helmet" in John Sutherland's *First Statement.* Perhaps the situation was partly due to the fact that Puritanism lingered long in Canada, yet I cannot imagine that before about 1958 *The Fatal Woman* would have been able to appear even in England in anything other than a private limited edition. Even now, I suspect, it is likely to remain "caviar to the general," but it is at least openly published, sold in suburban bookstores, and widely reviewed, none of which could have happened here, as Glassco's experience shows, a decade ago. The vaunted "permissiveness" of our age is only part of the explanation; the other part is that the erosion of philosophies of progress has liberated our minds to the validity of private worlds beyond the possible. Hence the growth of fantasy in fiction, the fact that many of our best novelists are also poets, and the final appearance of *The Fatal Woman* with a lucid but at times — one suspects — playfully misleading preface by its author.

John Glassco tells us that around 1934, after writing *Memoirs of Montparnasse* (another book which changing standards allowed to appear three decades after its completion), "I came under the renewed influence of Huysmans, Pater, Villiers, Barbey d'Aurevilly and others of the so-called Decadents, and decided to write books utterly divorced from reality, stories where nothing happened." He remarks later that, of the two paths which Edmund Wilson offered to those authors who cannot interest themselves in contemporary society, Axel's way and Rimbaud's way, he chose Axel's, which involved "cultivating one's fantasies, encouraging one's private manias, ultimately preferring one's absurdest chimeras to the most astonishing contemporary realities." This, he suggests, is what he has done in the three tales that form *The Fatal Woman*. And Axel, of course, was an invention of Villiers de l'Isle Adam; he can be taken as representative of the whole school called Decadent, for the adventures of the beings who populate the fictions of Huysmans, Pater, Beardsley, even Wilde, differ in detail rather than in kind.

When I try to find a word to define adequately the novellas that make up *The Fatal Woman,* it is *palimpsest* that comes immediately to my mind, and I think it can be more easily justified than the obvious alternatives. *Parody* indeed is there, but only as an element, and *pastiche* conveys too mechanical a process of arranging borrowed fragments. Palimpsest, with its concurrent image of taking something that already exists, partly erasing it, and then writing in fresh material that blends plausibly with the original and becomes a new work in its own right, is nearer to the process one senses at work. It is characteristic of the whole school of writers with whom Glassco here associates himself that they abandoned the romantic obsession with originality, realizing that in the world of private fantasy the patterns and the dominant figures are few and archetypal, the movement is hieratic, the end is a stasis of action resembling that of Keats's "Grecian Urn." The task, as Frank Davey said of Glassco's completion of Aubrey Beardsley's *Under the Hill,* is a "metamorphosis of life into 'pure form' and of sexuality into rigidly stylized forms"; it is not the content but the form that changes, since each time we dream of the same archetypal figure his disguise is different.

Fiction as palimpsest had appeared already when the Glassco-Beardsley *Under the Hill* was published in 1959. Beardsley himself had taken and worked into his own form the existing legend of

Tannhäuser, already exploited by Wagner, leaving the task incomplete at his death. Glassco picked up what Beardsley had done and transformed it into a complete work that retained his predecessor's borrowed framework and used what Beardsley had already written, but added his own material which completed the original and transformed without denying it. A similar sequence emerges when one considers the stories in *The Fatal Woman*. In "The Black Helmet" a divine pair of siblings, distantly reminiscent of Cocteau's *enfants terribles,* descend on a fantasizing onanist, Mairobert, in his decaying and debt-ridden house, and the female sibling, Miss Delarchet, traumatically ravishes (her sex grasps him "like the oiled fist of a wrestler") and transforms him. The tale, as Glassco explains, is "a re-telling of the Endymion myth," but there is more of the palimpsest here than the mere working over of a classical legend, for in the background of the story linger Mairobert's thoughts of his sadistic governess Miss Marwood, whose memory dominates his fantasy life until the arrival of Miss Delarchet. Miss Marwood, as Glassco does not tell us in the story, was the heroine of one of the books he describes as "aphrodisiac works which exploited the Fatal Woman as an article of commerce"; this was *The English Governess,* which he published in 1967 under the nom de plume of Miles Underwood, and again in 1976, as *Harriet Marwood, Governess,* under his own name.

The origin in Greek myth of the second tale in *The Fatal Woman,* "The Fulfilled Destiny of Electra," is as obvious in its action as in its title, despite the ironic background of a Canadian village concerned with tourist development, and the intervention of two policemen out of real life who serve mechanically to precipitate the destruction of the male victim. "Lust in Action," whose mode Glassco describes as "the satirical and ribald," is perhaps ultimately the least successful, but certainly not the least interesting of the novellas. It is an example of that genre rare indeed in Canada, the inverted utopia; women have taken over the earth and have subdued men, who are automatically castrated at the age of twenty, but are allowed a kind of grace period until then, during which any lapse into overt sexuality brings punishment and, in the worst cases, early treatment by the knackeress. The story centres on a rebellion in a prison for boys in which two of the more recalcitrant inmates take two wardresses hostage under the threat of exposing themselves and showing obscene papers. They even ravish an ancient lesbian guard; but are finally caught by troopers armed with lassos, and carried off for cutting.

The satire, at least superficially, seems to have topical targets; it would hardly have taken its present form except in a decade in which jail riots and militant feminism became familiar phenomena. Yet I suspect that Glassco has in mind, when he talks of the reader acquiring through laughter "a deeper and more disturbing vision of the fantasy as something close to reality," a dimension beyond or beneath merely transient phenomena. He is taking us to a level where private fantasies have public implications and — to borrow a Jungian terminology — the archetypes show their collective forms. The hideous vision of "Lust in Action" has after all been seen before, and, remembering John Knox and his "monstrous regiment of women," one realizes that the fantasies of Calvinists and their opposites can sometimes look amazingly alike. It is perhaps the detachment of sexuality from life in each case, and the essential pessimism both views sustain, that create this astonishing meeting of dissimilars. D.H. Lawrence would certainly have rejected Knox and Glassco with equal vehemence, yet while one might agree with him regarding the Calvinist prophet, one would find Glassco's supreme artistry sufficient cause to contend with Lawrence's indiscriminate vitalism. But the fact that the choice should even occur suggests what perils are involved when private fantasy takes to the satiric mode; for satire is essentially an activity for moralists, and the judgement of moralists is public.

[1975]

On Ethel Wilson

NOT VERY LONG ago Howard Engel of the CBC sent me, in connection with a program he was preparing, a series of questions on Ethel Wilson that had been formulated by William French. I found them useful in the sense that they stimulated memories and thoughts, and here and there in what follows I shall refer to them, but what emerged from considering them was not a series of answers, but rather a kind of memoir on a remarkable woman and a fine writer.

I don't know whether I can claim to have known Ethel Wilson well, and I certainly would not presume to describe myself as one of her close friends. I probably met her no more than a score of times, but as a personality she left as great an impression on my memory as my mind gained from her books.

I recognize the curious implications of what I have just said, of the choice of words, the defining of attitudes. In saying that I would not *presume*, I realize that I would not have used that Prufrockian word about any other writer I have known. Did I ever think of it in connection with Hugh Walpole or George Orwell, Dylan Thomas or Roy Campbell? Or in connection with Theodore Roethke or Denise Levertov or Norman Mailer, or with any Canadian writer except Ethel Wilson? Of course not. Then why does the phrase come to my mind when I remember my acquaintance with her?

Let me recall the first time I set eyes on Ethel Wilson. It was in the early 1950s at a writers' conference in Vancouver; in those days I still attended such functions. At one of the sessions I had been talking about the problems Canadian writers then experienced in publishing their work. I described the Canadian publishing situation, which was then appalling, and I went on to remark that the Canadian writer's chances of getting published in Britain diminished in almost geometrical ratio to his distance from London. Most of the writers present accepted my remarks without argument; after all, they'd sent their own manuscripts to London and heard no more about them or had them back with more or less polite notes of rejection. But a woman whom I remember as tall and very self-possessed, with clear-cut jawline and well-cut clothes, stood up and in very precise diction remarked that her experience had been much less discouraging; English publishers and editors had always been kind and considerate to her, and she felt I was doing them a notable injustice. She spoke without any obvious arrogance, yet there was a patrician assurance in her manner to which at the time I reacted rather acerbically; a little later in the day I was mortified to learn that she was Ethel Wilson, whose *Equations of Love* I had just been reading with admiration.

I met her afterwards—over the years—at occasional literary social gatherings, where she would pour tea with impeccable ceremonial grace and hold court with charming imperiousness. When I began to edit *Canadian Literature* in 1959, and she came forward with help and some very welcome contributions of her own occasional essays, I began to know her rather better, and though as I said I can claim no closeness of friendship, I did recognize the very sensitive being, her antennae tremulously open to every kind of perception, who lived within the public carapace of the Vancouver patrician. She and her husband Wallace, an abundantly likable man who was entirely devoted to her, would entertain one in their succession of apartments, which were always chosen so that they faced on English Bay and Stanley Park, with a view of the North Shore mountains and of the Gulf of Georgia out beyond Point Grey; it seemed, as one discussed her own books and the books of other Canadians, as if the scenery had been picked deliberately to give a background to the literature, though obviously it was the love of place that had come first. Strangely enough, I cannot remember visiting Ethel Wilson or her coming to our house, at any other time than high summer; perhaps it is not a coincidence that I also think of her novels as books of high summer, for indeed that is what they really are.

Ethel Wilson had the special kind of shrewd and mature alertness that often accompanies talents which emerge late in life. I found myself after a short acquaintance thinking of her as almost strictly a contemporary—perhaps five or six years older than I, but certainly not the twenty-two years that was the actual case. Her literary career, after all, had happened so recently. She had not begun to write at all seriously until the late 1930s. Her first novel, *Hetty Dorval,* did not appear until 1947, and then she herself was fifty-seven. For Ethel Wilson, one remembered with astonishment, had been born in 1890; she was eleven when the Great Queen died, twenty when the Edwardian age came to an end; when she reached Vancouver the city was still in its teens; she was four years older than Aldous Huxley and thirteen years older than George Orwell, yet to all intents and purposes her literary career belonged to a later generation than theirs. She was even, I have just realized with astonishment, four years older than J.B. Priestley!

And here, I began to understand after I had overcome the problem of reconciling mental and physical ages, lay the clue to the peculiar character of Ethel Wilson's novels—for I recognized them, as I still do, to be unlike anything else in Canadian writing. She had retained, I realized, an Edwardian sensibility, but she had developed a contemporary ironic intelligence, and it was the interplay of the two that gave her books their special quality.

At this point I must remark that I was unable to answer some of the questions that were included in William French's notes. I was asked if I could recall anecdotes about Ethel Wilson that illuminated her as a woman and a writer. All I can say is that Ethel Wilson in her private life was so deliberately uneccentric that anecdotes never crystallized about her. Which is not to say she was less than an interesting companion, for she had travelled far and seen many things, and could talk of them very well. I remember the particular vividness with which, one evening in 1961 when I was about to visit Egypt, she described her own visit to the Nile and the Valley of Kings in the 1930s. But, as happens with many writers who accurately note the behavioural oddities of other human beings, Ethel Wilson tended to adopt a protective guise for herself, to maintain a distance, and it was in her conversation rather than her behaviour, which was always held in the middle path of the wise, that one sometimes recognized the author of her novels.

I was asked also how I rated Ethel Wilson's contribution to Canadian literature. I think this is a pointless question. Writers do not set out to create a Canadian literature or any other literature. A literature—Canadian or other—is what emerges out of their efforts to express in imaginative terms their own very personal perceptions and experiences. There is, I agree, a distinctively Canadian character to Ethel Wilson's books, because of her sense of the history that she lived through, which in its most immediate form was British Columbian history, and because of her extraordinary sense of the geographical setting. No writer gives one a more lyrically authentic feeling of Vancouver's past—most of which she had experienced—than Ethel Wilson, and no writer presents in the body of her or his work a more comprehensive feeling of what it is to live with and to love the different faces of the Pacific landscape, from the mountains through the dry lands to the rain forests and the coastal islands and inlets. I could go further than that and admit that Ethel Wilson regarded herself very firmly as a Canadian and was interested in any critic who pointed out the nature of Canadian writing as an expression of the national psyche. Still, she never thought of her novels as primarily contributions to Canadian literature. She always felt that one should not fail to see the trees for the wood, and she viewed her own books—as the wise critic sees them—outside the categories that are invented by literary historians.

When I come to consider the special qualities of Ethel Wilson's fiction, I am tempted to embark on a long critical essay, which is obviously not at present called for. So let me draw attention to a few special points. I have already spoken of Ethel Wilson's historic sense, and of her inclination to write vividly of the landscapes she loved. If—as I am—you are especially fond of the stretch of inland British Columbia between Lytton and Kamloops, including long stretches of the Fraser and Thompson valleys, you will certainly find Wilson novels like *Hetty Dorval* and *Swamp Angel* congenial, quite apart from other qualities, for their precise and lyrical evocation of the sagebrush country and the mountain lakes.

For the rest, let me reflect on a few special facets of Ethel Wilson's approach. There is her extraordinarily wide range of irony, gentle enough when it shows us how the characters she loves deceive themselves and others, but modulating into somewhat savage satire when she is dealing with the kinds of stupidity that survive by armouring themselves with social conventions. (Remember the ironic double meaning of the title of her short story, "Mrs. Golightly and the Convention.") Then, as one can observe merely by noticing the titles of her novels, there is the emphasis on love. *The Equations of Love. Love and Salt Water.* And what love means here is not mere sexual amorousness, but the whole range of human tenderness, complete with its aberrations. For one thing of which we become certain when we read Wilson entire, novel by novel and story by story, is that in her view of the human soul there is no motive and no person wholly light or wholly dark, though stupid people are often shown as being pretty near to blackness.

This sense of the duality within all beings is illustrated by one of Ethel Wilson's favourite images which can be understood in its completeness only by those who have travelled the Interior of British Columbia and done so with a degree of imaginative perception. Just north of Lytton two great rivers, the Fraser and the Thompson, come together, and standing on a bridge outside the village one can see their dramatic confluence. The Thompson is a singularly clear river, its translucent waters deepening in colour from turquoise blue at the edges to deep malachite green in the centre. But the Fraser is muddy, a turbid stream, and within a few yards after their joining together the jewel-coloured limpidity of the Thompson is lost in the murk of the greater river. The sense that we are compounded of the clear and the dark and that in combination the dark of experience so often seems dominant over the clear of innocence, appears constantly in Wilson's novels; in fact in both *Hetty Dorval* and *Swamp Angel* the actual meeting of the two rivers is introduced strategically to alert us to the ambivalent emotions which the actions of her characters will reveal and also arouse.

The title of *Swamp Angel* of course emphasizes the same ironic dichotomy. The Swamp Angel is actually a nineteenth-century American pistol which one of the characters flourishes at crucial moments in the novel, but the phrase also invokes an image of rare incongruity, that of angelic qualities emerging in the swamp of human passions such as possessiveness and jealousy. The pistol is indeed the Swamp Angel, but Maggie Lloyd, the heroine, is the angel in the swamp, and like most angels she has at times to act with a decisiveness that appears to be brutal if she is to save herself from being submerged.

I would like, before ending these notes, to draw attention also to the repeated use by Ethel Wilson of the old tag from John Donne, "No man is an Island." She uses it always in contexts where it appears unhackneyed because it so precisely illuminates the failure of those who forget the mutuality of all existence and so become the victims of their own selfishness, and the triumph of those who remember that mutuality and so, even in misfortune, are vindicated. Hetty Dorval strives to be an island; we are left in no doubt of the ultimate tragedy she is creating for herself. Maggie Lloyd, by destroying a false human relationship to become involved in a cluster of new and true ones, recognizes her existence as being, in Donne's words, "a piece of the continent, a part of the main." Perhaps this is in the end what one remembers most not only of Ethel Wilson's novels, but about Ethel Wilson herself as a person and a writer; that radar of sensibility ever recording the complex shores of the human continent.

I am asked whether I have a favourite among Ethel Wilson's novels. I can answer that question only by drawing a distinction between what I admire and what I like. The book I *admire* most, because it is beautifully structured, because it uses the imagery of wild nature so effectively to reflect the human condition, and because it works out so well the polarities of personal relationships, is *Swamp Angel*. The book I *like* is *Hetty Dorval*. I suppose one can put a good case for its literary values. It is a tightly knit and economically written book, simple in plot, evocative in description, and very sensitive in its understanding of the adolescent mind of its narrator, Frankie Burnaby. On the other hand, Hetty Dorval, the central figure, is an improbable femme fatale, with her double faces of innocence and corruption. Yet if one makes the leap of credulity and accepts Hetty as a figure of allegory, the whole novel turns into a remarkable study of the process of growing up, in which Frankie herself, and not the enigmatic Hetty whom we see so much as the projection of Frankie's thoughts, becomes the central figure.

However, I do not really like to pick out any single Wilson piece in this way, since I find that her six volumes, which anyone can read in three weeks, seem best understood if one takes them together as parts of an imaginative chart of Canada beyond the

Great Divide and if at the same time one remembers that this chart with its mountain tops and valleys, its dry lands and its dripping coastal forests, is also a faithful map of the human heart.

[1974]

Armies Moving in the Night: The Fictions of Matt Cohen

AT THE END OF the 1960s, when native Canadian publishing developed a crusading fervour with the appearance of new avant garde enterprises like the House of Anansi and New Press, experimental fiction became a vogue in Canada in a way anticipated by only a few isolated works of earlier decades like Sheila Watson's *Double Hook* and Howard O'Hagan's *Tay John.* Perhaps the great publishing event of the waning decade, because it made us aware of a strong nouvelle vague of discontent among younger writers with accepted forms, was Anansi's launching of Spiderline Editions, an inspiration on the part of Dennis Lee, but in some ways a self-defeating one. It was a series devoted entirely to "first novels," and for a couple of years it tapped unexploited sources of imaginative energy, but then the flow of brilliant available material dried up and the series came to a quiet end.

The first batch of Spiderlines was a highly promising one, including Peter Such's *Fallout,* John Sandman's *Eating Out,* Russell Marois's *Telephone Pole,* and a translation of Pierre Gravel's *A Perte de temps,* all of them brief and highly experimental fictions and all of them worth attention; but certainly among the anglophone contributions to the series the best was Matt Cohen's *Korsoniloff,* and none of the later titles (though Rachel Wyatt's *String Box* and Michael Charters's *Victor Victim* were both highly interesting books) seemed so sure in technique or so original in insight. The impression was a lasting one because Cohen became the only one among the writers discovered and published by Dennis Lee during that brief creative springtime who has continued to write with a growing power, and who has developed in less than a decade into one of the most interesting and versatile among the younger generation of Canadian novelists.

Up to the time when I write this essay, Matt Cohen has published nine books in all. Two of them, *Korsoniloff* (1969) and *Johnny Crackle Sings* (1971) are experimental novellas; one, *Too Bad Galahad* (1972), is a fantasy for juveniles; two others, *Columbus and the Fat Lady* (1972) and *Night Flights* (1978), are collections of short stories of which the second largely duplicates the first; the remaining four are full-length fictions of which *The Disinherited* (1974) takes the form of a family chronicle, *Wooden Hunters* (1975) that of an elegy on dying peoples and cultures, *The Colours of War* (1977) that of a political fantasy in which the search for the future becomes a flight to the past, and *The Sweet Second Summer of Kitty Malone* (1979) that of a violent and tender study of love surviving age and degeneration.

Here I shall be concerned mainly with Cohen's four larger books as representative of his mature achievement and likely to point the direction of his writing from this middle point in his career. (He is now in his later thirties). At the same time, the two novellas and the short stories merit at least brief attention since they give first expression to some of Cohen's lasting formal and thematic preoccupations.

Night Flights consists of fifteen stories, of which four had appeared already in *Columbus and the Fat Lady* (including the title story). *Night Flights* shows perhaps better than any other volume the variety of Cohen's capabilities, his technical versatility, though to appreciate the scope of his fictional vision and the depth of his understanding of human predicaments one has to turn to his longer works. The stories vary in tone and approach from the mannered and decadent fantasy of "The Cure" and "A Literary History of Anton" to the near-realism of stories of rustic decay like "Brain Dust," "Country Music" and "Glasseyes and Chickens," small masterpieces of the darker comedy. But deep in all these stories, whatever their manner, is the sense of alienation that is equally strong in Cohen's novels. By alienation I mean more than Marx had in mind by the term — that a man's socioeconomic situation may detach him from his natural humanity. I mean also what the proto-psychiatrists of the early nineteenth century meant when they called themselves alienists: an inner division that splits a man's will so that in fictional terms he can be seen as schizoid, divided into two beings, of whom it is not always easy to know which is the real self and which the persona, or, for that matter, whether self or persona is dominant.

The problem occurs, in the sense of a division between role and personality, in "The Cure" when Eliot, the rich psychotic whose relationship with his senilely demented father forms the core of the story, "suddenly felt himself to be no more than an attempt by his bank balance to project someone human, an account book to live in, the living shadow of his own money." So far, so Marx; but we proceed into an alienation beyond the economic when Eliot "cures" himself in a hysterical scene where he transfers the sense of madness he feels rising within himself to his father: " 'I can't take you out,' he whispered, 'you're crazy.' And then he was shouting, 'You're crazy, YOU'RE FUCKING CRAZY.' " But in fact he has merely confirmed his alienation from his own self. He tells his doctor that the situation is "excellent," but:

The situation was in the centre of his mind, and from there he saw himself, absolutely inspired, so false he could have flown, raise one arm and place it, loose and familiar, on the shoulder of the doctor.

In another story, "Janice," there is a trio of Janice, the narrator Robert, and a mysterious Nicholas who is drowned, then survives to marry Janice, and finally fades into "Nicholas someone," half-forgotten; he is clearly Robert's doppelgänger, the feared other side of himself who must be destroyed.

In "Vogel," the shopkeeper Sam Vogel tries to escape from death by tuning-up programs and middle-aged sexual adventure, but does no more than change the form (not the way) of his death. He dies, essentially, from the split between the inner self represented by a twenty-five-year-old graduation photograph and the new self created when the doctor tells him he must become athletic to survive. The new self "existed solely in his mind and was not something that could be seen. It was a sensation. The feel of his own body in flight, running: one foot on the ground, taking his whole weight and springing it back, while the other licked out front, confidently reaching."

This image "in the mind" is regressive, so that Vogel lies like a child in his young mistress's bed, and dies from a heart attack on the running track, "curled up like a baby on the special composition surface of the track." Sam's death is like a journey into birth, just as his life had been a journey into death, a journey of forgetting the early self of the graduation photograph: "whoever had lived inside that picture, whoever had walked around with whatever forgotten obsessions, had been buried in circumstance."

Such stories relate very closely to Cohen's early novellas, *Korsoniloff* and *Johnny Crackle Sings*. Both of these are stories of inner alienation, of that division of the self which can end only in permanent loss. *Korsoniloff* concerns a failed teacher in philosophy, a schizoid who tells the story of his divided self — the separate lives of the cold "I" and the ineffectually passionate and amoral Korsoniloff.

Me cold? With my secret lusts and satanic nights, me, my career turned upside down by Korsoniloff — who is nothing but a bundle of super-charged impulses? Cold?

So at one point the narrator speaks, yet in another place declares:

I lead my life; Korsoniloff leads his. From time to time there is a shift in the balance of forces; the "I," as it were, switches to the new prevailing direction.

"I" is legally involved through the actions of Korsoniloff, who turns up at the marriage of their former mistress Marie, disturbs the peace, and is prosecuted. The incident is seen in terms of fantasy by Korsoniloff, of uncomfortable reality by "I." Marie had already sized up the situation:

She looked at me and told me that before she had met me she had known no one deeply and had felt alone within herself but that now she felt not only alone but isolated and that she wasn't sure but that she preferred the first.

And so we are not surprised, as the bathetic comedy of the trial goes on, to find "I" speculating, "Who was the master and who the pupil? I could see it both ways. For not only did I create Korsoniloff; Korsoniloff's existence transformed me." And behind this division of the self into alternately dominating personae, we find at the end the unconscious guilt, submerged in amnesia, of the child who sees his mother fall into the river, perhaps even pushes her, and immediately forgets. Korsoniloff is the uncon-scious self rebelling against the self-preserving censorship of "I," the ego.

Neither Freud nor Jung ever made a bad artist into a good one, and we can reasonably leave aside the possible sources in psycho-logical theory of *Korsoniloff* to remark that it owes perhaps more to Kafka and other European novelists in the essential terms of form and feeling than it does to either of the two great psychoanalysts.

It is a polished miniature masterpiece that—if it had not been set in Toronto—one could well have imagined in an ambience of Prague or Vienna or even, so sharply ironic is the moral edge, of Gide's Paris. Outside John Glassco's prose, I know few Canadian pieces of writing that so naturally demand a cosmopolitan connection. One can see *Korsoniloff* in the context of the nouvelle vague fiction that became so important in France a decade before, the novels of Marguerite Duras, Natalie Sarraute, Michel Butor. It has the same intellectual translucency, the same alabastrine un-emotionality, as these writers display.

Cohen's other novella, *Johnny Crackle Sings,* has a combination of stylistic brilliance and emotional detachment similar to *Korsoniloff,* and yet, in its eccentric way, it is as Canadian as its predecessor was European in feeling, and as temperamentally tied to the 1960s as Cohen's later novels have tended to move out of time, or at least out of the novelist's present.

The setting is rural eastern Ontario, the Ottawa Valley, with its old Upper Canadian order disintegrating under the impact of urban influences. Johnny Harper is a high school dropout built up by an unscrupulous and stupid local impresario into a pop singer doomed to failure, partly because he lacks talent but partly also because of the self-destructive urge that makes him take so easily to drugs. It is with a strangely sardonic tenderness that Cohen charts Johnny's erratic course, to hallucinatory triumph, to actual failure, to mental breakdown, to convalescence on a counter-cultural farm in the Ottawa Valley, and back to the singing circuit which will destroy him.

The manner of telling is oblique and deliberately discontin-uous; Johnny's inner fantasies alternate with the narrations of Lew Clinton, the civil servant turned farmer and shaman who both encourages Johnny in drug-taking and saves him after his worst excesses, and with the newspaper reports of the *Ottawa Citi-zen* columnist Frank Shaughnessy, who follows the highs and more frequent lows of Johnny's career. Always one is conscious of the inner division between Johnny the country boy who a genera-tion before might have been a happy farmer and the disoriented product of the modern educational system whose phony ambi-tions make him the victim of the kind of exploiters who preyed on and destroyed whatever creative impulses stirred in the youth cul-ture of the 1960s. *Johnny Crackle Sings* was an interesting jeu d'esprit when it appeared in 1971; now it reads as a bright period piece, less relevant outside its own temporal setting than almost anything else Cohen has written.

Yet the sense of living unhappily between two worlds, "one dead, the other powerless to be born," that one senses in *Johnny Crackle Sings,* is certainly one of the leitmotifs of all Cohen's major works, *The Disinherited, Wooden Hunters, The Colours of War* and *The Sweet Second Summer of Kitty Malone.* Orders that seem stable, like the agricultural economy of Upper Canada and the elaborately ceremonial culture of the British Columbian Coast Indians, collapse and leave their peoples disoriented, searching between a lost past and an unrealized future, until, in the third novel, the direction of progress becomes confused, and a search for the future becomes a journey into the past. It is in this confusion that the characters reveal their divisions of purpose, the essential alienations that warp their natures.

All these novels except *Wooden Hunters* are set in an eastern Ontario countryside where Loyalists, later American immigrants, and early nineteenth-century migrants from Britain cleared the forests, built towns of stone and farmhouses capable of lasting for generations, and established a stable and prosperous farming economy which seemed eternal — and lasted little more than a century before machine technology and urbanization changed it from a way of life into an industrial pattern. This countryside and its inhabitants are first introduced in three of the stories in *Night Flights,* all of them written before *The Disinherited* and all concerning two rustic drunkards, Pat and Mark Frank, who assume minor roles in *The Disinherited* and, in Pat's case, in *The Colours of War,* and major roles in *The Sweet Second Summer of Kitty Malone* in which parts of the early stories reappear in adapted form. The Malone family, whose various members figure in all three novels, is introduced in the story "Brain Dust," and in this story the town of Salem, the centre of this countryside, first appears: Salem, the old stone market town which in *The Colours of War* seems the epitome of rustic virtues and failings, and projects an eccentric sanity in a world of collective madness.

The world of Salem is one where, as a character in "Country Music" remarks, "people around here are awful liars" and where truth seems to shift according to the story and the teller. For in "Country Music" Pat and Mark are represented as being the sons of the widow Frank by a wandering single-day lover named John McRae, whereas in "Glass Eyes and Chickens," and later in both *The Disinherited* and *The Sweet Second Summer of Kitty Malone*, we learn that they were brought up by their widowed father, Terry Frank, a prosperous farmer who took to drink and whose farm, where Mark now lives by repairing decrepit trucks with bits of even more decrepit vehicles, serves as a paradigm of the land's decay and its submergence under the relentless invasion of the machine:

In the time of his father's sobriety, there had been a white frame farm-house surrounded by four barns, two hundred acres of only mildly rocky land, and a huge maple bush that backed down to the lake. Successive waves of alcoholism and fire had swallowed the land and burned down the original house. The new house was only the old pig barn in disguise; it was flanked by the two other remaining barns, which sat in front of it like twin warnings of disaster. Between them, leading from the house to the highway, was a hundred-yard driveway littered on either side with dead vehicles and spare parts, a true cornucopia of ancient and rusting cars and trucks. They filled the barnyard better than pigs or cows ever had. Like crops, they were planted from time to time and harvested when needed; but unlike crops, they demanded nothing, had no rhythms of their own, only the rhythm of his own days and whims.

This world of transition and decay is transposed, in *The Disinherited*, onto the screen of a novel in the classic manner, a family chronicle centred on the death of one of the family members and evoking a long past through the apparently erratic but really cumulative operation of memory. The action is rich, but it is seen through the inner eye.

Richard Thomas, a farmer in the Salem countryside and a neighbour of the Franks, goes out early one morning to inspect his property and is felled by a stroke; he is taken to hospital and there, when he is about to be released as at least partly cured, he dies of a second attack. As he lies in bed he remembers, and his memories and emotions are complemented by those of his wife, his son, and his adopted son. There is a chronological succession on one level — from Richard's stroke to his death and funeral, embracing the conflicts in the family over what will happen to the farm at his death. But the past appears sporadically, in fragments, as associations create it, and finally clusters into a completeness outside duration. The process Cohen uses is rather similar to the

134

process of recollective reconstruction I remember in my own experience when recovering from a brief amnesia; memories emerging apparently spontaneously and others being drawn in by association, so that blocks of the past were recreated rather haphazardly until in the end the whole jigsaw puzzle of lost time was filled in, leaving unremembered only the eight hours when I was actually in an amnesiac state.

The pattern that is recovered from time by the end of *The Disinherited* is one that justifies the title, since it presents the history of an Ontario rural family, founded by Richard Simon Thomas who came in the mid-nineteenth century as the ancestral earth-breaking pioneer. All in their differing ways vigorous and cunning and earthily amoral, Richard Simon and his son Simon and his grandson Richard carry on the farm in splendid style, each opening up new fields to satisfy his ambition, and in their century of occupation the holding assumes that illusive appearance of antique permanence the earlier-settled parts of Canada so quickly took on. But Canada was not in fact allowed the slow growth from the mediaeval into the modern world, the long maturing that made the peasant order of Europe a matter of centuries, even millenia, rather than generations.

By Richard's end in 1970, it is evident that the energy of the Thomas race is being sapped as surely as its land is being ruined by the creep of urbanization. Richard has held out obstinately against the tempting offers of land speculators who wish to build summer cottages and a resort-marina on the lake shore of his property. But his son Erik, through whose mind the novel is drawn to a close, is uninterested in following his example. Like Korsoniloff, he is a budding academic afflicted by a divided will, and the difference between him and his father is shown in a key conversation in the hospital as Erik tries to justify his choice of a university career instead of the agrarian life that would keep the farm in the Thomas bloodline. The passage is long, but it contains the thematic key to *The Disinherited*.

"You know," Erik said, "that just because I don't want to live on the farm, it doesn't mean I didn't learn anything from you."

"That's nice," Richard said.

"It's just that, well, there's a lot of important things going on in this country and so, you know, people have to be able to think clearly. And the university is the place where that happens."

"The rules . . ." Richard said, remembering a previous argument when Erik had claimed that all logical thinking had rules.

"Yes."

"You teach people the rules," Richard said.

"Yes."

"What about life?"

"What about it?"

"Who teaches people how to live?"

"I don't know," Erik said. Richard could tell he was starting to lose his temper. He had just put out one cigarette and was now lighting another, forgetting even to go and smoke it by the window. "People have to teach themselves how to live."

"God help them," Richard said.

"He never has." Erik up on his feet, pacing back and forth from window to door . . . . "People think well, all right, all they have to do is tend their own garden as best they can, never look beyond it, as if the world has stopped so they can do whatever they want, but it's not true, things have changed, the whole world is connected together."

"It was always connected together," Richard said.

"Politically."

"That's what Hitler wanted."

"God." Erik had sat down now, giving up entirely, looking as if he had decided he would sit there without speaking until either someone else came or Richard died, whichever came first, it didn't matter.

"I'm sorry," Richard said. "I'm just an old man."

"It doesn't matter."

"But I've always thought that there was more to life than rules and logic."

"Of course," Erik said.

"A man has to know his own destiny."

"Oh Christ," Erik sighed, starting to get to his feet again and then slumping back into his chair. "No one has destinies any more," he said. "They live in apartments and breed goldfish." It was early afternoon, just after lunch. The courtyard was emptier than ever, mid-August doldrums, and the sun shone flat and hot on the black asphalt. Around the edges of the courtyard, and slowly encroaching on the middle, were crumpled-up chocolate bar wrappers, old newspapers, crushed milkshake cartons. There were only a few cars parked there, all of them seeming dusty and familiar.

No matter how he had tried to change him, Erik always "seemed city to Richard, the way he avoided doing things with his body, wore his clothes as decorations, was always glancing nervously about him, as if there were something about to bite." The adopted son, Brian, disgusts Richard with his stupidity from boyhood, yet he is "stronger and more capable" than Erik and turns out in the end to be the only possible heir. But there are ambiguities even in this situation; Brian attacks Erik with a broken bottle at Richard's funeral even though the farm has been left for him to run as long as he wishes. For the line between the organically healthy and the alienated in *The Disinherited* is never so clearly drawn as it might first appear. The rural existence is no guarantee of a sane or serene way of life. Richard and his father Simon fight almost to the death over Katherine Malone. And if one seeks personifications of alienation they can be found not only in city-lost men like Erik but equally among the Franks and their companions, "drunken white witch doctors staggering around in the middle of winter passing through convulsions for this brief vision . . . ."

The Franks provide a kind of chorus of sad buffoons to the life of Richard and his ancestors, just as the night nurse in the hospital, with her tales of grotesque sicknesses and deaths, and his fellow patient Zeller, visibly shrinking with a rampant cancer and a stiff upper lip, provide the chorus to his death. The tragic and the bizarre, Cohen never ceases to suggest, are sibling conditions.

But to reduce *The Disinherited* to the Thomas men — even though that includes Cousin William C. Thomas, the mystic who seduces old Richard Simon's wife — is to diminish it greatly, for the women play the potent roles of reconciling the irreconcilables. Just as Richard Thomas's wife, Elizabeth, through lying in a barn with the poet, becomes the mother of the mad and exalted Frederick Thomas as well as of her legitimate son, the shrewd and vindictive Simon, so Katherine Malone is the mistress of Simon and then Richard, father and then son, and Miranda, whom Richard meets and marries when he too thinks of the city and spends a brief time at the university, provides the only true bridge between Richard and their son Erik. There is also a curious link between Miranda and Erik through the strange, self-contained Rose Garnett, who seduces Erik when he encounters her living in a decayed farmhouse on a backwoods road, and then surfaces as a well-connected fortuneteller whom Miranda recommends to her son.

If Katherine Malone, so fertile that any casual encounter seems to make her pregnant, is the earthmotherly symbol of other-containment in *The Disinherited,* Rose is the personification of self-containment, as perilously challenging as Jung's anima. As Erik sees her in her new role:

Whatever it was that had first made her seem so exotic had spread to her bones and muscles: now it was not only the way she held herself and dressed, but in every movement she made, like a fencer, parrying the world with swift invisible strokes, never straying from the tape. . . . When he asked her about the changes she just laughed, said that he had never appreciated her, now the complete jungle cat, sensuous and without even the most momentary of debts.

When Erik suggested to Rose that they live together, "she had ignored it, as if it was clear that he couldn't mean such a thing, that he was obviously incapable of letting anything pass in or out of his own boundaries."

And, indeed, when Erik does appear to achieve the kind of union with another human being that takes him temporarily out of himself, it is with an unnamed pregnant girl whom he meets and sleeps with casually and gives the ring of the mystic poet, though he knows they will never live together. In all his actions he shows himself taken up in the essential loneliness, the unrelenting alienation of modern man, from which the very precariousness of their way of life seems to shield the traditional farming people who gathered at Richard Thomas's grave and "mourned him without particular grief or feeling but as a necessary marking of their own passing."

The Disinherited is a work of unusual vigour and density. The sense of warring past and present is splendidly created, the characters swell to giants as they recede into memory, and the whole novel, though it is of no more than average length, has a largeness of texture that leaves a massive shadow on the mind. Up to now it is, I believe, Cohen's finest work.

But this is not to deny the special qualities of the later novels. The first of these, *Wooden Hunters,* leaves the setting of eastern Ontario for the new terrain of British Columbia's west coast and an island that seems very much like one of the Queen Charlottes, inhabited by the survivors of a great Indian nation, living side by side with itinerant loggers and a few lifestyle refugees from the straight world. It is a place where nature appears irrepressible, constantly self-renewing:

The alder silhouetted against the blue sky, the coloured leaves and frozen morning reminded him of the east but the wetness and fertility of this island, the newness of the air, the speed with which things seemed to grow and then be re-absorbed into the forest floor all made the east seem used and impossible to him, a place that could no longer renew itself, and now sometimes he imagined that whole section of the continent was a vast conglomerate city of doomed smokestacks and concrete.

In a way this sense of decay and everlasting renewal reconciles the characters with the setting, for all the people we encounter in *Wooden Hunters* — unlike most of the inhabitants of *The Disinherited* —have lost or forsaken their pasts. There are the Indians with their vanished extravagant culture, their old villages and mouldering totem poles, of whom the personification is Johnny Tulip, drunken, drug-soaked, dying and sustaining his last months playing old jazz tunes on the warped piano in the local hotel.

Johnny Tulip laughed his crazy broken laugh, laughed and then coughed again. It seemed impossible to Calvin that this man could have a past, at least a past other than what he carried with him, marked into his body and face, so much his own now that other people's mistakes could no longer touch him.

The pasts are there of course. It is by their converging pasts that such incongruous people as Calvin, the wandering white intellectual ("a weak and persistent moth," as he sees himself), and Laurel Hobson, his lover and once Johnny Tulip's, and the hotel manager C.W. Smith from Montana, with his undertaker's clothes and the hearse he drives around the island, have been brought together on this ultimate edge of North America, an edge beyond civilization where nature is still strong enough to threaten and where the old wars between traditions are yet unstilled. Smith thinks he has "slipped away from his past, eluded it in some secret and final way," but it is waiting to reclaim him, and eventually does, just as, despite Johnny's air of self-containment, he has never ceased to be an Indian.

Wooden Hunters, in fact, is constructed to take account of the reality of the past, even if ultimately to reject it, for it assumes a similar general forward movement in time punctuated by flashes into the past as *The Disinherited* does, though the time recovered is not so deep or rich as in the larger novel, since *Wooden Hunters* is not concerned with creating a dynastic record but rather with releasing the tensions of a violent present.

The memory patterns of the various characters differ considerably in intensity. Calvin has few memories except of how he encountered Laurel Hobson after he left his life in the east to discover a new existence, perhaps a new personality, in the west, and this limitation marks his sense of starting afresh, almost as ineffectual as a child, in this new and harsh environment where he feels he can survive only by a self-transformation he has not yet achieved. He is too involved in this immediate process to have much concern for his own past.

Laurel Hobson, who is his mentor as well as his lover, and in her self-containment somewhat resembles Rose Garnett in *The Disinherited*, has transformed herself and survived, a process that began with her first visit to the island six years earlier as an innocent, to be seduced by Johnny and then to break her spine falling down a cliff. Unlike Calvin, she can afford to remember because she accepts the apparent accidents that changed her life. Recovering in Vancouver from her almost mortal injuries, she finds middleclass life there so insipid that she returns to the island, takes over an abandoned cabin, and learns to become a ruthless hunter who sets a pattern of violence in the first pages of *Wooden Hunters* by initiating Calvin into the brutal West Coast custom of "pitlamping"—shooting a deer at night by holding it in the fascination of a flashlight beam. Laurel is wild and degenerate at the same time, scarred by long sessions of alcohol and morphine and cocaine, yet also surprisingly tough and resilient in both mind and body. It is almost as if the breaking and knitting of her spine were a symbol of the remaking of her personality, just as in shamanic myths the initiate is dismembered and reassembled to mark his inner transformation. (Interestingly enough, Rose Garnett, who seems in *The Disinherited* to have undergone her own kind of inner transformation, had also suffered and recovered from a broken spine.) "Despite everything that was animal about her—Calvin thinks—she seemed entirely rational to him, each action thought out and consecutive, one day following the other in some great inevitable framework whose shape was known to her, if no one else, its existence guaranteed by the absolute conviction with which she did everything. . . ."

In Laurel's learning to live with sangfroid in her cruel and tender world, where piano-playing Johnny presides like a shabby and self-destroying shaman, there is of course an exemplification of the theme of survival that would fit admirably into Margaret

Atwood's critical thesis. But at the same time one is also aware of the repetition of a pattern familiar in the novels of the European existentialists: the deliberate courting of extreme situations in which, by choices made in the face of death (one's own or other men's or that of creatures like deer and salmon brutally slaughtered), one recreates oneself. For there is a strangely triumphal quality to Laurel, with her scarred body and mind, that counterpoints the elegiac music of Johnny's inevitable decline, trapped as he is in the collective tragedy of his people. It is with Calvin that Laurel leaves, after the last encounter with Johnny and his mother who promises a "good future" seen through the luminous wooden eyeballs of her blindness: Calvin who has come west, his mind a tabula rasa, not to lose but to find himself. "In the spring they would explore the coast, live on mussels and clams, make salads of wild peas and plantains."

The Colours of War opens with Theodore Beam discovering, under the hard fists of police thugs, that the West Coast, where he had drifted like Calvin and like Johnny Harper at the end of *Johnny Crackle Sings* in search of a freer and perhaps more natural life, is engulfed in social war. War as a figure for the conflict of generations and ways of life had been present in *The Disinherited.* It had moved sharply towards concrete reality in *Wooden Hunters,* where Johnny one day greets Laurel with the mysterious remark, "It's a war," and takes her on an expedition to destroy the giant tractor which Smith and the logging company have taken into the woods to start a massive timber operation that will destroy the site of an old Indian village beside a deserted inland lake. This act is in fact the beginning of a miniature war that gives the novel its touch of melodrama when Smith retaliates by blowing up the mortuary poles at the lakeside village, and then is killed, on an evening when the Indians are about to riot in the hotel, by a psychotic youth who, ironically, has driven the hearse over from the mainland. That round of warfare, with its aspects of a revolt against the exploitative materialism represented by Smith and the logging company, subsides as the survivors go on with their personal lives and deaths. But the conflict of *The Colours of War* is no longer episodic; it has become a general condition of the times.

The immediate action of *The Colours of War* takes place in the future — but not too far in the future, since characters out of *The Disinherited,* like Katherine Malone and Pat Frank, have survived to take part in it. The plot is built around a bizarre journey which extends physically across Canada from Vancouver to Salem, Ontario, but the journey is also one through time. Theodore Beam is travelling in what, to the reader, is the future — on his way back to the past. Once again, it is a memory novel, and as he journeys, past, present and future mingle like the colours of a shaken kaleidoscope.

In Vancouver, where he lives the kind of easy existence without destination that is possible on the Coast, Theodore — the son of a Jewish newspaper editor in Salem — becomes dimly aware that social life is breaking down all over North America, for hunger has at last begun to afflict even the formerly affluent lands, and disorder follows hunger. Governments react in the only way that governments can:

Every day it seemed there were new declarations of emergencies and martial law. Not exactly a new law; things being the same as always but carried one step further.

One day the irrational hand of power reaches out to Theodore, when two detectives invade his flat, rough him up and ransack his rooms. He is not sure whether they have come in search of the packet of cocaine his Chinese landlady deftly removes from their sight, or for something mysterious which he does not in fact possess.

The day is his birthday and that night his father rings from Salem. Theodore decides to accept Jacob Beam's urgings to return home. But the journey that takes him back into his past, and in a sense also into Canada's past, goes by way of a future that may await us all. When he reaches the station he finds it packed with people responding to obscure fears and self-preservatory urges.

Not only were the departing trains completely booked, but the station was swollen with those who were arriving. For every one of us who was fleeing to some more certain home in the East, it seemed there were several who hoped that the mild wet winters of the Coast would be easier to survive. I was reminded again of old stories of the depression and the vast armies of the unemployed crisscrossing the country; when nothing else is possible, motion promises to fill the stomach.

Theodore finds eventually that the train on which he has managed to book a roomette is no ordinary train. True, there are coaches where bona fide travellers, unaware of the real purpose of the journey, are crowded together. But there are also sealed vans, filled with arms and ammunition, and in the control of a group of guerillas. Theodore has already met the partisan leader Christopher Perestrello by chance in the station restaurant. "His voice and features were so strong that he seemed almost dangerous, even cruel: not the careless cruelty of the police but something more purposeful."

Perestrello, like Katherine Malone and Pat Frank, brings in an echo from earlier Cohen writings, in particular from "Columbus and the Fat Lady." This is the story of a fairground performer who trades on his psychoses by living out on stage a tranced fantasy of having been Columbus, and who dies in the middle of his performance. His wife, like the wife of the original Columbus, is named Felipa Perestrello, and the wife of Perestrello (who bears the name of Christopher) in *The Colours of War* is also Felipa, while the town of Salem, we later learn, was founded by a descendant of the Francisco de Bobadilla who in 1500 arrested Columbus and his son Diego. It is a complex pattern of connection, for, as we shall see, Perestrello is obsessed with the consequences of the Columbian discovery of America and is dedicated to reversing them. He is a Columbus enlightened and repentant.

At his first encounter with Theodore, Perestrello is attacked by a stranger, and when the two are escorted out of the station restaurant by the police, Theodore picks up an envelope Perestrello has left on the table. It contains a map of the route the train is following, marked at certain points with sites of rendezvous, and Theodore's possession of it leads him into contact with the partisans, for in the bar car on the train he meets a girl named Lise who takes him to her room and later threatens him with a pistol and demands the map.

Theodore becomes Lise's lover, learns of her long connection with an underground group seeking to undermine the governments of North America, and realizes the true purpose of the train, which Perestrello has organized through his railway union contacts to distribute arms to partisan groups all over the country and to spread rebellion in its wake. Theodore is accepted into the partisan group, and is present when the citizen soldiers of Regina, mobilized by the government to preserve order, go over to Perestrello's cause; the one farmer who opposes is shot outside the hotel as Theodore watches.

And standing in this window, looking out at this scene, we might have been anywhere, in any of the dozens of cities that have seen revolutions and coups, reprisals and executions....

... I had always thought that the external world would plod along forever, unchanged, a comfortable and amorphous bureaucracy, surrounding my life like a giant marshmallow, a giant excuse. Now that was fading and I was beginning to feel responsible for every moment I lived.

The train goes on, stopping several times every night for crates of weapons to be hurriedly unloaded. Theodore feels "as if the train was now turning itself into a long metal arrow drawing together the endless years of strikes, shortages, summer riots, outbursts of violence, into one spectacular collision." He is not sure whether the partisans are involved in a general uprising in which the unions and the army may combine to take over the country, or whether Perestrello is merely hoping his journey will coincide with outside events to make a revolutionary situation, travelling like Columbus into a great unknown.

All through this journey, in dreams and reveries, Theodore is returning to the past that Salem — daily drawing nearer — represents for him. Perhaps his most evocative memory is of a childhood visit to his orthodox Jewish grandfather. He looks at the strange, gnomelike, ancient man, and sees shining out of a withered face "the pale blue eyes that I recognised as my eyes but a thousand years old, my eyes shining out of his face...."

As I lay in bed and waited for sleep, I held a secret in my mind — that grandfather and I were the same person, that I had seen myself in the mirror of the glass door, and then the door had opened and he stepped out: me in disguise.

Apart from the characteristic Cohen theme of the division of the self, the haunting doppelgänger, the interlude reveals the same intense concern with tradition and continuity that emerged in Cohen's earlier novel, *The Disinherited,* and it is significant that the grandfather's gift to Theodore should be one of time, objectified in a gold watch, thin and old.

Even Perestrello — and this assessment of the revolutionary mind is certainly one of the thematic notes of *The Colours of War* — is really entering the future to find the past. (And what else did either Marx or Bakunin attempt?) In the last scene in which he is actually present, Perestrello talks of "pure force," not merely as the urge of modern revolutionaries, but also as the urge that brought the people of the old world to the new world. Men had destroyed Europe; they came to the Americas where, this repentant Columbus tells, "before we came, men lived as true men, and every human being knew the meaning of his own life." The land was waiting, to "take for our own."

Perestrello shrugged and leaned forward over the table and the map this world had become. "Of course, we were wrong. The future was only the past in an elaborate disguise. The continent was ruined as easily as a child or a wife. With the slaves and the killings we poisoned ourselves. We began to realize that the new world had already become the old. There was no place to receive us. We could only go round and round, repeating ourselves.

"I still have hope," Perestrello said. "Somewhere inside us there's a place that has never been touched, and is still innocent, waiting to be discovered. When we've suffered, when the violence is over and the false governments have fallen, when we're simple men and women again, standing on the face of the earth, there'll be something we can reach for, something noble inside us."

In fact, Perestrello is a creature of the time of violence, and does not survive into an age of innocence regained. As the train continues on its journey, it becomes evident that all is not so completely in his control as once appeared. Felipa is attacked on the train by double agents; he himself is wounded by a sniper at the last rendezvous for delivering arms; news comes that government troops have suppressed the insurgents in Regina and Vancouver; finally, the train reaches a railway yard where army units are awaiting it with artillery, and in the battle Perestrello is killed. Theodore and Lise escape and so, independently, does Filipa.

Theodore and Lise make their way to Salem, which is filled with government troops whom Theodore fears. Nevertheless, there are some hilarious bibulous interludes with Jacob Beam, Pat Frank, and other town characters, before Theodore takes refuge in the Salem countryside in an abandoned church which belongs to Katherine Malone, now an octagenarian. When he goes to ask her permission to live in the building, Theodore sees a picture of Katherine on her twenty-first birthday, sixty years before, when, as we know, she was the mistress of both Simon and Richard Thomas.

In those days she had been immortal; her bones slender and long, her eyes tinted so they shone like bright beacons of rural confidence. The house in the background had been almost a mansion in that era of prosperity. Although now it shambled and sagged, the wood coming through the paint, in those days it was gleaming white with hedges and flower bushes that grew thick around the stone foundation walls.

Katherine still lives as a personification of a simpler world, the old house still stands, the old church even more solidly. There Theodore lives, after Felipa has appeared and led Lise away to become an urban guerilla. Hiding from the soldiers, he writes the book we are reading, hunting his food — like Laurel in *Wooden Hunters* — in the woods with an old gun Katherine has given him, until, in the last pages of the novel, Lise returns.

Once we dreamed of being citizens of a perfect state. The cells of our body ran wild with faith, pushing us through childhood to this place we have reached. I remember the dreams; but sometimes it can't be helped — I hear not music but armies moving in the night.

The earth will try to feed us, no matter how foolish we are. Soon Jacob Beam will sit out in the garden in the afternoons, feeling his eyes go blind, the sun crossing his face.

Old words flood through me. This hand records them — my hand, my father's hand.

The sky is clear and the sun is out. I can see Lise walking across the field, a rifle in her arms. For this day there is food again.

We will go on living here.

Theodore, in his inaction, has returned to the innocence Perestrello sought in vain through action.

There are features of *The Colours of War* that, if we consider the book as an ordinary novel, seem ineffectual. Perestrello is a figure we never enter; encased in his impeccable blue uniform, he is remote even from the other characters, and we do not witness his death, which is told of with offhand indirection. Lise and Felipa are types of naive and cynical radicalism, the sacred and profane poles of political enthusiasm. All three might be members of a dream of which the great train is a vehicle, and Matt Cohen has in fact been accused of populating his book with mannequins.

The criticism would be valid if *The Colours of War* claimed to be a novel in the ordinary sense. But by the same criterion, the King of Brobdingnag in *Gulliver's Travels* and even O'Brien in *1984* might also be dismissed as mannequins, because they are not developed and credible as human beings. But their function is quite different, and so is the function of Perestrello and the two women in *The Colours of War*. Theodore must be seen as a kind of latter-day Candide, set to wander as an innocent through the man-made jungles of the present, and to find that all the promises of the future are illusory in comparison with the rediscovery of roots and of Matt Cohen's wry equivalent of Voltaire's cultivation of one's garden. Despite appearances, it is, as Voltaire's was, a counsel of defiance rather than defeat, a statement of life continuing its tenacious way in the ruin of social order and of political idealism. Considered as a parable, which I believe is what Cohen intended, *The Colours of War* is direct and luminous and salutary.

While *The Disinherited* shows somewhat despairingly the flow of modernism that is dislocating the decaying agrarian culture of Canada and disinheriting its inhabitants, and *The Colours of War* shows a future where rampant progress has gone into retreat and men seek refuge in a defensive nostalgia, *The Sweet Second Summer of Kitty Malone* reaches, through its creation of an intensely living present, a brilliantly and rightly positive conclusion. It translates the myths of popular fiction by showing that splendid romantic passions can belong to the lifeworn and ugly as well as to the young and beautiful, and love can survive anger, defeat and degeneration and somehow squeeze from them joy.

The Sweet Second Summer must have been long in Cohen's mind, for two of the stories which in 1972 he included in *Columbus and the Fat Lady* find their way with very little alteration into the novel. These are "Brain Dust" and "Glass Eyes and Chickens," which introduce not only Salem and its declining farming country, but also three of the leading figures of the novel—Kitty Malone herself and the ageing twins Pat and Mark Frank, the "drunken white witch doctors" of *The Disinherited*. Kitty is the cousin of Joe Malone, whose wife Katherine was the lover of both Simon and Richard Thomas in that earlier novel, and her brother Charlie is the Frank brothers' closest friend.

Pat Frank is already an adult drunkard when Kitty, still a teenager, seduces him in the dreaming hayfields north of Kingston. In spite of her manifest infatuation, he refuses to marry her because he thinks that it will be her destruction; secretly he believes that his brain is shrinking and that the voids left in his skull are filling up with dust. Kitty goes off to Toronto and marries a city slicker, Randy Blair. But she never entirely sheds her infatuation for Pat

Frank, and inevitably the marriage fails. She returns to Salem to live in the house her grandfather built for his retirement before he fell to his death from the barn roof, and takes up again with Pat for another twenty years of haphazard shacking-up, from which she has a daughter, Lynn.

But it is only when she has finally surrendered the possibilities and illusions of youth that Kitty can really find herself. She goes into hospital to have a cyst removed in an operation that renders her sterile; at the same time Pat, at forty-nine already a skeletal alcoholic, fights the last battle of his belligerent career and is beaten up by Randy—her city-born son—and his father. It is now that they finally come together, lived-out wrecks by most standards yet filled with an inexplicable inner access of youthfulness, to marry and share the same decaying farmhouse, and Kitty can find herself, in the last words of the novel, "standing straight, ready to live out the warm endless summer ahead."

What gives *The Sweet Second Summer of Kitty Malone* its special sense of depth and authenticity, despite a plot that might easily have turned sentimental, is Matt Cohen's power of encompassing individual fates, and obsessive relationships like that of Kitty and Pat, within collective and ancestral patterns. In *The Disinherited* there is the lineage of the Thomases, from the original great-grandfather down to Richard's town-corrupted son Erik, to provide the background of a changing Canada within which the characters create and suffer and die, and the same applies to *The Colours of War*, where the scarcely credible adventures of Theodore Beam are given substance not by the Utopian visions of his doomed fellow conspirators but rather by the long family vista into the past provided by his father, Jacob, and his aged orthodox Jewish grandfather.

The age of a land, as Chinese and Melanesians well know, is validated only by the human ancestries with which it is identified, and so, in *The Sweet Second Summer,* it is the Malone ancestry—attached to the Malone lands—that forms the essential background to the strange romance of middle-aged Kitty and decrepit Pat, the ambiance within which these unlikely figures come to "calm of mind, all passion spent." The lineage extends from the grandfather who fell to death from the barn through Kitty's crazy mother, Ellen, who dies in an ecstatic vision of union with God as she is visiting Kitty in hospital (while in a kind of holy irony a drunken Pat shouts "Hallelujah!"), and down to Kitty's daughter by Pat—enigmatic Lynn who dreams always of places beyond the places where men live.

Against the quixotic world of Perestrello and his fellow conspirators in *The Colours of War,* Cohen presents in *The Sweet Second Summer of Kitty Malone* a kind of Sancho Panza world where survival is the great virtue. In that world men appear to be selfish, taken up with minor greeds, irrational prides and divisive longings, but the call of blood is strong, spreading out in great ripples from single passionate relationships to the strength of families and communities. In *The Sweet Second Summer of Kitty Malone* it is most dramatically illustrated in the funeral of old Ellen, who had so impressed the people of Salem with her eccentric presence that the cemetery is densely packed, and people come in hundreds to drink away her life insurance at the wake, which is also the wedding party for Kitty and Pat. Here at least, despite Hamlet, it is appropriate that the funeral baked meats should furnish forth the marriage table. For the strange ecstasy of Ellen's dying is not far removed from the strange ecstasy of Kitty's loving a man so doomed as Pat. Paradoxically, death at this point holds our minds in a celebration of life, a celebration few contemporary novelists have rendered so convincingly as Matt Cohen.

[1979]

Margaret Atwood:
Poet as Novelist

THE NOTES ON Margaret Atwood which follow this brief preface form a kind of many-headed essay that has developed on a roughly parallel track to her own development. In 1972 I published an essay in *The Literary Half-Yearly* of Mysore, entitled "Margaret Atwood" and dealing with her first six volumes of verse and her first novel, *The Edible Woman*. A year later, in 1973, I published in *Ariel*, a magazine of the University of Calgary, a second essay, dealing mainly with *Surfacing*, her second novel, and *Survival*, her book of criticism, which I called "Surfacing to Survive: Notes on the Recent Atwood." I had written the second piece as a complement to the first, with the idea of eventually combining them, and in 1974, when I was preparing my anthology of critical essays by various writers, *The Canadian Novel in the Twentieth Century* (New Canadian Library), I performed the splice and published the combined and largely rewritten version as "Margaret Atwood: Poet as Novelist."

Since that time Margaret Atwood has published another four books: a third novel *(Lady Oracle)*, a collection of stories *(Dancing Girls)* and two books of verse *(You Are Happy* and *Two-Headed Poems)*. After a great deal of thought I decided not to change in any substantial way the essay that was completed in 1974, since it stood as an effective statement of Atwood's achievement in her earlier phase; instead I would add a kind of postscript, which forms Part II of the piece that follows, dealing with the more recent works. Part I, of course, is a very lightly edited version of the 1974 "Margaret Atwood: Poet as Novelist."

I

Perhaps the most immediately striking of Margaret Atwood's eight books of verse is a collection of poems of sexual communion — for it is a relationship too acrid to be called *love* in the ordinary sense that she describes — entitled with mordantly analogical appropriateness *Power Politics* (1971). The opening poem is a terse and tense pair of couplets which not only set the acerbic tone of the volume as a whole, but also present an image that takes one by an amazingly short cut to the very heart of Atwood's kind of poetry and — what is largely the same thing — her kind of perception:

> you fit into me
> like a hook into an eye
>
> a fish hook
> an open eye

It is as sharp and disillusioned an expression as one could expect of the cruel inevitabilities of love: that what is so appropriate (fitting) should also be so painful. But look farther: Margaret Atwood is no mere black romantic, delighted only to uncover the horrors in what the polite world likes to dismiss as fortunate because it cannot be escaped. At least three essential characteristics of her poetic nature emerge from a closer look at this veritable caltrop of a poem — spiny in whatever direction you turn it.

First, there is her skill at the poetic booby trap — the sharp ironic inversion by which such an image of domestic bliss as the Victorian hook-and-eye — so secure a fastening until welcome hands undo it — is suddenly transformed by a shift to a related image which shuts out any thought of bliss, shuts it out like an eyelid, by its evocation of a pain one feels with an almost physical twinge, in one's own mind's eye.

But there is another, more intellectual kind of inversion involved; the poet proceeds from the metaphorical to the literal use of an image — that of the eye — and in this way reminds us of that world of resonant correspondences, of shading meanings and relationships in which our mental patterns as well as our physical perceptions exist. And yet, in that complex of symbolic relationships, our attention is still held by that vital image, the eye itself which holds so much that is significant in Margaret Atwood's poetry. For the eye sees, and is hurt, and so perception and feeling converge.

Perhaps more than any other Canadian poet of the younger generation, Margaret Atwood combines an extraordinary visual sensibility, the first requirement of any good poet, with a spare and laconic intellectual discipline. There is hardly a slack word in all her thin and rigorously selected volumes of poetry; there are no vague thoughts — everything is honed to sharpness; there is no avoidable obscurity. To make a comparison (which is not meant to be invidious in either direction) with another poet of comparable technical ability and intellectual power, one never finds in Atwood the essential difficulty of Margaret Avison's poetry, perhaps because Atwood's is a world where the complexities which exist are not spiritual. There is ambiguity indeed, but with the terms always clearly perceptible for those who have learnt her language; there is tortuosity of emotion, not of thought or expression. And always that limpidity of tone which tempts one to adapt a phrase of Orwell and talk, in relation to Atwood, of verse like a windowpane.

It is a question of poetic objectivity, for in the aspects that count Atwood is essentially an objective poet. This of course is not a matter of personality being absent; one finds it hard to imagine a poet's personality more astringently present than Atwood's in *Power Politics*. But personality, and personal experience, while they shape the content of her poems and infuse the style, in no way opacify the verbal surface, which is everywhere translucent; if among modern Canadian poets there is in spirit a true descendant of the imagists, it is Margaret Atwood. For her, as for all the really important modern poets, the visible world exists; her poems are, as all good poems must be, intensely visual, and through this quality the pervading mind and sensibility express themselves. And Margaret Atwood's accurate consciousness of the proper relationship between this visual sensibility — blending into the tactile and the aural perceptions — which dictates the substance of poetry, and the mental processes that shape its intent, explains why she is so remarkably good a critic, as her individual essays and her idiosyncratic survey of Canadian literature, *Survival*, have shown.

So much for the general view: the qualities in Margaret Atwood's poems that make one welcome the progress that brought her in a decade from her first publication to a position of recognition as one of the established Canadian poets and, in terms of current production, one of the best among them. Her first volume was a thin leaflet, now almost forgotten, and certainly never mentioned, entitled *Double Persephone,* which a little press brought out in 1961. For the next five years she published sparingly in little magazines; then, in 1966, appeared *The Circle Game,* a collection which served notice that a poet of stature had emerged. It won the Governor General's Award for that year, and, perhaps a surer sign of its genuine quality, A.J.M. Smith included no less than eleven pages from this volume — about a seventh of its entire length — in the definitive anthology, *Modern Canadian Verse,* which he published in 1967. Other books of verse followed at close intervals: *The Animals in That Country, The Journals of Susanna Moodie, Procedures for Underground, Power Politics.*

Atwood's poetic affinities are complex. Her highly articulate verses continue the tradition of sophisticated poetic utterance one associates with the poets who came into prominence in the 1950s, with Eli Mandel and Jay Macpherson, and, in another way, with Phyllis Webb. Her short-lined stanzas look superficially like those of the breath-counters and Black Mountain grunters who have won and lost so much attention in the past decade, but in fact they are the products of a very taut technical discipline in which the qualities of sound and statement are balanced tightly. It is poetry that — as true poetry must — stays on the page and in the mind when the voice has echoed into silence. Yet there are ways in which Atwood shares a great deal with the poets who are in terms of age her immediate contemporaries, like George Bowering and John Newlove, and also the late-blooming Al Purdy, for like them she is conscious of the Canadian land and of the Canadian past in a way the generation of the fifties, with the notable exception of Jeames Reaney, was not.

But before I enlarge on these aspects of Atwood's poetry, I think it is illuminating to consider her first novel, *The Edible Woman,* which appeared in 1969. It is a good novel, articulate, sophisticated, in which Atwood turns phrases and collates images in prose with the same assurance as she does in verse. It is as pungently expressive of a tantalizingly defensive individuality as any of its author's poems.

Some poets who turn novelists, and vice versa, show a curiously divided literary personality; one might be excused, for example, for failing to recognize that the same man wrote Roy Fuller's poems and his less-known novels. But there is none of this division in Margaret Atwood. The capillary links between her poetry, her fiction, her criticism, are many and evident. Indeed, the identity between the poems and *The Edible Woman* is so close that it was with a sense of déjà vu that I read *Power Politics* not long after a second reading of the novel, for both concern the cruelties of love, the Proustian impenetrability love encounters, and when I try to think of a quick way of saying what *The Edible Woman* is about, a verse from *The Circle Game* comes immediately to my mind.

> These days we keep
> our weary distances:
> sparring in the vacant spaces
> of peeling rooms
> and rented minutes, climbing
> all the expected stairs, our voices
> abraded with fatigue,
> our bodies wary.

The Edible Woman, too, is about the distances and defences between human beings. The distances and defences are necessary because human beings are predatory. *The Edible Woman* is a novel about emotional cannibalism.

This is the significance of the title, which also names the central image. The edible woman is a cake shaped like a woman and carefully iced for verisimilitude, which the heroine, Marian MacAlpin, eats at the key point of the novel, when she is released from the doggedly normal life she insisted on pursuing.

Having, cannibalistically, trapped a highly normal young man into a proposal of marriage, Marian has felt herself becoming in turn the victim of his moral anthropophagy. Seeking escape with a graduate student she meets in a laundromat, she finds that he too, if not exactly a cannibal, is a more insidious kind of parasite, a lamprey battening on her compassion to feed his monstrous self-pity.

Marian's recognition of her situation takes the form of a symbolic neurosis. She finds her throat closing first against meat, as she vividly associates a steak with the living animal. There comes the stage when she peels a carrot and imagines the soundless shriek as it is pulled from the earth. But this point, when she seems doomed to starvation, coincides with the point of climax in her personal relationships, when she runs away from her own engagement party to sleep with Duncan, the man from the laundromat, and, having discovered that there is no external solution to her problem, no solution in escape, returns and bakes the edible woman which, having offered it in vain to her outraged fiancé, she proceeds to eat. She has, of course, eaten herself, and in consuming the artificial "normal" being she tried to become, she is cured.

Such an account does far less than justice to a novel that is full of verbal and situational wit, and equally of ironic observation of human motives; as a comedy of manners the novel has to be read in detail to be completely appreciated. But it hints at the capable way in which Margaret Atwood uses the element of fantasy which has become so important a component of the New Fiction. She has indeed made Marian's improbable condition extremely plausible, and beside her handling of the fantastic, that of the average novelist seems crude and uncraftsmanly. One has only to compare *The Edible Woman* with the oafish obviousness of the fantasy in a second-rate Richler novel like *Cocksure* to realize this. But Margaret Atwood is a poet and Richler most clearly is not; evidently, a training in the poetic handling of images and myths gives an enormous advantage to any writer who aspires to fantasy fiction.

The virtuosity of Atwood's achievement becomes completely evident when one considers the other, more mundane aspect of *The Edible Woman*. For, among many other things, it is a social novel of high perceptiveness, and indeed, on second reading, I found the dense patterning of observed detail of human behaviour and of its physical setting perhaps more significant in relation to the writer's poetry than is the more obvious "poetic" element in the central fantasy. For here that pained eye of *Power Politics* is at constant agonized play, and the narrator—whether it is Marian herself in the first and last parts of the novel, or the objective third person of the middle section, seems an extension of that lover in the poems whose mind is constantly playing over her own emotions and mental condition, like the "third in the narrow bed" of A.S.J. Tessimond's poem of the 1930s.

Marian moves in a straight world of—to quote the author as quoted on the dust jacket—"ordinary people who make the mistake of thinking they are ordinary." By her occupation as a market researcher, she is kept in constant contact with the vast world of the unswingers (rarely celebrated in contemporary writing) who want nothing more than sheltered normality: the platinum blonde virgins who are more numerous than the sophisticated assume; the young men whose ambitions are bounded by a horizon of suburban retirement; the casualties of the graduate schools, obsessed with the detritus of scholarship; the inhabitants of the world of laundromats and supermarkets. In her own way, and for her own time and place, Atwood has done the kind of thing Jane Austen did for similar people almost two centuries ago; not that she is another Jane Austen nor, I imagine, would want to be. Except...

And here one takes a necessary leap back to the poems, for one volume of them extends temporally as well as analogically the web of correspondences that makes Margaret Atwood's imaginary world. That collection wherein a modern poet seeks to enter the mind of a pre-Victorian woman, *The Journals of Susanna Moodie*, takes us back in fact to an English writer of a generation and background very close to Jane Austen's. The difference is that Susanna Moodie came to Canada, extending thus the mental and physical dimensions of her life, and it is hard to imagine Jane Austen doing that. There is a static quality to the Austen view-point which was jolted loose by Moodie's experience, and this experience corresponds (in both the poetic and the common sense) with that process of dislocation and reassembling which typifies modern life and, since the cubists, has characterized more and more modern art and poetry. One senses it at the end of a poem like "The Immigrants" (from *The Journals*):

> my mind is a wide pink map
> across which move year after year
> arrows and dotted lines, further and further,
> people in railway cars
>
> their heads stuck out of the windows
> at stations, drinking milk or singing,
> their features hidden with beards or shawls
> day and night riding across an ocean of unknown
> land to an unknown land.

In such a poem one is aware of the strong historical sense that pervades the work of Margaret Atwood; the sense of a land and even a human culture which suddenly assume the quality of a vast age, even though its passage from the neolithic to the nuclear has taken little more than three centuries. But one is also aware of a kind of transference which gives much of the spiritual and compelling quality to Atwood's verse. In this case it is the attribution to a woman living more than a century ago of a kind of knowledge which only a poet in the present can have; there is an inversion of the situation in one of the poems of *Power Politics,* where that painful perceiver, the experiencing woman of the cycle, sees almost as in a lurid film the progression of feminine experience and herself at the centre of it:

> At first I was given centuries
> to wait in caves, in leather
> tents, knowing you would never come back
>
> Then it speeded up: only
> several years between
> the day you jangled off
> into the mountains, and the day (it was
> spring again) I rose from the embroidery
> frame at the messenger's entrance.
>
> .   .   .   .
>
> But recently, the bad evenings
> there are only seconds
> between the warning on the radio and the
> explosion; my hands
> don't reach you
>
> and on quieter nights
> you jump up from
> your chair without even touching your dinner
> and I can scarcely kiss you goodbye
> before you run out into the street and they shoot

But there are different transferences in the other poems, extending links between what is perceived and the perceiver, noting that the perception which seems objective can be subjective, that what we see is in ourselves as well as, or perhaps rather than, outside, and that, in all this, incomprehensible patterns exist. The poet sees the people looking at totem poles as the "other wooden people," and finds life only in the decay of a pole that has fallen on the ground; people handle Eskimo carvings, and when they have finished, the tactile experience has transferred to their hands the shape of the stone. The mental landscapes and the real landscapes interpenetrate, and solid and tangible as objects seem in Atwood's poems, their very materiality can suddenly be seen as a quality of the immaterial, though not dissolving or insubstantial for all that; it remains solidly, visually and sometimes tangibly there, striking its resonances in the mind, which form themselves into the final reality. The reader becomes like the man in "Progressive Insanities of a Pioneer":

> By daylight he resisted.
> He said, disgusted with the swamp's clamourings and the
> outbursts of rocks,
> > This is not order
> > but the absense
> > of order.
> He was wrong, the unanswering forest implied:
> > It was
> > an ordered absence.

What Margaret Atwood gives us, however, is not exactly an ordered absence; it is rather that ordering of apparent chaos through the search for analogies and correspondences which is the modern poet's historic task.

There is obviously much more to be said about Atwood as a subtle and complex and powerful poet, but perhaps the most important thing I have left unsaid she has implied herself in one of the poems of *Power Politics:*

> Beyond truth,
> tenacity: of those
> dwarf trees & mosses,
> hooked into straight rock
> believing the sun's lies & thus
> refuting / gravity
>
> & of this cactus, gathering
> itself together
> against the sand, yes tough
> rind & spikes but doing
> the best it can

Here is not merely an attitude to life that is evident in all Atwood's writings — an attitude appropriate to an age when survival has become the great achievement. Here is also the metaphor that expresses a personal poetic, even a personal ethic. To be (tenacity) is more certain than to know (truth); one does the best one can, shapes one's verse like one's life to the improbable realities of existence ("the sun's lies"), and in this age and place the realities impose a defensive economy, poems close to the rock, poems spiny as cactuses or caltrops.

When I read Atwood's second novel, *Surfacing,* and her topography of the Canadian literary consciousness, *Survival* (published almost simultaneously in the autumn of 1972), what impressed me was the extent to which these recent books developed in more discursive forms the personal ethic, linked to a personal poetic, which I had found emanating from the poems of her latest book of verse (though assuredly not her last, for so many of her poems have appeared recently in journals that one expects a new volume most seasons). I found the continuity, the sense of an extraordinarily self-possessed mind at work on an integrated structure of literary architecture, not only interesting and indeed exciting insofar as it concerned Margaret Atwood herself, but equally interesting and exciting as an index to the development of our literary tradition; a generation or even a decade ago, it would have been impossible to think of the Canadian literary ambience fostering this kind of confident and sophisticated sensibility.

The titles of Atwood's most recent books are themselves of immense significance. *Surfacing; Survival.* In each case the soft French prefix in place of the hard and arrogant Latin *super*, and in each case a word that suggests coming out to the light with gasping relief. Margaret Atwood's confidence lies in continuation, not in triumph. She has not written — and is unlikely to write — a book called *Surmounting* or *Surpassing*. "We shall overcome" is a hymn of the American resistance, an underdog's paean to Manifest Destiny; it has no place in the Canadian resistance.

Thus, while *Survival* is certainly a polemical work, it is concerned with elucidating and perhaps eventually changing states of mind rather than with directly provoking action. It is really an application to the whole field of Canadian writing of the ethic worked out in Atwood's poetry, though the ethic is modified: "Beyond truth, / tenacity," indeed, but tenacity becoming a kind of truth, since ultimately it teaches us the reality of our condition; by being resolutely what one is, one comes to know oneself.

This is not evident on first opening the book, for *Survival* is one of those mildly exasperating works in which a brilliant intelligence has been unable to put the brakes on its activity and has run far ahead of the task it has undertaken, so that all readers get more than they bargain for, and the disappointed are probably as numerous as the gratefully surprised. It was planned, originally, with the utilitarian intent of presenting "a teacher's guide to the many new courses in Canadian literature," and vestiges of that intent survive in the lists of recommended texts, "useful books" and research resources which in themselves form a survival course for one's interest, intruding as they do on the ten essays on aspects of the Canadian literary persona which form the essential substance of the book.

Atwood presents, and supports with much shrewdly chosen evidence, the proposition that our literature is still scarred and misshapen by the state of mind that comes from a colonial relationship. All Canadian attitudes — she suggests — are related to the central fact of victimization imposed or at least attempted, and she lists and grades these attitudes, from *"Position One: To deny the fact that you are a victim"* (which objectively considered is the ultimate in victimization), to *"Position Four: To be a creative non-victim,"* the position of those whom Atwood tells, "You are able to accept your own experience for what it is, rather than having to distort it to make it correspond with others' versions of it (particularly those of your oppressors)."

Such numerological schemes, even when they are propounded by serious authors (e.g. Jung's Psychological Types and Toynbee's and Spengler's lists of cultures and civilizations), have always a flavour of perverse absurdity, as if the author were aspiring to Pythagorean guruhood, and Margaret Atwood's inclination to carry her propaganda for Canadian literature, as a form of national salvation, into the schools and lecture rooms suggests that the suspicion might not be wholly unjust. But the absurdities of the intelligent are always worth observing for the serious matters they reveal, and there is plenty of sound argument, together with a proportion of rather splendid nonsense, in *Survival*.

The colonial situation, Margaret Atwood suggests, has made Canadian writing, whether it springs from the denial or the acceptance of experience, a literature of failure; it reflects an attitude to life that aims no higher than survival. The French Canadians recognized this situation, and turned it into a self-conscious way of life, with its doctrine of *La Survivance* as the national aim; the English Canadians recognized it explicitly in their pioneer literature and implicitly in their literary identification with animals, whom typically they see as victims, and whose triumph can never be other than survival, since they cannot surmount their natures to be other than animals who live on to face another danger and, if they are fortunate, another survival.

In her argument—which, of course, is much more intricate than this very brief paraphrase could suggest—Atwood has indeed isolated a familiar Canadian syndrome. We have no heroes; only martyrs. (Any other people would have written an epic about Dollard at the Long Sault rather than about Brébeuf; would have made a folk hero out of Gabriel Dumont, not Louis Riel.) We pride ourselves with puritan smugness on our ironic modesty. With an inverted pharisaism, we stake what claim to moral superiority we may offer, not on our successes, but on our failures. All this, of course, has been recognized and commented on in a desultory, somewhat embarrassed way by other writers, but none of them, before Atwood, has stoically gathered these scattered insights, and, in a manner now becoming customary among Canadian critics, built them into a scheme which provides an alternative, or perhaps a supplement, to those constructed by Northrop Frye and D.G. Jones. The main difference between her and Frye or Jones is that their maps are descriptive, charts for explorers; hers are tactical, tools in a campaign, charts to help us repel a cultural invasion.

In developing a thesis that fits so many facts of our life and literature, Atwood presents a salutary view of a people who express their nature mainly in struggle against frustration of one kind or another. It is a vision that cannot be accepted in literal totality. There are Canadian writers who do not fit the pattern in any real way, like Robertson Davies; others, like Purdy and Layton, only partly belong. And preoccupations—even obsessions—with survival and failure are not peculiar to Canadian writing. Survival is the core of a recurrent mythic pattern, exemplified in many literatures and a multitude of works from *The Odyssey* and the *Book of Job* down to such classics of a colonizing (not a colonized) culture as *Robinson Crusoe*, *The Coral Island* and *Kim*. Any number of modern writers in countries of all kinds display the survival-equals-failure syndrome. It dominates most of Orwell's novels for example, and Orwell showed himself a model Canadian—according to Atwood's scheme—by remarking that every life, viewed from within, is a failure.

Margaret Atwood—I am sure—would answer that it is survival without triumph as the only way out of failure that is the characteristic Canadian predicament and the characteristic theme of an astonishingly high proportion of Canadian writing. And, even if we must deny universal application to her thesis in Canada, it is impossible to dispute that the poets and novelists of failure and survival are too haunting and too numerous not to give a special flavour to our literature.

Yet criticism is such a protean activity, so necessarily conditioned by the need for empathic understanding between the critic and every single author he discusses, that no critical map of the literary terrain of a country or a time can be accepted as more than a frame of reference, a usable hypothesis, at least insofar as we are seeking enlightenment in the books and authors which are its nominal subjects. Once we recognize that criticism is as much about the critic as it is about what he criticizes, we realize that even our best Canadian critic, when he is not directly reacting to a book or a poem, is merely offering an apparatus constructed so subtly that in itself it is a work of literary artifice, relevant mainly to the creativity of Northrop Frye. In the same way, the prime importance of *Survival* to the reader—if not necessarily to the writer—is perhaps not what it says about Canadian books, much of which we can learn in other places, but the fact that it develops in another form the themes and insights that have emerged from Atwood's practice of poetry.

For when we read *Survival*, when we seek to distil the spirit that inspires it, we go down below the polemics, and come to a mental toughness and resilience that resembles the dwarf trees of Atwood's poem in all their predictable tenacity; we come to a defensive strength very much like that of "this cactus, gathering / itself together / against the sand," and this tenacity, this defensive strength are, in Atwood's vision, the reality one begins by recognizing. But beyond this recognition there is the journey of self-discovery. Recognition, self-exploration, growth. This is the pattern of hope that at the end of *Survival* Margaret Atwood holds out for Canadian literature, and, through its literature, for the awareness and the life of the Canadian people. Let me quote two passages:

I'm not saying that all writing should be "experimental," or that all writing should be "political." But the fact that English Canadian writers are beginning to voice their own predicament consciously, as French Canadian writers have been doing for a decade, is worth mentioning. For both groups, this "voicing" is both an exploratory plunge into their own tradition and a departure from it; and for both groups the voicing would have been unimaginable twenty years ago . . . .

The tone of Canadian literature as a whole is, of course, the dark background: a reader must face the fact that Canadian literature is undeniably sombre and negative, and that this to a large extent is both a reflection and a chosen definition of the natural sensibility . . . . When I discovered the shape of the national tradition I was depressed, and it's obvious why: it's a fairly tough tradition to be saddled with, to have to come to terms with. But I am exhilarated too: having bleak ground under your feet is better than having no ground at all. Any map is better than no map as long as it is accurate, and knowing your starting points and your frame of reference is better than being suspended in the void.

And let me end with the two questions that Margaret Atwood leaves her readers:

Have we survived?
If so, what happens *after* Survival?

One could dip through *Survival* picking up many other passages that have roughly the same intent as these: what seems to me important about them is that they present the process of thought out of which *Survival* developed as a kind of journey of exploration and realization; an attempt to come to terms with the reality of the writer's environment, or rather the reality of her culture, which means also the reality of herself. And once that reality is established, once the darkness has been recognized and the eyes have become accustomed to it, then, as Margaret Atwood also says, one can see the "points of light — a red flower, or a small fire, or a human figure . . . in contrast to their surroundings: their dark background sets them off and gives them meaning in a way that the bright one would not."

Thus, in *Survival* we meet, stated in expository terms (and with a personal narative implied in the exposition), the ideas we have already absorbed osmotically from reading her verse, and we recognize that *Survival* is at least in part a work of self-examination, an attempt to reduce to rational terms—almost to homiletic terms—the emotions, the insights which Margaret Atwood had already expressed metaphorically in the poems and in *The Edible Woman.*

It is with this almost Buddhistically self-examinatory inclination of Atwood's in mind that we have to consider her second novel, *Surfacing.* In every way—complexity of action, range of characters, variety of themes, use of metaphor and fantasy—it is a much sparser and more concentrated book than her first novel, *The Edible Woman*; more than ever one is reminded of the "cactus, gathering/itself together/against the/sand." The large screen of urban Canada, with its obvious possibilities of farce and caricature, is abandoned; so is the Gothic fantasy through which the theme of emotional cannibalism is enacted in the earlier novel. The social criticism is less diffuse, more pointed. And thematically, there is a surface resemblance between *Surfacing* and *Survival* at which the reader is tempted to grasp, perhaps at his peril.

Certainly *Surfacing* concerns survival, and like the book *Survival* it is concerned with Canadian victims to such an extent that one can identify among its fauna a majority of the types of victim described therein. As major characters, or drifting but ominous shadows, there appear victim animals (a heron and some fish and frogs), victim Indians (it is too far south for victim Eskimos), victim sham pioneers (it is too late in history for real ones), victim children, victim artists (the chapter heading "The Paralyzed Artist" in *Survival* perfectly describes Joe, the frustrated potter, in *Surfacing*), victim women and victim French Canadians. That leaves out victim explorers, victim immigrants, victim heroes and victim jail-breakers, all featured in *Survival,* but it may be significant that the novel's narrator assumes all these missing roles, since she is an explorer of her own past, she is a migrant into a new self, she is as much a heroine—and a martyred one—as the novel admits, and she is breaking the jail of her imprisoned self.

A further link between *Survival* and *Surfacing* is, of course, the fact that in both books Canada is the victim of a sickness of colonialism, symbolized in the first paragraph of the novel by the white birches which are dying, as the elms have already died, from a disease that is "spreading from the south." That disease is personified in the Americans who are ravaging the Canadian wilderness, but its pervasiveness is only revealed to us completely when we realize that the heron whose death is central to the action has been wantonly killed, not by Americans, but by Canadians who have become indistinguishable from Americans.

One can overstress these didactic elements, which obviously arise from Atwood's absorption, at about the same time, in the ideas she expounded in *Survival*. One might invert the comparison and suggest that certain personal elements in *Survival* are there because of the ficitional preoccupations that carried over from the writing of *Surfacing*. For, like *The Edible Woman, Surfacing* is the account of a rite de passage; it is a novel of self-realization, hence of life-realization. Yet it also appears to possess what has so far missed the critics — at least those I have heard discussing the book with a degree of solemnity I find hard to associate with the Margaret Atwood I know — an element of self-criticism, almost of self-mockery. But let me leave that point while I sketch out the general scheme of *Surfacing*.

The narrator is a young woman who has heard of the disappearance of her botanist father from his cabin on a lake somewhere in the Laurentian Shield country, and who goes there with three companions — her lover Joe and two self-styled *émancipés,* David and Anna. It is a journey into her past; she has not been to the lake for nine years, and has been estranged from her parents — except for visiting her dying mother in hospital — for that long; it is also a journey, though she does not realize this to begin with, into her real self. She is significantly nameless; she names the other characters, and they name each other, but all of them refer to her only as "you" or "she." She is a failed pioneer, as Joe is a failed potter, David a failed rebel and Anna a failed wife.

"I" is indeed in the state of final atrophy which Marian reaches in *The Edible Woman* when she loses the power to eat, a condition closely resembling that known to medicine as *anorexia nervosa;* whereas Marian cannot assimilate physical food, "I" cannot either absorb or generate feeling. She describes herself as being nothing but a head, untouched and untouching. And yet, through the events that explode out of her return to the scene of her childhood, she is able to recover her real self as a whole being.

It is a process of surfacing, but also — before that — of submersion. The metaphors of drowning and near-drowning recur constantly. Her brother almost drowned as a child; her father, she finally discovers, has drowned accidentally in searching for Indian cliff paintings on the rock walls that fall sheer into the lake; her own point of crisis occurs when, diving in an attempt to locate the paintings, she encounters the floating corpse of her father, weighed down by his camera. The surfacing in this instance becomes almost literally a rising from death into life.

By this time other realizations have surfaced in the narrator's mind: about her childhood as she has relived it through returning to the lake island, reshaping it and reordering childhood characters nearer to true relationships as she calls them up into memory; about her companions, whose pose of liberation is reduced to a cluster of behavioural clichés borrowed from the Americans they pretend to despise; about the pollution of every kind that man takes with himself into the wilderness; above all about that monstrous indifference to the suffering of other living beings which echoes through Atwood's poems as the greatest of human crimes. Faced with the dead heron,

I feel a sickening complicity, sticky as glue, blood on my hands, as though I had been there and watched without saying No or doing anything to stop it: one of the silent guarded faces in the crowd. The trouble some people have being German, I thought, I have being human. In a way it was stupid to be more disturbed by a dead bird than by those other things, the wars and riots and the massacres in the newspapers. But for the wars and riots there was always an explanation, people wrote books about them saying why they happened: the death of the heron was causeless, undiluted.

"I" must shed all she has acquired, must unlearn adulthood, must return through her childhood and beyond humanity, must become like the victim animals, as she does in the crucial chapter of the book, when, having fled from her companions and allowed them to depart, she lives naked on the island, surviving like a beast on wild roots and mushrooms, until the delirium that in a dual sense is panic passes away from her. Then she returns, like Marian after she has eaten the cake that is her surrogate self in *The Edible Woman,* to a consciousness beyond beasthood, beyond the animistic world of primitives and children. The gods have departed; she is alone, with the child she now wants growing in her womb. "The lake is quiet, the trees surround me, asking and giving nothing." One senses, as the novel ends, that benign indifference of the universe of which Camus speaks. There is not hope; the narrator has gone beyond that recourse of the weak. But there is sanity. Doug Fetherling has reproached me for not appreciating the mystical in Atwood. But I find no mysticism here, any more than I find it in the purest, most intellectual forms of Buddhism. What I do find, as I find in that true Buddhism, is a courageous coming into the light of reality.

So there is sanity in this ending, and there is no mockery in it, of self or of other. Yet at the same time there is mockery in all that part of *Surfacing* where "I" is still a detached observing head which feels nothing and has prejudices but no passion. "I," as head, detects with a bitter satiric eye the shams of her companions, the fact that under their anti-American skins they are Americans. But "I" as ultimate narrator, who we must assume is the "I" of the final sane pages of *Surfacing,* and who is perhaps nearer to the author than the unregenerate "I," implicitly mocks her own attempt to fit a nationality to the villainy that is universal where man survives. And in so doing she casts an ironically oblique light on *Survival* itself, which is indeed a work with a villain, colonialism.

So, if we consider *Survival* and *Surfacing,* and observe them in relation to Atwood's poems, and especially to *Power Politics,* we see the versatility with which her intelligence plays over the horizons of her perceptions. In the poems these perceptions are expressed with metaphorical tightness and conciseness; they become sharp goads to the feelings. In the essays that form *Survival* they are transformed into discursive nets that entrap the reason. In *Surfacing*, the perceptions are projected in a strange winter light of feeling, until, passing through the destructive element of satire, they are etched with the lineaments of myth. No other writer in Canada of Margaret Atwood's generation has so wide a command of the resources of literature, so telling a restraint in their use.

[1974]

II

Of the four books published by Margaret Atwood since the first part of this essay was written, *Dancing Girls* — her collection of stories — provides the most obvious continuity with her earlier writing. Eleven of the fourteen stories it contains had been published beforehand in magazines varying from James Reaney's recondite and long-defunct magazine, *Alphabet,* to *Chatelaine* and *Ms.* Except among Atwood's growing group of admirers, they aroused little attention when first printed, and it was only when they appeared in book form that the reviewers began to take notice of them.

There is a certain justice to this kind of reaction for, compared to, say, Alice Munro or Hugh Garner, Margaret Atwood does not excel as a writer of short fictions. Reading the stories in *Dancing Girls,* one realizes that, however variously her talents may seem to be distributed, Margaret Atwood is successful primarily as a novelist and a poet. When she writes a novel she is handling the kind of theme and the kind of human situation that cannot be dealt with adequately in the extremely condensed kind of verse she writes. But her stories often deal with mental conditions not unlike those she handles so superbly in verse, and too often one feels that she takes excessive time over a theme that might better have been wrapped into the laconic poem. Pieces like those in *Dancing Girls* are too frequently not merely prose; such stories as "Polarities" and "The Man from Mars"—tales of psychotic and possessed personalities—tend to be prosaic as well, clogged with longueurs of an earnestness one recognizes as perhaps belonging to the author of *Survival,* but which does not fit well with the impeccable certainties of Atwood's poetry.

Such statements as these are of course meant comparatively. In terms of the Canadian literary culture, Atwood must be considered a major novelist and poet, but she is—in a country where the short story flourishes—a minor practitioner of that art. Her stories repeat, often rather tediously, the situations of sexual incompatibility that are better handled in her novels or in verse like that of *Power Politics.* They are perhaps most telling when they contain a clearly autobiographical element, like the title story, "Dancing Girls," or "Hair Jewellery," which contain echoes—and doubtless no more—of Atwood's period as a graduate student at Harvard, or like "The Grave of the Famous Poet," whose background at least—Dylan Thomas's village of Laugharne on the Carmarthenshire coast—she observed during a period in England in the early 1970s. But even here one feels that the heart of these stories is not appropriate to semi-realistic fiction, though it might eventually become material for the kind of personal memoirs a writer so sensitive to time and place as Margaret Atwood should eventually write.

There are many ways in which *Lady Oracle* (1976) resembles its predecessors, *The Edible Woman* and *Surfacing*. Joan Foster, alias Louisa K. Delacourt, is as obsessively concerned with food, and as morbidly dominated by her parents, as the heroines of the two earlier novels. Whereas Marian MacAlpin and "I," at critical stages, suffer drastic revulsions from food, Joan is so attached to eating that in childhood she becomes a classic fat girl, almost beyond shape, and in later life reverts to gorging whenever she becomes especially unhappy. Furthermore, like the lives of the earlier heroines, her life exemplifies the abrasive nature of sexual relations, and during the whole present of the novel Joan is in flight from her husband, hiding in a sordid Italian coast resort town, pretending to be dead, while her memories range back over the panorama of a grotesque existence.

Where *Lady Oracle* does differ from the earlier novels is in the sureness of its comedy and the accurate intensity of its satirical representation of Canadian bourgeois life — in both its philistine and its bohemian aspects. Joan lives a double life, recognizing that her fat and thin personalities are quite distinct, though they tend to influence each other. Learning to live with her fatness, to use it as a weapon against her hated mother, and to turn it to her advantage in gaining popularity at school, is the process that dominates Joan's earlier life. But when her aunt, the original and true Louisa K. Delacourt, dies and leaves a useful nest egg to Joan on condition that she lose a hundred pounds, her desire for freedom from her mother inspires the effort that transforms this fat and apparently asexual girl into a slim, red-haired near-beauty whom men desire for a mistress or, in the case of the dull left-wing intellectual, Arthur Foster, for a wife.

During this period of flowering, when she is living as his mistress with a minor Polish nobleman in London, Joan begins to follow a thoroughly double life. She finds that money is to be made out of writing historical romances for the popular market, and for this purpose she takes her aunt's name, Louisa Delacourt. Long passages of *Lady Oracle* in fact consist of sections of Joan's overblown romances, which Atwood — herself a student of the Gothic novel — writes with a superb parodic flair, and which, counterpointing as they do the rather tawdry melodrama of Joan's own life, give *Lady Oracle* a special flavour of pretentious unreality.

Joan happily earns the comfortable income from her pulp romances while carefully concealing this side of her life, especially after she meets Arthur, with his resolute earnestness and his sanctimoniously left-wing friends. But Aunt Louisa's legacy consists not merely of a couple of thousand dollars and a nom de plume. At one period she has trailed Joan with her to spiritualist séances, and a vestige of this period is a lingering interest in automatic writing. Joan attempts it, goes into a trance, and produces a sequence of Gothic-surrealist poems which she publishes under the title of *Lady Oracle*. Now she is living a double life in literature as well as personally. Nobody except a rather inefficient blackmailer recognizes the links between Joan Foster the psychic poetess and Louisa K. Delacourt the writer of historical romances. But fame in her own name leads Joan into a series of ludicrous encounters in the literary and artistic worlds, including a stormy affair with the Royal Porcupine, a talentless artist named Chuck Brewer who gimmicks his way to fame by exhibiting mutilated pets, the quick-frozen victims of traffic accidents. *Lady Oracle* is in fact a roman à clef, incorporating figures from the Toronto literary world, and there is at least one characterization, that of Fraser Buchanan the blackmailer, in which Atwood is clearly paying off a well-known and deeply held grudge against a fellow writer.

What is perhaps most impressive about *Lady Oracle* is the way Atwood has reused old themes and devices, the divided personality, the resentment of child against parent, the fatal abrasiveness of long relationships between man and woman, leading to physical escape from an intolerable situation, and has raised them to a higher level through a remarkable adeptness in the devices of comedy which her early writings had hardly led one to expect. True, a wry ironic wit often surfaces in the earlier poetry, and a good deal of sardonic fun is poked at institutions and human types in both *The Edible Woman* and *Surfacing;* in both novels grotesque and fanciful situations are used to enhance the absurdity of the central predicament. But it is the sustained and uninhibited comic tone that secures Atwood's fictional achievement in *Lady Oracle* from any doubt as to whether she can sustain her role as a novelist and avoid being caught in a groove of merely poetic fiction.

Similarly, Atwood's two most recent books of verse demonstrate the mutability and the steady maturing of her talents. *You Are Happy,* which appeared in 1974, is a book in which the mythological is carefully balanced against the actual. Partly these are poems about life in the countryside of Loyalist Ontario, to which Atwood had recently retreated, and which can offer the kind of physical experience that inspires the sense of total detachment expressed in the title poem, "You Are Happy":

> When you are this
> cold you can think about
> nothing but the cold, the images
>
> hitting into your eyes
> like needles, crystals, you are happy.

But the larger part of the volume is taken up with two groups of poems linked with the Circe myth, particularly as recorded in *The Odyssey.* The "Songs of the Transformed" are about beasts who were men before they were changed by Circe. They are observed in their bestial natures, yet through these natures they paradoxically reflect the aspects of our humanity which we most try to conceal, and often in their last lines these poems make reflections which are totally human in their implications, as when the pig declares:

> I am yours. If you feed me garbage,
> I will sing a song of garbage.
> This is a hymn.

Or when the rat says:

> You'd do the same if you could,
>
> if you could afford to share
> my crystal hatreds.

Or when the crow remarks, in the voice of a tired leader:

> Watching you
> my people, I become cynical,
> you have defrauded me of hope
> and left me alone with politics. . .

Transformation, and especially transformation in which the core of being remains unchanged, is of course a constant

Atwoodian theme, and so is that of the "Circe/Mud Poems," the other complete cycle in *You Are Happy,* which develops the paradoxical combination of need and conflict that dominates male-female relationships, and the threat of departure that always exists because for both sides the cost of continuation is intolerable. As Circe says to Odysseus:

> To be feared, to be despised,
> these are your choices.

But the myth — the story "which is ruthless" — raises one above the scarred present, and it is into this present that the poet descends in the later poems of *You Are Happy:*

> We're stuck here
> on this side of the border
> in this country of thumbed streets and stale buildings
>
> where there is nothing spectacular
> to see and the weather is ordinary
>
> where *love* occurs in its pure form only
> on the cheaper of the souvenirs
>
> where we must walk slowly,
> where we may not get anywhere
>
> or anything, where we keep going,
> fighting our ways, our way
> not out but through.

Again, we are with the poetry of endurance. But another aspect of the unavoidable present is offered in *Two-Headed Poems,* published four years after *You Are Happy* — four years of literary success for Margaret Atwood, and perhaps of greater personal happiness, exemplified in love for the young daughter who more than any other personality dominates these poems; the old theme of sexual conflict is diminished, reduced largely to the thought that: "What defeats us, as always, is the repetition." It is a collection of poems much more closely linked than *You Are Happy* with the actualities of existence. When the myths do appear in *Two-Headed Poems,* they are incorporated in the symbols of daily living, like dolls or Hallowe'en heads made of paper bags, and the process acquires a sense of endless potentiality.

Paper head, I prefer you
because of your emptiness;
from within you any
word could still be said.

With you I could have
more than one skin,
a blank interior, a repertoire
of untold stories,
a fresh beginning.

There are two whole series of "Daybooks," which are poetic notations, as concrete and as suggestive as Robert Frost's, on the meaning of a way of life — country life in Atwood's as in Frost's case. Typical is "Apple Jelly," in which is demonstrated an unexpected opening out of Atwood's viewpoint, and even her manner of writing, from the tight simplicities of *Power Politics* and other poems of the earlier period.

No sense in all this picking,
peeling & simmering
if sheer food is all
you want: you can buy it cheaper.

Why then do we burn our hours
& muscles in this stove,
cut our thumbs, to get these tiny
glass pots of clear jelly?

Hoarded in winter: the sun
on that noon, your awkward leap
down from the tree,
licked fingers, sweet pink juice,
what we keep
the taste of the act, taste
of this day.

Here, at last, is something more than tenacity. There is, as in *Lady Oracle,* a lifting of the spirit into a level of writing in which the themes of the past are already being discarded, as attempts at liberation that have become imprisoning in comparison with the recognition of realities that are both human and universal, as in the last lines of *Two-Headed Poems,* in which the poet tells her daughter:

This is your hand, these are my hands, this is the world,
which is round but not flat and has more colours
than we can see.

It begins, it has an end,
this is what you will
come back to, this is your hand.

[1978]

Remembering Roderick Haig-Brown

WHEN RODERICK HAIG-BROWN died, it was quietly and suddenly in the garden of his house on Vancouver Island, beside the river he had loved and about which he had written so often in his books on fishing and in his discursive essays. To us who knew him, as a man of quiet wisdom, as a good friend, as a fellow in the craft of writing, it seemed a fitting passage.

Through the craft of writing we shared I came to know Haig-Brown, and I remember vividly the unusual combination of humility and assurance with which he approached it. His emphasis was always on the craft, on the primary need to perform the task in a workmanlike way. "And if one practices the craft with diligence," I remember him saying as we sat one night years ago in his great study beside the river, "then the moments of art come to one gratuitously, as a reward."

I believe that in the thirty-odd effective years of Roderick Haig-Brown's writing life the moments of art in fact came quite often. Yet his name has not been one spoken loudly by Canadian critics during the recent upsurge of interest in the writers of our country, and this neglect, this lack of critical perception, has seemed to me particularly unfortunate, since I can think of few Canadian writers who have developed a more subtle and adaptable prose or have responded with a more immediate sensitivity to the texture and feeling of the Canadian land. Recently there has been a pronounced turning by younger poets, particularly in western Canada, towards an almost topographical verse in which a direct response to the land and its qualities is emphasized, and among novelists since Margaret Laurence there has been an equally pronounced turning to a kind of local historical fiction into which physical landscape qualities enter very deeply. In all this I feel the poets and the fiction writers are actually building on the work of essayists who have developed a Canadian version of the kind of rural writing one associates with the great line of English country writers from William Cobbett down to W.H. Hudson.

Prominent among such Canadian writers have been Frederick Philip Grove, who remarkably rendered the look and feel of the prairies in books of essays like *Over Prairie Trails* and *The Turn of the Year,* and Hugh MacLennan with books like *Cross Country,* his collection of travel essays, *The Rivers of Canada,* a rich group of historico-geographical vignettes, and *The Other Side of Hugh MacLennan,* a very recent collection of his nonfictional writings.

It is in this company that Haig-Brown should have found a high place, for he has been for thirty years one of our best essayists, yet his widest repute has developed not among writers, who should have responded naturally to his mastery of a difficult prose form, but among outdoorsmen — hunters, fishermen and environmentalists — who read him primarily for the subjects he treated, which on the most obvious level were mainly fishing, hunting and conservation. Yet I am sure that many such readers sensed the artistry of Haig-Brown's prose, and that his success among them was due very largely to his literary quality, to his extraordinary power of making one experience not only the feel and smell and look of the natural environment but also the sheer excitement the angler feels when he has made a catch with proper skill, using his wits against an adversary he respects and, in strange, oblique ways, loves. I will return to that point about the beloved adversary, for Haig-Brown's books tell us some very interesting things about the curious relationship that exists between the hunter and the hunted.

But for the moment I am still concerned with the question of why Haig-Brown was not widely accepted by Canadian literary critics. I think it springs less from his subject matter than from the curious paradox that, though Canada has produced a remarkable succession of fine essayists from Joseph Howe down to MacLennan and Haig-Brown, there has never been a wide Canadian readership for their work. As a consequence, the sheer economics of making a living by writing has forced natural essayists to concentrate in other fields, so that both MacLennan and Grove became not entirely successful essayists in fiction, while

Haig-Brown swerved away from the purely literary essay when he found that the fishing and hunting, which had been his passions since boyhood, provided him with a readership outside the perimeters of the orthodox literary world.

What the critics missed was that in the process Haig-Brown achieved some very interesting effects in reconciling his expositions of the craft of fishing with his inclination to reflective and evocative prose by becoming something of a twentieth-century North American Isaak Walton. For, like Walton, Haig-Brown quickly learnt the ability to give the reader a feeling of total experience when he wrote of fishing, a feeling that someone who was not a fisherman, even someone theoretically opposed to fishing, could sense and respond to. This was partly because he wrote so often in terms of personally experienced episodes, and partly because, like Isaak Walton, he always regarded fishing as a "contemplative man's recreation," with the consequent fringe benefits. "A man," he said in *Fisherman's Summer,* "should think when he is fishing, of all manner and shapes of things, flowing as easily through his mind as the light streams along its rocks." Some of this free and flowing thought Haig-Brown introduced into his writing, so that his fishing books, like the central tetralogy, *Fisherman's Spring, Fisherman's Summer, Fisherman's Winter* and *Fisherman's Fall,* contain many things that have no place in an ordinary angling textbook. In fact, of course, they are not textbooks, but books of experience, and out of experience comes reflection, and out of reflection, distilled and processed, comes what one recognizes as the art of prose.

And indeed, by the time you have finished the four books I mention, you recognize that thinking about his experiences while fishing has made Haig-Brown a great deal more than a fisherman only. Among other things, it made him into what, if he had given a slightly different form to his books, we would call a very evocative travel writer, for many a British Columbian lake and stream comes to life as he takes us to its waters. Then there is *Fisherman's Winter,* dealing with a journey Haig-Brown made in the early 1950s to investigate trout fishing in Chile and Argentina, the southern Andean chain of mountains, lakes and rivers. There emerged a travel narrative reminiscent of the Victorian naturalists' books, which Haig-Brown admired so much. Just as the best of those writers, like Charles Darwin in *The Voyage of the Beagle* and H.W.

Bates in *A Naturalist on the Amazons,* rendered vividly the physical look and native life of the countries whose fauna and flora they investigated, so Haig-Brown, in describing the game fish of the Andes, gave an unforgettable picture of the mountains and rivers of Chile and of the Chilean people at a period which the country's recent history makes seem poignantly idyllic. Similarly, in what is perhaps the best of all his books of essays, *The Measure of the Year,* Haig-Brown wrote an unusual kind of static travel narrative, in which he takes one through time rather than space as he tells the yearly cycle of his life in the then small village of Campbell River on Vancouver Island, where he functioned not merely as a writer and fisherman but also as the local magistrate and a highly respected community leader.

But even more than making him an unusual kind of travel writer, Haig-Brown's passionate interest in fishing also turned him into a fine naturalist in the same style as the Victorian field naturalists he admired, carefully observing in their proper settings the creatures that fascinated him. He did not neglect modern biological discoveries; in fact, he was well-read in them, but he never sought the total objectivity of the professional scientist, and he distrusted the temptations of specialization. What intrigued him in his observations, as in the practice of fishing, was — as he expressed it — "the strangeness and beauty of the fish, their often visible remoteness, their ease in another world, the mystery of their movements and habits and whims."

There were some striking changes in Haig-Brown's attitudes over the years towards the wild creatures which he had pursued ever since his boyhood fishing in the chalk streams of the England where he was born, and here we come back to that interesting question of the beloved adversary.

The theme emerged in a public way when Haig-Brown became an ardent conservationist and did so — like Aldous Huxley — many years before environmentalism became a radical fashion; there are statements printed as long ago as 1951 in *Fisherman's Spring* that would have seemed freshly contemporary coming twenty years later from the pen of a young ecologist. In the 1950s Haig-Brown fought publicly, and often with very little support in the community, against many of the hydroelectric and industrial developments in British Columbia which he argued would be harmful to wildlife and to the environment in general. In almost every case events proved him right, and a lot of harm was done to the environment to very little real advantage by governments and corporations that did not heed his warnings.

Of more intimate interest than Haig-Brown's public actions as a conservationist was his growing empathy with game animals and fish which he evinced in the succession of his books. At first he appears to have hunted and fished with zest and without much apparent reflection on the implications of his acts. Then he gradually became conscious of the strange sense of identity with the quarry that so often comes to hunters, and at this point he grew close in sympathy with the native Indians of British Columbia, whose hunting magic was based on a belief in the bond of affinity between man and the creatures his needs lead him to pursue. This sense of the link between the hunter and the hunted was shown in what I think is the best of Haig-Brown's several novels for children, a book called *The Whale People,* which portrays the life and the hunting methods of the Nootka Indians of western Vancouver Island, who went out in canoes to chase the whale and, with great skill and courage, using elaborate sympathetic magic, often succeeded in killing the gigantic cetaceans and towing them home to their tribal beaches.

As early as *Fisherman's Spring* in 1954 Haig-Brown remarked: "It is the imponderable and the unpredictable in the ways of wild creatures that unites us and makes our common ways. We try to become one with the creature we pursue, to know and anticipate its actions." In Haig-Brown the recognition of this process led not only to a sense of identification with the quarry which many hunters experience, but to an acceptance of the atrocious-seeming fatalities which natural life cycles often involve. Like anyone who sees it for the first time, he was appalled by the apparently meaningless waste of lives that takes place when the Pacific salmon, having ascended the river and spawned, almost invariably dies. But once one has developed an empathy with creatures whose strange fate it is to die through the process of giving life, then acceptance can come. "Now," says Haig-Brown in *Fisherman's Fall,* "I have lived so long with this fact of collective, simultaneous death that I no longer resent or question it. Instead I find it fitting and beautiful, certainly useful in ways that are not entirely clear, and a yearly occasion of high drama. I am still curious about the manner and meaning of it, but I do not question that it has manner and meaning."

What one observes in all these stages of Haig-Brown's changing attitudes is the steady shedding of barriers between the human and the animal world. The final stage comes in the extraordinary terminating chapters of *Fisherman's Fall*, Haig-Brown's last important book, in which he tells of his experiences when he took to scuba diving and began to spend hours underwater in the familiar river outside his house which hitherto he had known only from the other side of the surface film. He found that in fact he was not only seeing the fish's world with a fish's eye, but that he was also experiencing in a tactile way the sensations of being a fish. The experience turned the fish from an alien being inhabiting the other side of the water surface into the denizen of a shared environment. "I find," said Haig-Brown in what is an unexpected confession for a lifelong fisherman, "that I have practically no desire to go out and catch the fish I have seen when diving; I would rather go back and have another look at them. By the time I have watched the same fish twice, he is an old friend and I wouldn't dream of going out to kill him; I would even hesitate to disturb him by catching him and putting him back."

At the end of *Fisherman's Fall*, Haig-Brown tentatively raised the question whether this book, published in 1964, would be his last writing about fish and fishing. It was in fact the last book written with the special sense of total involvement that had marked his fishing books up to this time, and the final decade of his life was — for his admirers — disappointingly scanty in terms of literary creation. It was not inactive; in fact, it tended to be filled with community service of many kinds. But Haig-Brown's true vocation was writing, and the reason he finally became almost silent on paper must be found in the way his writing developed, moving constantly towards that point of empathetic identification with the subject which meant that writing no longer seemed necessary.

Such considerations circle one back from Haig-Brown the fisherman, the naturalist, the environmentalist, the servant of the community, to Haig-Brown the writer, which, as he himself well knew, was his central role. And as a writer there is one more important thing to say about him. He wrote for a wide audience, and probably had more readers in the United States — and presumably more in Britain — than he had in Canada. But his appeal was based on his intense apprehension of a particular locality. He did not write about streams or lakes or forests in general. There was never any doubt that he was writing with a specific vividness about certain actual rivers, mainly in British Columbia, though occasionally in childhood England or the traveller's Chile. In other words, he made the vital connection between regionalism and universalism, and this in part is why he has been misunderstood by Canadian critics who have been bemused by nationalist myths. Haig-Brown was never in the narrow sense a nationalist, though he was a good Canadian patriot. But he realized that patriotism had its roots in the intimate locality, the *patria chica* or little fatherland, as the Spaniards call it, and once he said: "I am not at all sure that provincialism is such an evil thing at that. No man becomes a great patriot without first learning the closer loyalties and learning them well; loyalty to the family, to the place he calls home, to his province or state or country . . . ."

Even in the way he forged his craft, Haig-Brown was an intensely local writer. He began to write in his teens while he was working in Pacific Coast logging camps. Unlike many other writers, he never served an apprenticeship in the literary world of some capital city; he remained on the Pacific Coast, immersed in its local life, and there he became the writer we have all known. But when as an editor I once asked him for an essay on the writer in isolation, which appeared as the first item in the first issue of *Canadian Literature* twenty years ago, he came to the conclusion that even his remoteness from the grand cultural centres did not mean that he had ever been in a real sense more isolated than other writers. Like them he had been influenced by books and by the people he met and the experiences he underwent, and like them he faced the ultimate task of creation — as one faces birth and death — on his own. Or, to put it in his words: "In the end, all writing is isolation. A man observes and absorbs readily enough among his friends. He may test ideas or sharpen argument or search for encouragement in talk. But he must mature his thought, develop and control his emotions, plan his work, alone. And he must write alone."

Yet at the same time Haig-Brown felt that a writer was perhaps better off if he added just a little more to this inevitable isolation of creation, and there is one passage from his *Canadian Literature* essay which I have always felt singularly timely in our present generation when writers are constantly tempted to become public exhibitionists, signing their books in bookstores, appearing on television, and doing everything but write. "Any writer," said Haig-Brown, who has the necessary minimum of integrity can readily afford to expose himself to influences of all kinds without fear of loss and with some real chance of gain. Yet talk is a danger to writers. More than that, talk is a positive, ugly menace. Talk is much easier than writing, its satisfactions are so immediate, that some of the need to write is all too easily lost in it. It may be true that no man can talk himself out of being a writer if he has it in him to write, and no doubt some men have capacity for both. But I think the frustration of enforced silence is good for most of us.

I remember now the good sense of these words, and of much else that Roderick Haig-Brown wrote, and even spoke, though mostly in private, and I realize once again that he was not only a good writer; he was also that much rarer kind of being, a man made wise by the patient observation of nature and of life.

[1977]

Callaghan's Toronto:
The Persona of a City

ONE SUMMER, TRAVELLING through France, from Chartres towards the Loire, I drove into one of those grey and rather inhospitable small French towns which exude an atmosphere of frustrated mediocrity. It was called Illiers, and there I first realized the full extent of the transforming power of the literary imagination. Proust would have put it a different way and talked of the transforming power of memory. And this was Proust's town, the original of his Combray. As I stood there, the iridescent outlines of the place I had constructed in the mind dissolved, as soon as they were called up, into the dull and dusty reality of that August afternoon between the ugly houses in the stench of bad French gasoline. I had not Proust's transforming memory to link Illiers, which was the detestable here and now, with Combray, which was a past crystallized (in the full Stendhalian sense) in a writer's imagination. But once away, it was Illiers I almost forgot. Combray remained in the mind as I had always seen it.

In a similar way, over visits at increasingly long intervals during the past twenty years, I have come to a vague knowledge and a rather active dislike of the post-1950 city of Toronto. Yet there is another Toronto, which I have never seen except as a mental construct, but to which I am deeply attracted. Something like it perhaps did exist in reality, in a dead age, but as it comes to me it is entirely the product of Morley Callaghan's literary imagination and his memory in creative interplay.

The great attraction of Callaghan's Toronto, of course, is that it is lodged in that almost totally vanished past; one can never pay it a visit at risk of comparing the fictional city with its original and being disappointed. It is the Toronto of the twenties and the thirties, of Prohibition and the Depression; from his first novel, *Strange Fugitive,* to his sixth, *More Joy in Heaven* (if one can indeed assume that the unnamed city of that novel is in fact a version of Toronto), Callaghan builds up the picture of a small city changing and growing, darkening and losing innocence, during those decades between the wars when Canada began to emerge out of colonialism in the direction of nationhood.

One senses in the novelist a parallel change to that which he sees within the city, and it may be indicative of Callaghan's attitude towards a later Toronto that he has written no novel that is creatively perceptive about his city since 1939. He turned for two books to Montreal (*The Loved and the Lost* and *The Many Colored Coat*), for another to Rome (*A Passion in Rome*), and though his two most recently published novels (*A Fine and Private Place* and *Close to the Sun Again*) have been set in Toronto, the city he shows in them is not the kind of living entity that Toronto seemed in his earlier books. Also, in his volume of memoirs, *That Summer in Paris,* he wrote about the haunts of the Lost Generation, and only in recreating that Paris of his youth did he render the feeling of a city with a lyrical intensity comparable to that of his six early Toronto novels, and even then it was obviously a strange city he was portraying, a city he saw as an outsider condemned to being nothing more. But Toronto he saw from the very heart, and I doubt whether any of its citizens, except perhaps Raymond Souster in verse, has presented so coherent and so illuminated a picture of a city now as submerged as any *cathédrale englouti* under a towered mirage of prosperity.

Reading these Callaghan novels, whose publication covers a mere decade from 1928 to 1937, one enters a world whose tempo is reflected in the means of transport its inhabitants adopt. The characters in *Strange Fugitive* (1928) walk great distances over the city, and when they do not walk they go by streetcar. Except in criminal business, the automobile is still far from universal, even among lawyers (who swarm in Callaghan's Toronto), though Canadians are already addicts of the telephone. When Harry Trotter goes out to the country to see his parents' grave, he does not hire a car at the station nearest the village; he gets a horse and buggy from a livery stable. A little later, in *A Broken Journey* (1932), we move among people who do own cars, for this novel is concerned with the moneyed middle class and the rebellion of their children; by the time of *They Shall Inherit the Earth* (1935), the Depression is on, and everybody walks because poverty has slowed down technological progress.

This city where people go on foot and by streetcar, and encounter the horse-drawn carts of milkmen and bakers and Italian vegetable peddlers, and sniff the sweet smell of horse piss, has already passed out of the rusticity some characters remember from yet another past, before the First World War, but it is still a place where the lake and the ravines on the city boundaries are much more important than they now are to the majority of Torontonians. Callaghan's characters are always walking by the lake, or taking the radial car to the edge of town, where the pavement ceases as if one were entering foreign territory, and one descends into secretive dells threaded by slowly running rivers, or climbs the high hills where on summer days people "lay on the grass waiting for a breeze. Farm land was farther back from the bluffs, fields of corn and peas behind low fences." Don Mills Road—hard now to imagine—leads "through small farmland."

This green country, duplicated in the parks within the city, often seems intended to convey the sense of a natural innocence, contrasted to the depravity of human beings; sometimes it brings an emotional renewal to the characters. But there is at times a rather sinister underlying quality to this element in the novels. It is in a prison in a park that the hanging takes place in *It's Never Over* (1930), and there is an affinity between these partly tamed enclaves of wild nature within and on the edge of the city, and the real wilderness which, in *A Broken Journey* and even more emphatically in *They Shall Inherit the Earth,* is shown as a cruel and pitiless place, a home for wolves and no Utopia for men, though its harshness is natural and splendid and unrelated to the man-made evil that can exist in the cities.

In Callaghan's Toronto there are many dreaming, scented gardens, and these mirror the latent sexuality of those who walk or sit within them; there are many streets like that which Callaghan once describes as "all a small, simple, orderly world." But towering over these sheltered privacies loom the few great buildings of that age: office blocks which we would now regard as of modest height, and the two so-often evoked towers of the cathedral and the city hall, which exemplify the poles of spiritual and temporal power. The cathedral spire is most often shown illuminated by the natural light of the sun above the town's darkness, whereas the municipal tower is most often revealed against a night sky by the artificial illumination of a searchlight or a spotlight. In the shadow of these towers lie the business streets, and the streets where show-girls walk between the theatres, and the streets without women of the Chinese.

Callaghan's Toronto is predominantly a place of WASPS and Irish Catholics, church-ridden in either case. Overshadowing society is the world of "the influential people" who "all worked together as though belonging to the same lodge"; in *Such Is My Beloved* (1934) we see how ruthlessly that world can move to destroy a young priest who appears to challenge its basic moral assumptions, and in *They Shall Inherit the Earth* how clubmen and church ladies can unite to reject one of their own when luck turns against him. Keeping up position and appearance counts more than character or integrity in that moneyed world, and its values filter down into the lower-middle class, where one still talks about "nice people" and regards the old radicals who hang around the Labour Temple as "not respectable."

In such a world, though immigrants are fewer than they are today, they are made more prominent by the baleful light of prejudice. Pre-Hitler Torontonians speak slightingly of Jews in a way few would—at least publicly—today; they talk of "Chinks"; towards the Greeks who run restaurants and the Italians who keep fruit stores and go in for bootlegging the attitude varies from patronizing to hostile.

One could draw from Callaghan's books a very interesting map, perhaps not street by street, but reasonably complete in its essential detail, of the Toronto he knew a third of a century ago, illuminated with descriptive vignettes of each locality. But more important than this physical topography is another aspect of his novels which is more germane to their role as imaginary projections of the city's spirit.

This aspect is the concentration that takes place in the novels, in the triple sense of (a) an increasing density of collective emotion, (b) a deepening flow of feeling between the individual and the community, and (c) an actual tendency for action to move into the city's centre. In the earlier novels, especially *Strange Fugitive* and *It's Never Over,* life tends to go on in the residential periphery where the leisurely pace of an Ontario town continues, and in both these novels of violence or of intended violence the protagonists move *against* rather than *with* their backgrounds. But later, and especially in *Such Is My Beloved* and *They Shall Inherit the Earth*, the characters seem much more aware of the city both as a human continuum in which they are passionately involved, and also as an abstract collectivity that mysteriously threatens them. They are on the verge of what we now call urban alienation.

Father Dowling is brought by chance from the ordinary life of a Catholic parish where a few rich people linger among the poor Italian immigrants, into unexpectedly intimate contact with the seedy half-world inhabited by pimps and prostitutes; he is overcome by a troubling sense of incomprehensible darknesses moving in the life of the city. "There was much he did not understand, there was a whole economic background behind the wretched lives of these girls." And yet the young priest can also identify himself joyfully with the city where he sees so much unhappiness:

Father Dowling felt suddenly that he loved the whole neighbourhood, all the murmuring street noises, the street cries of newsboys, the purring of automobiles, and rumble of heavy vehicles, the thousand separate sounds of everlasting motion, the low, steady and mysterious hum that was always in the air, the lights in windows, doors opening, rows of street lights and fiery flash of signs, the cry of night birds darting around the Cathedral and the soft low laughs of lovers strolling in the side streets on the first spring nights.

There is a similar lyrical evocation of the city at its best season in the beginning of *They Shall Inherit the Earth,* when Alexander Aikenhead and his son walk in the street "amid all the murmuring city noises, the cries of little boys shouting on the corners, and the shrill calls of little girls alleeooing to each other in the streets...." An almost unurban feeling is stirred, as if the noise and harshness of the city at normal times have been somehow mitigated by the luminosity of a summer's evening. But, as the book continues, and the characters gain experience and self-knowledge in a world where economic insecurity and pharisaical moralism come into evil conjunction, a different sense of the city is felt by Michael Aikenhead in the days before he is finally reconciled with his father.

When he was passing through the streets among those with faces full of discontent, or passing by the long lines of men outside the soup kitchens, and among the evictions of families of men who wanted to work, or when he read the police court news in the papers and read of brutal crimes and vicious punishments, he felt that the life of the city was like a turbulent riot in which there could never be any order or justice, in which you had to hold fast to any little thing you loved or it would be snatched from you.

Throughout these novels the cathedral appears as a dominant symbol, acting often as an emblem of hope, or faith, but at other times as a sign of foreboding, and at last in *Such Is My Beloved* as the visible manifestation of an invisible tyranny. We are not always told that the cathedrals in the various novels are Catholic, and their symbolic relevance seems to be universal as they stand with their walls in shadow and their spires in light, just as the church's aims are illuminated but its works are often dark. The most dramatic of all the appearances of the cathedral is in *Strange Fugitive*. There has been a fire in winter, and the cathedral stands, its beams charred and its roof collapsed, all coated with ice, and from this crystal church the bells are ringing and seem to urge Harry Trotter back from the self-destructive life on which he has embarked. (On the significance in Callaghan's novels of Toronto's bells—church bells, city hall bells, railway bells—as warning knells on the road to tragedy, one could write another essay.)

The recurrent appearance of the cathedral in Callaghan's novels is also important for the way in which it enables the writer to fuse his own experience as an Irish Catholic in Toronto with the wider experience of other citizens to whom the tower may be merely a landmark yet for that very reason—in a city still unskyscraped—a focal point in life and movement. But perhaps the most vital of all the cathedral's functions is to unite the visible world which Callaghan portrays with the moral fable to which, as I have suggested in another essay,[1] all his novels of that period approximate. The moral qualities permeate the setting and give it symbolic resonances, at the same time as the imaginative authenticity of the setting gives the necessary plausibility to characters and actions which we are not meant, ultimately, to interpret naturalistically.

Callaghan's Toronto, then, is a construct of the mind that fulfils three functions. It is an impressionistic view of the city's past

---

1. "Lost Eurydice," in *Odysseus Ever Returning* (Toronto: McClelland & Stewart Ltd., 1970).

which is certainly more attractive than the historian's and perhaps more subjectively true. It provides the verisimilitude of background which, from the days of Swift, fictional moralists have always sought, to give an authentic ring to the simplified characters and motives and actions necessary to their fables. And, insofar as Callaghan the artist exceeds the moralist, his Toronto lives in its own clear light of memory transmuted as a city of the mind, which one revisits with curiosity and, where the sense of his autonomous vision is most complete, with delight.

[1972]

This Fall in Toronto:
A Late Callaghan Novel

CLOSE TO THE SUN AGAIN (1977) is, in my view, the best book Morley
Callaghan has written since *That Summer in Paris* fourteen years
before, and the best novel since *More Joy in Heaven,* forty years
before. Callaghan has had such repeated returns and renewals
that it would be rash to suggest that *Close to the Sun Again* may be
his swan song. But if it is, after so many summers the swan is
singing superbly.

There is a majestically cyclic movement in Callaghan's career.
It spreads over half a century, beginning with the gauche, ten-
tative, implausible books written in the 1920s, like *Strange Fugitive,*
A Broken Journey, and *It's Never Over.* It moves to the ascendant
during the 1930s when Callaghan finds himself as a fictional
moralist and produces those three splendid novels-as-allegories:
Such Is My Beloved, They Shall Inherit the Earth, and *More Joy in
Heaven.*

After *More Joy in Heaven* in 1937, Callaghan moved into a long
zone of silence; in the 1940s it was widely believed he had written
himself out. But then, after fourteen years, there appears another
trio of novels: *The Loved and the Lost* in 1951; *The Many Colored Coat*
in 1960; and *A Passion in Rome* in 1961. Callaghan is attempting
something different in these books, moving away from the terse
manner and simple construction of his fictions of the 1930s into a
lusher style and a more complex and decorated form—that of the
classic realist novel.

But he does it with the equipment of a writer of short stories
and of those long and simply constructed novellas that the French
call *récits* as distinct from *romans.* In every case the adjustment
means a corruption of style, an offending of credibility. *The Loved*

and the Lost and *A Passion in Rome* both fail in the unity of conception and the force of moral passion that distinguished such books as *They Shall Inherit the Earth. The Many Colored Coat* is the nearest of these three post-1945 novels to the successful books of the 1930s, at least in spirit, but Callaghan has laboured a true and simple theme, sufficient perhaps for a novella of 150 pages, into the tedium of an overwritten narrative 318 pages long.

The wheel continues in its revolutions. *A Passion in Rome* — up to that time Callaghan's most ambitious and most disastrous book — is followed by another fourteen years of fictional silence, though during this period his autobiographical volume, *That Summer in Paris,* challenges comparison with John Glassco's *Memoirs of Montparnasse* as one of the few Canadian accounts of the great Left Bank days.

Then, in 1975, appears the book we all knew was due sooner or later, that sad and unnecessary novel of self-justification, *A Fine and Private Place.* Callaghan, praised more than most Canadian writers, overpraised by Edmund Wilson in a moment of reminiscent generosity, has always harboured the illusion of being neglected or unjustly condemned by his fellow countrymen. Writers sure of their own worth are rarely troubled by such situations — real or imagined; they write what they must and are happy if even a few people recognize them. Others attempt to redress the "injustice" by writing about it, and in *A Fine and Private Place* Callaghan presents a flattering self-analysis, and a situation in which the blind characters who clearly represent his critics are made to bear the blame for destroying his fictional persona.

Books of this kind are embarrassing to many readers, and to most critics, who feel they are being morally blackmailed; ultimately, one imagines, they must be embarrassing to the author himself. Yet certainly in Callaghan's case having a go at his real and imagined enemies in *A Fine and Private Place* has had an extraordinarily liberating effect. The wheel of his creativity has swung again to the top. Here, at last, in *Close to the Sun Again,* is the Callaghan book we have been expecting for thirty years, the completing fourth to *Such Is My Beloved, More Joy in Heaven,* and *They Shall Inherit the Earth.* It hasn't a fine biblical title like the others, but the sun, after all, is a universal image of deity and also of the brightness of going over into death. ("They are all gone into the world of light," as the seventeenth century's Henry Vaughan had it.) And *Close to the Sun Again* is a story about death as the completion of life.

In many curious ways it is a recapitulative book so far as Callaghan is concerned. It is brief and terse, a true *récit,* with a simple one-directional plot like the Callaghan novels of the 1930s. And essentially it has only one character, since the whole novel revolves around the way the moral disintegration of Ira Groome, a model of organizational impersonality, almost predestines the accident that brings him — shattered beyond recovery — to a hospital bed where the barriers to memory are all released. Then Groome remembers the strange experiences that withered his life and turned him into the rigid figure of the Commander, as all men know him. (And here, whether Callaghan intended it or not, one remembers the stony Commander who guided Don Juan into death in Lorenzo da Ponte's libretto for *Don Giovanni,* though Callaghan's Commander is in fact his own guide.)

The echoes multiply as one reads through *Close to the Sun Again.* The plot — and some account of the action is necessary to appreciate Callaghan's intentions — shows the Commander, Ira Groome, returning from a distinguished executive career in Brazil to take over the police commission of a Canadian city, presumably the half-mythical Toronto of Callaghan's earlier novels. Slowly we realize that under the imperturbable surface everything is wrong. The Commander, whose wife died alcoholic and whose son has rejected him, is haunted by expectation; he is awaiting the reawakening of some crucial memory. He begins to drink, and to slip away every few months to a nursing home to dry out. He becomes more reckless and more desperate; there is a ludicrous scene in which he spews gin over his fellow members on the police commission. The Commander goes for the last time to his nursing home, and here the horsy rich-bitch who is in his present mistress makes a remark that suddenly gives the clue to the memory he has been seeking. He walks out, starts to drive back to the city, is crushed in an accident, and, dying in the hospital, remembers like a drowning man the events that have turned him into the stony statue of the Commander.

What follows — the great Proustian area of memory recovered — is the kernel, the best part of the novel, and the most direct and uncluttered writing Callaghan has done in years. Ira Groome (the novel is full of the kind of orally clumsy names Callaghan has always delighted in, such as Leo Cawthra and Jethroe Chone) is lieutenant on a corvette escorting an Atlantic convoy in the Second World War. The corvette picks up a boat of survivors from a wrecked merchant ship, including a striking pair, the beautiful semidebutante Gina Bixby and Jethroe Chone, a self-assured thug whom her rich father (mixed up in gangland and himself in flight) has appointed her guardian and who, according to Gina, has raped her. Ira falls in love with Gina, but her relationship with Chone troubles him. Is she in the man's power, or does she want to keep him in hers until—when they land in England—her father can avenge her dishonour?

The corvette is torpedoed, and Ira comes back to consciousness on a float that eventually picks up Gina and Chone. Mortally hurt, Chone eventually drops over the side of the float, and Gina, with an agonized cry of "come back, you bastard," leaps into the water and is lost with him and to Groome. Picked up by the packet—and this is the frailest passage of the book—Groome sees the "world of wonderfully impersonal relationships" that a naval career offers, and decides that "there could be relief in forgetting the voices of his own heart." But can one really forget voluntarily the voices of one's heart, heard in full manhood? Is it plausible that Groome should have put the dramatic incident of Chone and Gina so completely out of his mind that only the approach of death releases it? Could you? Could I?

But the difficulty of believing such things literally may mean that we are back with the essential Callaghan, who at his best was not greatly interested in realism, but rather in presenting moral drama. *Close to the Sun Again* is nothing if not such a drama—an allegory on the way the will to power develops among men only when their natural impulses are suppressed and their personal defeats come to dominate them. Touch a powerful man and you find an emotional cripple. That is the tale of Ira Groome.

But there is another point to make before leaving *Close to the Sun Again*. It is the resemblance between Gina Bixby's equivocal situation and that of Peggy Sanderson in *The Loved and the Lost*—though Gina, more consistently enigmatic, is more fictionally convincing than Peggy. And a final link. As Ira lies in his hospital bed, near his end, he hears Gina's voice calling over the water and "he saw a sunlit clearing on the edge of a jungle and into that clearing came a white leopard to sit in the sun, and then he was dead." It is, of course, in association with a leopard and an old church that James McAlpine remembers Peggy in *The Loved and the Lost*. But McAlpine and Peggy are far less realized beings in one's mind than Gina and Groome. Callaghan, at seventy-four, is at the top of the wheel again. Long may he remain there! Long may the old swan sing!

[1977]

The Own Place of the Mind: An Essay in Lowrian Topography

THINKING OF MALCOLM Lowry, one is often tempted by the familiar Miltonic tag, "The mind is its own place, and in itself / Can make a heav'n of hell, a hell of heav'n." The mind is its own *place* not its own *person*, for Heaven and Hell alike exist, in the grand Miltonic and Dantesque topographies, as realms where personality has reached its end. Lowry, as I shall suggest, is a writer for whom personality, the common concern of the novelist, becomes increasingly less important and less attainable in fictional terms outside the author's imprisoning self, but for whom place, not merely as a reflected state of mind but also in its physically apprehensible sense, becomes increasingly important.

At its most intense, the visual imagery of Lowry's fiction takes on such a super-real quality of inner illumination that it is easy for those not familiar with the actual Mexico of *Under the Volcano* or the actual fragment of Canada where "The Forest Path to the Spring" is set to believe that everything is the invention of a brilliantly fertile imagination, presenting a series of dream landscapes where nightmares can be enacted without relationship to the world of here and now. But when one knows the places, such an assumption is impossible. Like other great writers on Hell and Heaven, Lowry never fell into the error of dividing in man the physical from the spiritual, either in his apprehension of existence or in his presentation of it, and so he did not merely take convenient images from his Canadian setting to create the state of mind—the elegiac mood—of "The Forest Path to the Spring"; the actual experience of the setting as Lowry lived himself into it shaped the novella, and the cougar is a physical beast as well as an inner terror. In the case of Mexico, I have already, in *Odysseus*

Ever Returning (1970), examined the detailed way in which Lowry describes the actual environment so that it emerges not merely as a natural background but also as a present and active element in the tragedy of Geoffrey Firmin.

The inclination among critics to neglect the importance of the perceived environment, of place in its most direct and concrete sense, in Lowry's work has been encouraged by the accounts of some of his acquaintances who failed to understand his eccentric ways of perception. James Stern, who wandered with him about Paris and New York, thought Lowry was totally lacking in a sense of place. "Unlike mine, his bump of locality on land was erratic." And his French translator, Clarisse Francillon, disappointed with Lowry's unenthusiastic response to her efforts to show him the sights of her beloved Paris, concluded, "He preferred his own inner landscape and orbit, sampling the cantinas," and "Sun and trees, these he no longer knew how to appreciate—he never looked out of the window."

Clarisse Francillon's remarks—which no one who had seen Lowry within the landscape of "The Forest Path" could have made—referred to a visit to Paris in 1948, when he had still a great deal of writing ahead of him which showed an almost hypersensitive responsiveness to the places where he lived. Such assumptions of Lowry's imperceptiveness of his immediate physical surroundings as she and Stern made, on the basis of his apparent lack of reaction to them, fail to take into account Lowry's extraordinary ability to absorb visual and aural data in an almost subliminal way, so that at times, when he appeared to have passed out from drinking, he could give an exact account of incidents that had happened when he seemed to be unconscious to the world. Lowry's physical antennae were extraordinarily highly developed.

In fact, as Hilda Thomas remarked in her essay on "Lowry's Letters" (George Woodcock, ed., *Malcolm Lowry: The Man and His Work,* 1971), one of Lowry's most attractive characteristics was his "humble regard for the natural world." Had we not learned to see him through *Under the Volcano* as the modern prose poet of damnation par excellence—a kind of flawed Dante—we would almost certainly be inclined to find a place for "The Forest Path to the Spring," with its accurate and limpid perceptions of wildlife in its proper setting, beside the classic nature writing of such men as

W.H. Hudson, H.D. Thoreau and Lowry's fellow adoptive Canadian Roderick Haig-Brown, as a work that reflects — even if with sometimes frightening ambiguity — a pantheistic sense of environment in which God, and Devil as well, are wholly immanent. Paradise exists in such writings (it is only *hoped for* in *Under the Volcano*) and it is a paradise that can be apprehended directly through the senses, almost as if Lowry were following Ruskin's injunction, in *Modern Painters*, that "the whole power, whether of painter or poet, to describe rightly what we call an ideal thing, depends on its being thus, to him, not an ideal, but a *real* thing." But, like all paradises, that of the "The Forest Path," despite the almost pre-Raphaelite particularity with which it is presented to us, is precarious and its inhabitants are under perpetual threat of eviction (Lowry's habitual synonym for damnation). The hell that threatens, one is often led to assume, is what emerges out of man's nonphysical life, out of the world of mind and soul. It is the fruit of the Tree of Knowledge as distinct from the Tree of Life.

Half conscious I told myself [says the narrator of "The Forest Path"] that it was as though I had actually been on the lookout for something on the path that had seemed ready, on every side, to spring out of our paradise at us, that was nothing so much as the embodiment in some frightful animal form of their nameless somnambulations, guilts, ghouls of past delirium, wounds to other souls and lives, ghosts of actions approximating to murder, even if not my own actions in this life . . . .

What Lowry means here is all that makes the human karma, beyond and behind instinct, innocence and joy, insofar as it can be separated from the realm of nature.

Lowry's extreme sensitivity to place outside the mind can be seen in the kind of constant revision that he applied to the series of unfinished books on which he worked after completing *Under the Volcano*, in the hope of creating a great interlinking oeuvre — "The Voyage That Never Ends" — that would equal Proust's great masterpiece, *A la recherche du temps perdu*.

Proust, of course, was as expert as Lowry at inducing in his readers a vivid multisensual apprehension of place. Lowry shares both spatial preoccupations and stylistic tricks with Proust, and one can make an interesting comparison between the French writer's treatment of the changing relationships of church spires seen from winding lanes near Combray in *Du côté de chez Swann* and Lowry's treatment in *Under the Volcano* of mountain peaks seen from a circling Mexican hill road on the bus journey to Tomalin.

Indeed, there are passages of Lowry that read almost like pastiches of Proustian description, as in the early pages of *Under the Volcano*, when Jacques Laruelle — in Mexico — remembers with preternatural clarity the first time "he had seen, rising slowly and wonderfully and with boundless beauty above the stubble fields blowing with wild flowers, slowly rising into the sunlight, as centuries before the pilgrims straying over those same fields had watched them rise, the twin spires of Chartres Cathedral."

But there is an essential difference between Proust and Lowry in their treatment of place. Proust retreats to the cork-lined room of his final years, and what he presents through the voice of his namesake narrator is place conditioned by time and particularly by memory; that no experienced scene is ever so vivid as the involuntarily remembered scene is a central axiom of Proust's philosophy and of his method. His constant revision is aimed at making more perfect the presentation of scenes filtered through memory.

Lowry, on the other hand, was not concerned with conforming to the Platonic model offered by an irradiating and modifying memory of the past. He set out to draw significance from the experience of a lived present, and especially the lived present in a place that had acquired for him a peculiarly paradisial quality, the shores of Burrard Inlet at Dollarton, a few miles east of Vancouver and under the slopes of Seymour Mountain. The attempt to render that paradisial quality and exercise its hellish counterpart in prose engaged and baffled him all the later years of his life. Only in one work, "The Forest Path to the Spring," did he wholly succeed in this task.

Lowry's attitude to place, and the ways he tried to express it, changed constantly during his career. *Ultramarine* is a novel that seems subjective to the point of solipsism, yet even here place is an important element. One is aware of it not so much in the perfunctorily described harbours of the China Coast — "What did another port mean to him? Only another test of his steadfastness" — as in the vast spaces of ocean, so that a seaport evokes emotion only in nighttime stillness when one remembers the great waters beyond, as in the description of the *Oedipus Tyrannus* docking in Hong Kong harbour.

But the sun spun round in its might towards the evening land of clouds, the atmosphere turned to evening with the burning of pale red stars — that night the *Oedipus Tyrannus* had reached another port, Hong Kong. She glided in silently at four bells in the evening. Lanterns were swinging at the water's edge, an army of lights marched with torches up the slope to the barracks, a few natives came on board wearing enormous cymbal-shaped hats, but on the ship was dead silence, save for the hiss of the darkness. Oh God, oh God, if sea life were only always like that! If it were only the open sea, and the wind racing through the blood, the sea, and the stars for ever!

And, at the end of *Ultramarine*, in a passage whose imagery makes it read like a prose complement to the poetry of James Elroy Flecker, the desert and the sea are equated as scenes of unending journey and search:

The Suez Canal! All around is the desert save where a cluster of palms struggle in the noonday fire; the eternal stream, which once was lost but lives always in the dreams of men. The anchor weighed, to be released, to glide slowly through the grey, sun-bleached land where the desert men kneel in still, confident peace, where the darkness draws in in a moment. Where the wild mysteries of the desert nights gleam in everything, in the sand garden's waste, in the palm's breath, in the starlight's cold, and in stars in motion on the dark stream. Then at last again to be outward bound, always outward, always onward, to be fighting always for the dreamt-of harbour, when the sea thunders on board in a cataract, and the ship rolls and wallows in the track of the frozen sea's storm....

Place in *Ultramarine* is essentially unbounded space, the endless ways of the sea or the desert where the suffering immature spirit can at once escape from an unendurable present and continue into the future on the never-to-be-fulfilled Golden Journey of all youthful romantics who, like Flecker's pilgrims, search

> Beyond that last blue mountain barred with snow,
> Across that angry or that glimmering sea...

in the "lust of knowing what should not be known."

If *Ultramarine*, insofar as it is conceived in spatial terms, ends in a yearning for infinitely receding ocean or desert distances, *Under the Volcano* is dominated by the immuring mountain horizons that form the physical correlative of the Consul's imprisonment in his private hell of destiny. Even that inner hell, too, is seen — symbolically — in terms of space. In the never delivered letter to Yvonne which Laruelle finds between the pages of his dead friend's copy of *Dr. Faustus,* Geoffrey writes: "And this is how I sometimes think of myself, as a great explorer who has discovered some extraordinary land from which he can never return to give his knowledge to the world: but the name of this land is hell."

Under the Volcano is much closer than Lowry's later and uncompleted long works of fiction to the conventional novels of his time. The plot is elaborately structured; the characters are fabricated out of observing many people instead of being merely direct fictional projections of the author himself. And—what is more germane to the subject of this essay—fictional place is related closely to actual place, so that the imagined town of Quahnahuac is created by grafting real-life Oaxaca onto real-life Cuernavaca, in both of which Lowry lived out experiences remembered with an intensity that was more than Proustian; Lowry was never content with recollections but sought literally to relive the past, with the disastrous consequences described in *Dark As the Grave Wherein My Friend Is Laid* and the unpublished "La Mordida," which tell what happened when he was drawn back to the places out of which he had constructed the setting for *Under the Volcano.*

When we turn to that novel, we see the special deliberateness with which the landscape is used as a setting, in a cinematographic rather than a theatrical sense. It is no static stage set that we perceive, for example, in the very first pages of the novel, when—a year after the Consul's death—Jacques Laruelle, himself a filmmaker, looks out over the scene of his friend's last hours with an eye as dispassionate as that of the universe itself. The knot of mountains and their volcanoes is set in the mind's eye on the world map, and then the focus narrows to the town of Quahnahuac, and then to the tennis players, Laruelle and Dr. Vigil, sitting on the terrace of the Hotel Casino de la Selva, and finally to Laruelle's memory which sharply narrows our attention to the Consul and his tragedy.

Thus we begin with a sense that place is vital to the novel, and this sense never leaves us as we watch and live within the constantly varying scene of the last days in the Consul's journey to damnation. There is no doubt that Lowry observed Mexico carefully, noted down his observations in the memorandum books he kept almost to his death, and retained a memory of his experiences exact and vivid enough to enable him to compose the final and successful version of *Under the Volcano* when he was already living in British Columbia, the *Paradiso* of his personal Divine Comedy. The terrain of Mexico had not only been seen; it had also been felt, in all its dramatic beauty, in all its latent menace. Had it not been felt in this way, its impact throughout the novel would not be so portentous, and we would not remember the novel so vividly in the mind's eye in terms of people in an infernal landscape.

So we can assume that Lowry, in Mexico, responded intensely to Cuernavaca and Oaxaca as places—as natural and urban settings for the violent and death-obsessed Mexican way of existence, even before he decided to use them—in the brilliant cinematic manner he borrowed from the classic German filmmakers—as the physical correlatives of his hero's inner experiences. The volcanoes, the neglected garden, the decaying palaces, the deep and dense *barranca*, all are more than the features of a natural background. They reflect the Consul's inner condition—the own place of his mind—and in this way they force him into self-recognition and the reader into a dispassionate recognition of the Consul's condition. Yet at the same time they continue to be there objectively, just as Milton and Dante meant us to perceive the physical features of Hell objectively, and even as we try to isolate the symbolic elements of *Under the Volcano* we are forced to remember that this is the story of what happened in a material way to a man who dies. That man's inner life, for all its fancies and illusions, is nevertheless given its final expression in the foolish and sometimes splendid physical action that ends in his being shot and thrown into the *barranca* like a dead dog; in fact, with a dead dog. The Consul's hell may be internal, but the ministers of evil who kill him are part of the external Mexican world. The mind as its own subjective place can exist only in an objective place, and when the mind subjectively has gone into the hell of personal disintegration, then the outer world becomes hell, too.

The constant interplay of human fantasy and of the fantasy of the external world, mind and matter perpetually reflecting each other, and manifested in such phenomena as coincidence and the near-coincidence Jung called synchronicity, always fascinated Lowry. We can only understand *Under the Volcano* if we understand the kind of continuities or at least of correspondences that such a view implies. Mountain and *barranca* may symbolize the heaven and hell within the Consul's heart, but they play their essential role in the novel—that of correlatives—only by being their solid selves: as solid as symbols, to be effective, must always become.

That Lowry used these elements of landscape—and of setting generally—quite deliberately and on several levels is clearly shown in the letter to his English publisher, Jonathan Cape, of 2 January 1946, which answered the readers' objections to the final version of *Under the Volcano* and preceded its ultimate acceptance. Lowry argues in this letter that the "Mexican local colour," whose abundance one of the readers criticized, is "all. . . there for a reason," and stresses the vital importance of his "use of Nature." When, later in the letter, Lowry describes the intent of the various chapters, the centrality of place to his concept and his structuring of the novel becomes quite evident. He maintains that the first chapter is necessary "more or less as it is, for the terrain, the mood, the sadness of Mexico," and, going into more detail, he continues:

The scene is Mexico, the meeting place, according to some, of mankind itself, pyre of Bierce and springboard of Hart Crane, the age-old arena of racial and political conflicts of every nature, and where a colourful native people of genius have a religion that we can roughly describe as one of death, so that it is a good place, at least as good as Lancashire or Yorkshire, to set our drama of a man's struggle between the powers of darkness and light. Its geographical remoteness from us, as well as the closeness of its problems to our own, will assist the tragedy each in its own way. We can see it as the world itself, or the Garden of Eden, or both at once. Or we can see it as a kind of timeless symbol of the world on which we can place the Garden of Eden, the Tower of Babel and indeed anything else we please. It is paradisial; it is unquestionably infernal.

As we read on through the novel, with these hints from Lowry in our minds, we see that he not merely persists in laying on a thick impasto of vivid aural and visual detail, which accentuates the melodrama of the action in much the same way as the meticulous representation of incongruously gathered objects accentuates the fantasy of a surrealist painting. He also carefully relates everything seen and heard and felt to the Consul's inner predicament which changes form as rapidly and dramatically as the views of volcanoes seen from the panning perspectives of the precipitous

Mexican roads. And dominating the scene that is established with such portentous clarity in the imagination are the great mountains, which touch heaven and at the same time plunge their craters into the inner fires of the earth; and the great *barranca* and the dark wood, both linked specifically to the Dantesque inferno; and the dishevelled and neglected gardens—the Consul's own and those in public parks—which are the physical tokens of a lost paradise, even bearing notices which the Consul interprets as threatening the eviction of those who destroy the gardens—a warning often to be repeated in his later writing.

The scape of wild nature which so persistently attracts our attention in *Under the Volcano* must necessarily be shown as massive and spectacular and powerful if it is to bear the burden of the preternaturally strong emotions which the various characters project onto it, often consciously, as reflections of their various natures, or perhaps more accurately of their various stages on the way to self-destruction. For the Consul that scape can be cruelly indifferent:

The sun shining brilliantly now on all the world before him, its rays picking out the timberline of Popocatepetl as its summit like a gigantic surfacing whale shouldered out of the clouds again, all this could not lift his spirit. That sunlight could not share his burden of conscience, or sourceless sorrow. It did not know him.

But the same view can also be diabolically complicitous:

He lay back in his chair. Ixtaccihuatl and Popocatepetl, that image of the perfect marriage, lay now clear and beautiful on the horizon under an almost pure morning sky. Far above him a few white clouds were racing windily after a pale, gibbous moon. Drink all morning, they said to him, drink all day. This is life!

Enormously high too, he noted some vultures waiting, more graceful than eagles as they hovered there like burnt papers floating from a fire which suddenly are seen to be blowing swiftly upward, rocking.

And in the end the mountain scape seems to preside with a knowing menace as the Consul, with drunkard's cunning, lightly but fatally puts the final touches to his half-conscious plot for his own destruction.

He was running, too, in spite of his limp, calling back to them crazily, and the queer thing was, he wasn't quite serious, running toward the forest, which was growing darker and darker, tumultuous above — a rush of air swept out of it, and the weeping pepper trees roared.

He stopped after a while; all was calm. No one had come after him. Was that good? Yes, it was good, he thought, his heart pounding. And since it was so good he would take the path to Parián, to the Farolito.

Before him the volcanoes, precipitous, seemed to have drawn nearer. They towered up over the jungle, into the lowering sky — massive interests moving up in the background.

For Hugh, on the other hand, retarded in adolescent romanticism, there is, as he looks at the same landscape, a reaction that seems like an echo of *Ultramarine* and of Dana Hilliot's longing.

There was something in the wild strength of this landscape, once a battlefield, that seemed to be shouting at him, a presence born of that strength whose cry his whole being recognized as familiar, caught and threw back into the wind, some youthful password of courage and pride — the passionate, yet so nearly always hypocritical, affirmation of one's soul perhaps, he thought, of the desire to be, to do, good, what was right. It was as though he were gazing now beyond this expanse of plains and beyond the volcanoes out on the wide rolling blue ocean itself, feeling it in his heart still, the boundless impatience, the immeasurable longing.

And, a final example of the Mexican landscape reflecting states of mind, and projecting as well as conspiring in destiny, there is the late passage describing part of the walk that Yvonne and Hugh take in search of the Consul.

They had reached the limit of the clearing, where the path divided into two. Yvonne hesitated. Pointing to the left, as it were straight on, another aged arrow on a tree repeated: *a la Cascada*. But a similar arrow pointed away from the stream down a path to their right: *a Parián*.

Yvonne knew where she was now, but the two alternatives, the two paths, stretched out before her on either side like the arms — the oddly dislocated thought struck her — of a man being crucified.

If they chose the path to the right they would reach Parián much sooner. On the other hand, the main path would bring them to the same place finally, and what was more to the point, past, she felt sure, at least two other cantinas.

They chose the main path: the striped tents, the cornstalks dropped out of sight, and the jungle returned, its damp earthy leguminous smell rising about them with the night.

This path, she was thinking, after emerging on a sort of highway near a restaurant-cantina named the Rum-Popo or the El Popo, took, upon resumption (if it could be called the same path), a short cut at right angles through the forest to Parián, across to the Farolito itself, as it might be the shadowy crossbar from which the man's arms were hanging.

The noise of the approaching falls was now like the awakening voices downwind of five thousand bobolinks in an Ohio savannah. Toward it the torrent raced furiously, fed from above, where, down the left bank, transformed into a great wall of vegetation, water was spouting into the stream through thickets festooned with convolvuli on a higher level than the topmost trees of the jungle. And it was as though one's spirit too were being swept on by the swift current with the uprooted trees and smashed bushes in débâcle towards that final fall.

Here, the features of the landscape project the themes of sacrifice/victimization and choice/free will, which are inevitably part of a novel so oriented towards damnation. The arrows are images of martyrdom and also signs offering a choice; the paths cross in ways that suggest to Yvonne on two separate occasions a crucifixion. The choice of paths leads one either to the falls or to the Little Lighthouse, ironic source of light where the Consul will find darkness. But it is the path to the falls that Yvonne takes, and the choice is underlined by the fact that miniature cascades are already ploughing down beside them as they walk in the direction of the final fall towards which Yvonne feels her spirit being swept away. This of course is a premonitory image of the death that awaits her, but it is also a sign that this is a novel not only about eviction from paradise, but also about the Fall, in theological terms. And, of course, if anyone in the novel is unwilling victim and needless sacrifice, it is Yvonne.

Place in *Under the Volcano,* as manifested in the Mexican setting, is grandiose and indifferent or, subjectively seen, grandiose and menacing; the very scale of the natural phenomena intensifies the pettiness, the hopelessness, above all the eventual depersonalization of human endeavours, just as the scale of Dante's inferno emphasizes that ultimate wretchedness, beyond the human condition, beyond personality, in which its dwellers neither live nor truly die. As Lowry said of his Mexico, "It is paradisial; it is unquestionably infernal."

A paradise that was not infernal did find its way into the final, published version of *Under the Volcano;* the Consul, Yvonne and Hugh all think and talk about it, and we first encounter it in the Consul's letter which Laruelle finds in the copy of *Dr. Faustus* at the start of the novel:

I seem to see us living in some northern country, of mountains and hills and blue water; our house is built on an inlet and one evening we are standing, happy in one another, on the balcony of this house, looking over the water. There are sawmills half-hidden by trees beyond and under the hills on the other side of the inlet, what looks like an oil refinery, only softened and rendered beautiful by distance.

Just before his fatal encounter with the neofascist vigilantes who kill him, the Consul's thoughts turn again to that northern land so different from Mexico — and yet so familiar in its cloud-topped mountains:

British Columbia, the genteel Siberia that was neither genteel nor a Siberia, but an undiscovered, perhaps an undiscoverable Paradise, that might have been a solution, to return there, to build, if not on his island, somewhere else, a new life with Yvonne. Why hadn't he thought of it before? Or why hadn't she?

And almost at the point of death one of Yvonne's last visions is of a northern house burning on a seashore: "Their house is dying, only an agony went there now."

Now, as anyone who has read the recent biographical literature on Lowry will know, he did find that "undiscovered, perhaps . . . undiscoverable Paradise," at Dollarton, British Columbia, which he called Eridanus in his later fiction; the view from his porch was that which the Consul envisaged, and his house burnt down, which led him in June 1944 to write a poetic "Lament," beginning with the lines, "Our house is dead / It burned to the ground / On a morning in June / With a wind from the Sound," and ending in the laconic words, significant to a man who thought often of Hell, "But our house is gone / And the world burns on."

From this time onwards a clear polarity of place appears in Lowry's writing, related to a corresponding polarity of joy-and-despair, heaven-and-hell. While Mexico remains infernal, the paradisial is transferred to British Columbia and specifically to the foreshore at Eridanus, but the salvation which this paradisial place seems to assure is only conditional, and eviction always threatens its inhabitants, as it threatened — in the Consul's misreading of the Spanish notice boards — those who entered the gardens of Mexico. The real, the material basis for this fear was that

Lowry lived as a squatter on the foreshore, and was periodically threatened with expulsion by the harbour authorities; that threat corresponded to his haunting fear that the happiness and the creativity which he enjoyed at Dollarton were only temporary, a fear which he saw confirmed on the one occasion when he ventured back into Mexico, in 1945–46, and underwent a' series of misadventures (described in his letters and in the biographies) in which that country appeared only in its infernal aspects.

The Dollarton-Mexico polarity appears in one way or another in almost all of Lowry's writings after *Under the Volcano,* though there is one manuscript, "In Ballast to the White Sea," of which we know almost nothing, since it was destroyed in the fire that burnt Lowry's cabin in 1944.

Of the three unfinished novels that have survived, two — *Dark As the Grave Wherein My Friend Is Laid* and the unpublished "La Mordida" — were based on the journey back to Mexico in 1945-46, when he failed to discover an old friend who he learnt had been killed in a drunken quarrel; when he himself became embroiled in difficulties with the immigration authorities which led to his being deported from the country; and when, to complete the psychic failure of the expedition, he allowed himself to sink into a morbid reliving of his first marriage, which had collapsed in Mexico. He retained from this journey an even more negative picture of Mexico than he had created in *Under the Volcano.* Now it had become unrelievedly infernal, its paradisial aspects burnt away, its landscapes always threatening and its towns always sinister. It existed for him less as a memory than as an obsession, less as a place seen objectively in all its visual splendour than as Milton's Hell in the own place of the mind.

But if Mexico had become all Inferno, then Eridanus-Dollarton, notably recorded in *October Ferry to Gabriola,* the remaining unfinished novel, and in "The Forest Path to the Spring" and other stories of *Hear Us, O Lord from Heaven Thy Dwelling Place,* became in compensation all Paradise. In personal terms this was because, as Douglas Day has said in his *Malcolm Lowry,* it was "the only place where Lowry ever felt at ease, able to work, able to exercise some control over his drinking." It is true that there were other elements besides place which contributed to the fugitive tranquillity, existing like a deep calm pool in the midst of the torrent of Lowry's life. The comparative success and stability of his second marriage, the withdrawn life among simple fishermen and boat builders, the occult studies he pursued under the old Golden Dawn devotee, "Frater Achad," all contributed, yet his letters and his last writings leave no doubt at all that this combination of fortunate circumstances would not alone have made Eridanus-Dollarton into a precarious paradise. The dominant element of place was needed, the world of nature that so dramatically yet so intimately surrounded him, the world in which he immersed himself both bodily and spiritually, the world of the tide that sucked under his floorboards and the mountains that towered behind him, of the birds and cougars in the forest, of the killer whales and the gulls and the mergansers populating the sound in which he daily swam.

At Dollarton Lowry attained some interludes of peace, a fleeting sense of fulfilment, yet the consciousness of paradise has rarely in itself inspired great art, and whatever personal benefits Lowry may have gained from the years at Dollarton, the effect of the experience on his writing was mainly detrimental. It is probable that Lowry's life was prolonged by this interlude of relative happiness, but prolonged mostly for a succession of unresolved attempts at literary creation. Except in "The Forest Path to the Spring," Lowry never again achieved the extraordinary melding of place and person, of symbol and spirit, of the external world and the inner drama, of artifact and artist that he had attained in *Under the Volcano.* In the end, therapy took over from art, and in Lowry's last works the artist—in ways I shall shortly show—became more urgently important than his creations. Even therapy failed in the final, fatal weeks at Ripe, a third of the world and three years away from Dollarton, and Lowry's letters written during those final stages of his life illustrate the obsessional identification with place—at times the virtual identification of place and person—that characterized his attitude towards Dollarton.

Lowry and his wife Margerie had built a crazy, insecure pier to their squatter's cottage. It survived winter storms that knocked more solid structures awry, and in the end Lowry began to feel a peculiar affinity with this brave, fragile structure which seemed, like him, so threatened and yet so enduring. In the spring storms of 1956, by which time he had reached England, it was destroyed, and he learnt of its end in the summer of the same year with a sense of shock, as if an old friend had died, as if the bell tolled now for him.

I cannot believe our poor pier has been swept away: that pier that gave so much happiness to many and us, *was us* in a sense; . . . we risked our lives building it, and I am broken hearted it has gone.

The personalization of place seems to be carried even a step farther in the strange reference in one of Lowry's last letters — 29 April 1957 to the Canadian poet Ralph Gustafson — to "the waterfront shack on Burrard Inlet which I still have that I loved or love more than life itself."

These references, made in the creatively barren months of Lowry's life, might be dismissed as merely of biographical significance if they did not echo strikingly similar sentiments which are expressed by the central characters in two of the unfinished novels written at Dollarton. Sigbjørn Wilderness, travelling down to Mexico on his portentous journey in *Dark As the Grave Wherein My Friend Is Laid,* recalls with epiphanic intensity the first time he saw his first cabin in Eridanus, and remembers the later cabin as "their poor beloved rainy house in Eridanus, British Columbia." He remembers the great December storms that sweep up the inlet ("joyful, tremendous" yet at the same time fearful), and then it is "unbearable to think of their new little house, alone, in the sea, and unprotected"; only a few pages afterwards he sees "the unfinished house standing there helpless, all but unprotected, at the mercy of the shipwrecks, and battering weather, something indeed like their own lives."

Since Ethan Llewellyn, in *October Ferry to Gabriola,* is involved in the desperate search for a new house because he is threatened with eviction from Eridanus (a threat from which he is reprieved before the book ends), it is natural that memories of the inlet and the cabin, memories of the place should be even more poignantly and extensively recorded than those of Wilderness in the other novel. And, indeed, we find him thinking that

their cabin seemed to possess a kind of life . . . that couldn't have been called forth wholly by its owners, or its past owners. One had come to love it like a sentient thing (and here it was more like a ship) with a life of its own, not that one just imagined as living, or that it flattered and amused one to consider doing so, because one had given it life oneself. . . . And the trouble was that Ethan felt it still did live, after they'd abandoned it . . . . Well, this was animism certainly . . . .

And from this, Ethan concludes:

That among other things, between the cabin and themselves was a complete symbiosis. They didn't live in it, Ethan said, they wore it like a shell.

Such passages confirm one in the feeling that during the years at Dollarton Lowry not merely received a kind of physical therapy from the way he lived, but also that, on a less obvious level, his writing after *Under the Volcano* became a therapy, so that he reversed the traditional progression of the novelist, which tends to be from the autobiographical to the invented. In his later work, in fact, Lowry was quite incapable of detaching his characters from himself or clearly distinguishing their experiences from his. Perilous as it is to identify any fictional character with a living person, it is difficult to avoid — in discussing *Dark As the Grave* — the admission that Sigbjørn Wilderness returning to Mexico *is* in a peculiarly intimate way Malcolm Lowry following the same quest, and that Ethan Llewellyn and his wife setting off in *October Ferry* to find a home on Gabriola Island *are* likewise Lowry and his wife who undertook precisely the same quest for the same reason. *October Ferry* and *Dark As the Grave* are in fact failures both in fiction and in autobiography; Lowry is so possessed by his personal quests that his characters become unconvincing as fictional creations and also as projections of his inner self; there is an immense inhibition at the point of revelation, and episodes which one knows actually happened take on an air of unreal fantasy in these splendid failures, his incomplete books.

It is, in fact, only in the visually live and stimulating descriptions of places — whether Mexican uplands or British Columbian coastland — that these books really detach themselves from their dominating, obsessive inhibitions and fears. Thus one can say that in his final phase Lowry's sense of *place* was stronger and truer than his sense of *person,* which as I suggested at the beginning of this essay, places him among the poets of damnation and salvation, who wrote of a realm where personality had reached its end.

This is what makes it appropriate that "The Forest Path to the Spring," that slight novella in which the leading character is so neutrally sketched that we cannot even clearly define him as a persona of Lowry, in which the action is shifted away from a melodramatic Lowrian search for an impossible grail into a flimsy plot of psychic experiences while carrying water through a wood to a foreshore cabin, should assume in Lowry's later career the role of a key work which *Under the Volcano* assumes in his earlier career. The reason why it makes its special appeal, why it seems uniquely successful and consummated among Lowry's later works, is precisely that it has admitted and accommodated his growing sense of the precedence of *place*—including "own place"—over person.

From the very opening lines—"At dusk every evening, I used to go through the forest to the spring for water"—a tone is set, and the characters and the action are quietened as the picture of a place and the fragile way of human existence within it are created. Out of that creation emerges a sense of unity with nature, in its destructive as well as its regenerative aspects, as near the paradisial as Tartarus-haunted Lowry ever came.

And the rain itself was water from the sea, as my wife first taught me, raised to heaven by the sun, transformed into clouds, and falling again on to the sea, while within the inlet itself the tides and currents in that sea returned, became remote, and becoming remote, like that which is called the Tao, returned again as we ourselves had done.

If we think of *Under the Volcano* as Lowry's Paradise Lost, "The Forest Path to the Spring" is his Paradise Regained, and it is appropriate that, like the original *Paradise Regained*, it should be both briefer and less dramatically striking than its Satanic counterpart. But, as in Milton's great epics, *place* is essential. Heaven and Hell are to be conceived, in Ruskin's terms, as *real* before they can be ideally apprehended, and this happens in Lowry's magical forest harbouring the spring of salvation as much as in his shadowing volcanoes presiding over damnation. In the classic cosmogenies Hell and Paradise had their fixed and proper and actual places. One must be able to locate the *own place* of the mind as surely as these other places, and in his two most fully achieved works Lowry does this.

[1978]

The Novel that Never Ends: David Watmough's Reminiscent Fiction

Into my heart an air that kills
From yon far country blows;
What are those blue remembered hills,
What spires, what farms are those?
A.E. Housman

ONE OF THE MOST skillful and one of the best fiction writers of western Canada is a teller of stories that are centred largely on a distant land of childhood. David Watmough's fiction, as it has appeared in book form up to now, consists of one novel, an open-ended work entitled *No More into the Garden,* and three collections of shorter pieces. Two of these, *Ashes for Easter and Other Monodramas* and *Love and the Waiting Game,* were published in Canada and contain some twenty-one items; the third, *From a Cornish Landscape,* was published in the Duchy of Cornwall and contains nine pieces, all of which appeared in one or other of the Canadian volumes. Other stories and monodramas have appeared in periodicals or have been broadcast over radio without being collected. Watmough has published other kinds of writing, including plays and reviews and a study of the French worker-priests, but the story and the monodrama and the loosely knit novel are the forms he has chosen for the most intimate expression of his inner life.

It is perhaps in the monodrama that he has spoken most evocatively, and I use the word *spoken* deliberately, for Watmough is greatly concerned with the way in which writing in our generation has returned towards the speech, the oral process, from which it originally emerged. The fictions which he calls monodramas — and which constitute a large proportion of his works of imaginative prose for he has written at last fifty of them—appear on the page to be short stories, but they are written to be spoken, to be played, as it were, by a single actor who serves as a narrator and who also plays all the parts in the dialogue. Much of Watmough's time is in fact spent wandering like an airborne trouvère reciting his monodramas to audiences wherever he can find them. He also reads his stories, but the difference between the stories and the monodramas is made clear by the method of delivery. The stories, being written for the eye and the mind, are read. The monodramas, being written for the ear, are rendered dramatically; it is a matter of acting out with inflections and gestures, as Homer probably did and as bards in contemporary oral cultures certainly do, tales that were composed for speaking. As the form of an originally oral epic like *The Odyssey* suggests, oral literature may be formally highly sophisticated, and this is the case with Watmough's monodramas. But Watmough lives in what, *pace* McLuhan, remains the Gutenberg age; his monodramas are composed so that they can be rendered dramatically by the author, who mimics the individual accents and voice tones of his characters, or can be read with equal effect as stories on the printed page. One of the criticisms that has justly been made of much recent experimental writing is that it sounds well when spoken but does not survive commitment to print. A few contemporary poets have indeed solved the problem of writing poetry that appeals equally to the physical ear and the mind's ear; Watmough is the only writer who to my knowledge has deliberately set out to make this double appeal in prose other than that intended for theatrical production—and has succeeded. What he has done is something quite different from the achievements of novelists like Peacock and Meredith, who became subject to the influence of the stage and wrote novels that consisted of sections of vigorous conversation and sections of narrative, alternating and not integrated, so that their books read as if they were mythical literary monsters, part play and part novel. In Watmough the dramatic and narrative elements are brought together, are harmonized, since both are written for the rhythms of speech.

Watmough is a Cornishman, a member of a Celtic people politically and linguistically trapped within the borders of England; he has lived for the past quarter of a century in North America, and in Canada—in Vancouver to be precise, a place as sea-bitten and westward facing as Cornwall—for almost twenty years, but he has not severed his Cornish links, and every year he returns to the native duchy where his roots run deep into the rural life.

Watmough came to the monodrama and also to the particular type of reminiscent short story which he writes through long toil in more orthodox forms. He wrote drama in the generally accepted sense, for several actors, and his plays were performed on radio and television. He also wrote, before *No More into the Garden,* what he himself describes as "nine or ten bad novels." But he would argue that he never in fact abandoned either drama or the novel; he was merely seeking his own form in each.

Perhaps one of the main functions of the monodrama in Watmough's development has been to impel him towards complete candour even at the cost of complete self-revelation. His monodramas are always couched in the first person, and so, instead of telling the tale of some invented hero or some figure from racial memory, as the bards did, the narrator is in fact baring himself, so thin the membrane between his public persona and his real self in these highly autobiographical fictions. As Peter Hay remarked, in his introduction to *Ashes for Easter,* "Each Monodrama, regardless of subject matter, becomes a strange form of public strip-tease." It depends on a process of identification even greater than that required for a stage play, for not only does the listener have to reconstruct in his mind's eye the scene the narrator evokes, but he has to do so by empathizing with the narrator, for there is no other channel of comprehension. As Peter Hay quotes Watmough, the members of the audience "are embarrassed because they feel my embarrassment."

In the stories, as well as in *No More into the Garden,* this direct confrontation between monodramatist-narrator-actor and audience does not take place, yet there is no doubt that the appeal through candour is made here also. Each story, each chapter of the novel, is a confession of ambivalent acts, ambivalent motives. And together, as Watmough sees them, the monodramas and the stories and the one published novel become sections of a great continuing work that is fiction in the same way as Proust's cycle on the involuntary memory is fiction.

The main character—and the narrator—of all the stories and monodramas, and of *No More into the Garden,* bears an invented name, Davey Bryant, and the details of his Cornish boyhood, the

214

centre around which the tales cluster, are in certain ways different
from Watmough's own farmhouse childhood in the Duchy. They
even differ slightly among themselves in terms of family structure
and relationships.

Yet the whole work is in the classic tradition of modernist fiction, a portrait of the artist as a young man, dog or—as
Watmough might Cornishly prefer—badger. The episodes out of
real life have been irradiated by the imagination, modified by the
memory, subsumed within art, but in the true sense they are the
products of invention. Watmough is invoking, even more than
evoking, childhood in all its aspects and dimensions; and it is seen
not always with the eye of the present, but often through the recollective vision, as when in the monodrama "Shipwreck," Davey
returns home and encounters the son of a homoerotic companion
of twenty years before, or when, as in the story "Cousin Petherick
and the Will," the disputed testament of a maligned old relative (a
male virgin falsely accused of homosexual passions) sets in motion
the wheels of memory as the narrator reads in Vancouver the
letters from Cornwall that bear the news to him filtered by
distance.

There is even, at least once, in the story "Fathers and Sons," an
almost classically Proustian awakening of the involuntary
memory. Davey Bryant sits on a rock over Burrard Inlet outside
Vancouver, and the smell of the blossoming salmonberry acts as
his *madeleine* and suddenly evokes the smell of primroses in springtime Cornish lanes. He is taken back in memory to his
grandmother's funeral, when he was a small boy walking behind
the coffin down a narrow farm lane and picking primroses from
the hedgebank as he went. A remark by his father, about the kind
of mother the old woman (whom Davey knew only in the daftness
of her senility) had been, leads the boy to understand suddenly
the way in which each generation repeats the experience of its predecessors, for this is how Davey sees his own mother; there is a
link of insight between son and father which had not existed before. But then comes the spark of association that makes this realization of long ago re-emerge into the present of a memory so
vivid that it seems exact. They are beside the grave, where the
Anglican burial service has just ended.

Suddenly I feel a firm hand on my shoulder. I know that touch. It can
only be Father.

I'd almost forgotten the flowers I'd been clenching for so long. I looked down at them. Do you know those wild primroses and violets had already begun to wilt!

I peer down into the grave at the pale oak coffin lid with the dry earth scattered atop of it. Then I throw in my offering. Sticking together from the clamp of my clutch and the sweat of my palm, they land with a dull thump in one piece.

Then I do what I am so often scolded for doing by Mother; I sniff my hand. And that's it. That's the connection.

Primrose stalks, bruised vegetation. A lifetime later, eight thousand miles from where Grandma Bryant yielded her body to the life of the churchyard, I take the cup of my hand that is holding a sprig of salal, a leaf of salmonberry, again to my nose. And it is the simple vegetable matter that blends with my own scent to ring bells of memory.

I look out across the Pacific to where the Lions Gate Bridge is just a charcoal line in the distance, Vancouver a haze smudge beyond that. Then I stare and stare until my eyes mist with the effort and I cannot say any more whether my blurred sight is just a physical thing or the fruit of remembering a bunch of wildflowers and discovering fathers were also sons.

A passage like this illustrates the kind of stylistic tightrope Watmough is always walking between his oral and his written aspects. This is a story not intended for dramatic presentation, but it is clear that even here the process of the monodrama, with its heightened effects, has operated. Read straight, the passage has more than a faint reek of sentimentality. But examine it more closely, and it becomes evident how — even here where the dramatic reading is not contemplated — the words have been carefully ordered and the sentences balanced for the sake of sound. It is this acute sense of sound that, in stories and monodramas and novel alike, enables Watmough, through the voice of the narrator or equally through the verbal arrangement of the page, to control the impact, so that what at first seems like sentiment makes its final effect as feeling, and the lushest of descriptive passages can conceal the bleakest truths about human motivation.

Watmough's stories, indeed, are all essentially ironic, with the initial nostalgia of the vision always underlaid by the nagging memory, the jarring truth, that provokes the nostalgia. We tend to dwell more on disturbing than on comforting memories, and among the monodramas some of the most telling are those which evoke moments of folly or unworthiness that stir the same shameful recollections in the audience or the reader as the narrator experiences or, alternatively, make him uneasy because of the perilous closeness to the possibilities of his own life of the predicaments—frequently homosexual predicaments—that are delineated.

In "Scar Tissue" Davey Bryant, drawn into the Royal Navy by Britain's national service laws rather than by any patriotic feelings, is picked up in a London park by a couple of detectives and charged with importuning and soliciting. That Davey is homosexual we are left in no doubt; whether the specific accusations are entirely unfounded is never fully resolved, and so an essential ambiguity hangs over the monodrama right to the end, and gives a poignancy to the magnificently rendered bits of dialogue between prisoners, or between Davey and the chaplain, or Davey and the court psychiatrist, that form the virtuoso points of the monodrama, in which the narrator reveals his ability to reproduce accents and to create characters with no better visual aid than the listeners' or the readers' imaginations. In "Black Memory" (like "Scar Tissue" one of the comparatively few entirely non-Cornish episodes in Watmough's fictions), an encounter in a New York john with a gigantic and remarkably endowed black leads Davey for the first time into genuine danger of death at the hands of muggers, and he is lucky to escape, in a marvellously suspenseful confrontation scene between two of his robbers, with his life and a ten-dollar bill. The shift from the comic to the sinister in "Black Memory," as we move from the furtive peepings at Grand Central to the threats in a Harlem room, is splendidly crafted, and Watmough indeed is extremely skilled in such transitions between the opposites, in mood and situation alike.

Death is as perilous a terrain in Watmough's stories as sexuality, as the abundance of pieces about dying great-aunts and grandmothers and cousins reveals. It is not death itself that is the obscenity, as in the writings of the existentialists, for Watmough is a believing Christian, but rather our own human reaction to the facts of ageing and mortality, and again there is a rich area of irony between such phenomena, represented as part of a natural cycle vividly described in environmental terms (landscapes, vegetation, wild animals), and the shameful reactions they provoke in the survivors, such as the falsehoods uttered at funerals, the character assassinations of the dead that can be provoked by unpopular testaments (as in "Cousin Petherick and the Will") or the mixture of shame and callousness we are inclined to show towards the perishable remains of those we have loved, as in one of the best of all Watmough's monodramas, "Ashes for Easter."

In this piece Davey Bryant, now a grown man getting on in his forties, returns from Canada to visit his widowed mother, who involves her rather unwilling son in the task of scattering his father's ashes on the farm that is the scene of so many of the boyhood stories. In a sense it is — on a miniature scale — the parallel to the great recapitulative reunion scene at the Guermantes ball in *Temps retrouvé*, the concluding volume of Proust's great masterpiece.

Twenty minutes later found me parking the car in the gateway of Pol'garrow farm. I'd be in no one's way I realized, as I switched off the ignition, for that track led only to that empty farmhouse where my Dad had first discovered the world — and where he'd subsequently brought his wife and sired the three of us.

I had always thought it was the most beautiful farm in all of Cornwall, but for the past fifteen years that once child-teeming farmhouse had been silent. All the farmers in my family, you see, have died off.

Even five years of uninhabitation can be fatal to a domicile in that moist and fecund Cornish climate. I wasn't surprised, then, to note a daintier version of a jungle sprawl had been at work. Ivy and periwinkle swarmed over windows, tiny saplings sprouted amid the mossy hillocks of a perpetually damp roof, tongue ferns flourished in clogged gutters — and, imprisoned in unheated rooms behind dank cob walls, I could imagine the Cornish mustiness, smelling like yeast and stale cheese.

With my bulky package clutched under my coat, I tiptoed carefully over the moist ground. Though Pol'garrow stood empty, a neighbouring farmer had use of the land. It was his scarring treads that had churned up the soft grass approach.

If it hadn't been for the sunny brilliance of the morning, the rich mosaic of greens in the freshness of spring growth, then the dilapidated farmhouse with its caved-in roof, which for centuries had housed the yeoman history of my father's family, would certainly have depressed me. But now I experienced a not unpleasant melancholy over the relation of Pol'garrow, at this stage of its dissolution, to the parcel I clutched tightly out of sight and which I was about to open.

But the luxuriation in melancholy ends when Davey is faced with the physically disagreeable process of wrestling with the carton containing the ashes, and trying to get rid of his father's remnants in a muddy farmyard on a windy day while singing the

Nunc Dimittis, the only appropriate tune that comes into his head. There is a brief interlude of glory when he wanders to the edge of a quarry and looses a good share of the ashes to the wind as Easter bells ring out below. And then:

I opened my eyes. The bells had stopped. A large cloud was trespassing on the blue space the sun occupied. In a moment, I realized, the land would be in shadow. I looked at my hand still stretched out and at the carton held in it. I gave the thing a jerk. It rattled. There were still a few bits left in the bottom. For some reason they gave me the creeps in a way the ashes in my hair and on my face had not. Perhaps it was some fragments of bone that didn't incinerate? Anyway, something unpleasant. I wasn't going to peer in to find out.

The whole dusty cycle does not come completely to an end until much later, in Vancouver, when Davey finds in his pocket the label from the carton containing his father's ashes:

I rolled it into a tight ball with the palm of my hands. Then I flipped it lightly with forefinger and thumb out across the water. My basset hound, Wendy, saw it, and made as if to retrieve it. But the rippling tide put her off. She never has been that keen on water, nor even with retrieving, come to that.

To divert her I ran quickly along the flat sand to the beach, calling to her. Soon she was baying at my heels and we ran 'till we were both puffing.

I never did look back to see whether that scrap of paper had finally sunk below the small waves . . . .

So, in this trivially grim duty, with all its revelations of the general human fear of what reminds us of our inevitable ends, the past is closed off from obligation, but not from memory, as the great corpus of Watmough's recollective stories and monodramas show. They build up into a kind of living novel of which the book he treats formally as a novel, *No More into the Garden*, is in fact a part more closely organized in a chronological sense than the preceding episodic fictions.

Yet, for all its chronological continuity from Davey Bryant as farmboy to Davey Bryant as middle-aged writer in Vancouver, *No More into the Garden* preserves the episodic nature of all Watmough's fictional writing. The succession of chapters creates an inner development other than that of cause-and-effect, so that each chapter is self-contained and yet presents Davey at a stage of growing awareness of the nature of existence, of the character of his own life and—by an implication Watmough never lets us ignore—of the author's life as well. In the brief interludes between chapters, David actually addresses Davey, to assert the autonomy of a fiction whose links with its creator are tenacious but also elusive. "Davey," he exhorts, "you will persist in the freedom from your progenitor and reveal the power of your subjective liberation from me." Yet he also talks of "author and character, touching and dividing," and so emphasizes—as poignantly as Proust—the deviousness of links between creator and creation, the strange oscillations between autonomy and dependence in the man who acts through his writing persona (already a stage removed from his everyday banking and boozing self) to produce that second remove from himself who is the character.

No More into the Garden is not in any chronological way an extension of the earlier stories and monodramas in which Davey Bryant is the experiencing narrator, centre of attention and consciousness alike. It goes back over the time from Davey's late childhood to his middle age, and the episodes, though different, are drawn from periods of his life that have already been presented in other fictions. To some of its episodes (e.g. Davey's experience in a naval psychiatric ward) his earlier stories (such as "Scar Tissue" with its account of his arrest for alleged importuning) provide an illuminating background. And there is no doubt that at the very moment of its completion *No More into the Garden* becomes an integral part of the great interconnected fabric of Davey Bryant's life that will keep growing so long as memory fascinates David Watmough. Until the well of the past runs dry, there will obviously be continuations, so that *No More into the Garden* is likely to find its eventual place in a sequence as monumental in its own way as that which contains *A côté de chez Swann* and *A l'ombre des jeunes filles en fleur.*

Yet *No More into the Garden* has its own internal rhythm and structure, proceeding as it does from the seemingly innocent pastimes of youth (a happy Christmas on a Cornish coast where war throws up corpses and more profitable flotsam) to the middle-age realization that the atrocity of death shadows all our pleasures. There is a geographical progression from Cornwall via London and Paris and the Côte d'Azur, to the final destination where author and character meet again, conscious of "the return of the snows to the peaks of the North Shore and the sense of immense relief that for us in Vancouver the white shutters of winter were upon us." But it is also an experiential progression, with its brilliantly ironic juxtapositions. In chapter nine, for example, Davey goes on a pilgrimage to Victoria to see once again the woman who in her forties ravished him so mistressfully when he was fifteen; he finds her prematurely old in her sixties, and only his boredom and pity are aroused; he flees, because "I don't think I could stand learning from such aged lips that life had been a terrible mistake." And in chapter ten, teaching at a summer school in the Okanagan, he — a forty-year-old homosexual — is gently seduced by a fifteen-year-old girl, whom he then sends away in panic.

I could read her face in spite of the gloaming. On it was the expression of resignation, of bowing to the inevitable, that I see so often on the faces of today's young, and which I had thought, in my own youth, belonged only to such people as Arabs, bent by the rigours of implacable climates and terrains.

In a sense, we are all "bent by the rigours of implacable climates and terrains," and in our society, perhaps, this applies to none more than those who in some way depart from the norms of our culture, as Watmough suggests with an almost relentless honesty in the chapters of *No More into the Garden*. He shows Davey as the victim of ludicrous circumstances, as when the filthy Archimandrite Alexei leads him in Paris into an alarming encounter with a mad American giantess from which he nevertheless gains enough cash to tide him over financial crisis; he also shows him as the perpetrator of petty moral atrocities, as when out of jealousy he lies in order to destroy the relationship between a girl student and a man he loves. The victim is impelled perpetually to seek a changed role as the victor, and all but one of Davey's homosexual relationships in *No More into the Garden* are marred by some element of cruelty that degrades one or other of the participants.

Apart from such unifying factors, which bind the chapters in a structure more organically cohesive than the sequences of an obviously conventional plot, there is a pervading elegiac consciousness that deepens as the novel proceeds. The longed-for garden that is never re-entered is in one sense the Cornwall of Celtic childhood happiness, but in another sense it is the state of collective innocence and safety to which all men, like Davey, seek a way back. Yet, as Davey remarks: "Things happen to you, without asking. They just steal up. And one day you wake up and realize you're cut off from everything you once thought would be there for ever." And so, in Blakeian terms, Davey's life moves on from innocence to experience, symbolized by the continent and the ocean which he puts between himself and "that hurting Cornish terrain" of childhood. The garden finally becomes "a harvest of threats," and, by the novel's end, the fullness of life is revealed at the same time as the ever-presence of dying, for as the mind expands its borders, so in any life the physical possibilities narrow. Here, for Watmough, is the irony, and the elegy also; in his best work they are always coterminous.

[1977]

Diana's Priest in the
Bush Garden: Frye
and His Master

NORTHROP FRYE IS a critic with an immense reputation, in his native Canada and beyond as well. He is credited with having created a whole mythopoeic school of criticism; he is even, in Canada, credited with having created a school of poets without himself having published a single poem.

None of these claims, be it noted, has been made by Frye himself, and often one wonders whether his reputation, like the less durable reputation of his fellow Canadian, Marshall McLuhan, cannot be largely credited to the almost hypnotic fascination which in our age is exercised by those rare individuals — equipped of course with the necessary charge of talent and originality — who pursue their goals with single-mindedness and preternatural self-confidence.

The perceptive critic of critics can find many things in common between Frye and McLuhan, but the most striking of them is undoubtedly the extraordinary assurance regarding their own special theories with which these two ornaments of the University of Toronto have faced the world. Yet there are significant differences, and since these help to sharpen our view of Frye, they should be brought out.

McLuhan, beginning with an intellectual elitist attitude derived directly from the Great Panjandrum Wyndham Lewis, which he projected in some of the most unreadably pedantic critical articles ever published in scholarly journals, later transformed himself from a highbrow distrusted by the Philistine establishment into the Court Jester of the Electronic Age, eager to betray the literary culture from which he sprang if by that means he could win to his eccentric Utopia, the Global Village, the support of men with political and economic power. McLuhan reminds one of Charles Fourier, the equally eccentric and woolly-headed utopian socialist of the early nineteenth century (who envisaged his own Peaceable Kingdom in which anti-lions would lie down with anti-lambs beside seas of lemonade). Having published his view of a future no stranger and no less likely than that with which McLuhan hypnotized his readers during the 1960s, Fourier announced that he would be present in his rented room at a set hour every morning so that any rich man who was interested in financing his plan for a pilot phalanstery or model community could appear, with cash in hand, to discuss how the earthly paradise might be funded and brought into being. Fourier's capitalist never came, but eventually, at one of those morning hours, there was a less substantial visitor, and Fourier was afterwards found dead beside his bed in the attitude of prayer, his integrity uncompromised.

McLuhan in his turn expounded his utopian message of the Global Village, with the less fortunate result that the rich men came, so that he enjoyed his hour in the blaze of publicity, his glory as a public relations consultant, and his brief illusion that the world was changing to his touch. In the end the rich men turned out to be merely Fourier's visitor in another guise; having betrayed art and the life of the intellect, having attempted to subvert the literature that had fostered him, McLuhan faces the living death of those who have enjoyed false fame. His vogue is ended. His works will survive, as Fourier's have done, among the curiosities of intellectual history. But unlike Fourier's, they will have lost the bloom of unbought innocence.

In contrast to McLuhan's disastrous fame, Frye's much more durable repute has developed undramatically, and largely as a result of the refusal to co-operate, not only with the world beyond literature, but even with the world beyond the academy. Like Sir James Frazer, whom he has admired consistently since his undergraduate years and who may well have been the largest single influence on his work, Frye has remained a denizen of the academic world. Just as Frazer never ventured upon a single field trip into the actual haunts of primitive man, but compiled that dazzling masterpiece, *The Golden Bough,* entirely from what came to him in writing (and usually published writing), so Frye has never ventured into the world of literary creation (or at least has never admitted it) and has outspokenly dissociated himself from what he calls "public criticism."

So far as I have been able to discover, Frye's main foray into the nonacademic world was his period of editing the *Canadian Forum,* and the *Forum* has always been so dominated by university teachers that it can fairly be regarded as an organ of the Canadian academic establishment rather than, like such magazines as the *New Statesman* in Britain and the *New Republic* in the United States, an expression of a widely diffused liberal opinion that has no necessary connection with educational institutions. Frye has also, and notably in the significant lecture on Frazer which I shall later discuss more elaborately, given talks on the networks of the Canadian Broadcasting Corporation, but always in scholarly series in which the other speakers were almost without exception fellow academics.

Otherwise, Frye's life as a critic has been circumscribed by academic walls. His books have appeared under the imprints of university presses — Princeton, Cornell, Toronto, Columbia; when *The Bush Garden* was published by the House of Anansi it seemed a break with the past, for Anansi was a little press devoted to publishing avant garde fiction and poetry, but the break was not so clear as it first appeared, since when Anansi accepted the book it was mainly under the control of writers who had been Frye's students and were themselves university teachers. Quite apart from their publishing history, Frye's books have consisted largely of collections of lectures delivered at universities or in academic symposia, for Frye is singularly adept at producing the occasional paper whose importance transcends the occasion, at turning the graceful academic exercise into a statement weighted with momentous generalizations.

Frye has also been careful to sustain his status as an exclusively academic critic by avoiding participation in critical journals whose policies are eclectic or which maintain the tradition of "public criticism." I have to record, not without sadness, that in the eighteen years during which I edited *Canadian Literature,* Frye contributed only one piece, and that not a critical essay but a brief reminiscence of the late E.J. Pratt. He was invited freely and frequently; he invariably eluded participation with the greatest politeness and geniality, but — which strikes me as the most interesting fact — he was the only Canadian critic of any significance who did so. It seems evident that Frye "voted with his feet" against the one Canadian journal that over this period strove to give expression to every critical viewpoint. This may reflect no more than the difference between his dissenting tradition of election and my Anglican latitudinarianism, but it cannot be omitted from the data on which my view of him is based.

I think that in Frye's voluntary isolation from the world of letters, if not from literature (an isolation remarkably different from McLuhan's willing immersion in the destructive side of commerce and communications), there have been two shaping elements.

The first is an extraordinary and laudable loyalty — the kind of loyalty one finds rarely outside the old universities of Europe and New England — to the academy in which his mind was shaped and his career has been encapsuled. It is hard for anyone who has merely read Frye to appreciate how deeply he is dedicated to the process of teaching. The teaching of many critics who are also university men is merely a by-product of their writing (and as such often a tedious distraction), but in Frye's case the criticism emerges from the teaching.

And this leads us to the second of the reasons for Frye's isolation from the actual world of letters. For the elaborate and beautiful structures he builds out of his insights into literature are, as practising critics usually find, of little help in the work of criticism. Anyone imagining that he has found in *Anatomy of Criticism* a critical handbook or a guide to appreciation is sure to be disappointed. What he will actually encounter is a great and intricate structure of thought in which works of literature are transformed in the alchemy of the critic's mind so that they become components of an edifice whose true purpose is its own existence. Frye has carried to its ultimate conclusion Wilde's theory of the Critic as Artist, for he has gone beyond what he calls the "aesthetic view of the work of art as an object of contemplation" to the creation of critical works which themselves are objects of contemplation independent of the works that may be mentioned or categorized or interpreted within them. Thus *Anatomy of Criticism* is not really an anatomy at all in the sense of describing something that exists; it is an autonomous structure of the imagination. And here, paradoxically, lies its educational value, for it teaches, by precept and example, how to perform that reduction of the inspired and irrational to an inspired rationality which is the true purpose of the academic study of literature. Academic criticism, even at its best — and there is none better than Frye's — always runs parallel to the creative processes of more originative writers. It is a modifying mirror rather than a clear lens, and writers who are puzzled by the discrepancies between their intentions and what is found in their works by university wits, should be content with the thought that, in the hands of an academic critic like Northrop Frye, their work becomes the content of art which, as Frye tirelessly preaches, takes its true existence, which is its form, not from life but from other art.

There is, of course, another kind of criticism whose relation to the work of literature is more direct and whose intent is to assist the reader in his understanding or at least his appreciation of the book or the poem he reads, or of the writer's relation to his work and his world. This, as we have seen, Frye somewhat disparagingly calls "public criticism." "It is the task of the public critic," he tells us, "to exemplify how a man of taste uses and evaluates literature and thus show how literature is to be absorbed into society.... He has picked up his ideas from a pragmatic study of literature and does not create or enter into a literary structure." Apart from remarking that the public critic also shows how literature emerges out of society, I would accept this as a fair description, particularly since it emphasizes that if the public critic does not "create or enter into a literary structure," the academic critic certainly does, and in doing so distances himself from actual literature. It fairly delineates the functions of critics of the calibre of Edmund Wilson and V.S. Pritchett, of George Orwell and George Steiner, and the only real objection one can make is that Frye has himself performed an act of evaluation (which he has frequently declared to be an uncritical function), since the intent of his remark, taken in its context within *Anatomy of Criticism,* is clearly that the practical critic and the academic critic are of two different kinds, and that true criticism is to be found only within the kinds of "literary structures" that are constructed in the academy.

Given this austere withdrawal, it may at first seem strange that Frye should attract the degree of attention outside the academic world which he in fact commands. It is not the fame of the best-selling popular writer or of the intellectual who becomes the public clown; inside or outside Canada, far fewer people know of Frye than of Farley Mowat or Marshall McLuhan. But it is the kind of fame that leads to feature articles in Canadian popular magazines like *Saturday Night* which do not usually pay much attention either to literary critics or to academic hermits.

The reasons for this fame are, in my view, threefold, and each is linked with Frye's interest in Sir James Frazer and *The Golden Bough*. First, because of the ramifications of his interests, Frye is much more of a "public" critic than his own avowals may suggest. Secondly, he is at heart a creative artist, interested in detecting the essential forms in the works of other men and incorporating them into the edifice of his own theoretical visions of the nature and origins of art, so that his major works are in fact as much imaginative creations as are great synthesizing works in other fields, like *A Study of History* or *The Decline of the West* or, of course, *The Golden Bough*. Thirdly, he has been fortunate enough to advance his own theories on the mythopoeic elements in literature at the same time as a mythopoeic trend appeared in Canadian writing, just as Frazer introduced his vast work on the significance and universality of the myths of the sacrificial king and the dying god at a time when British writers were exploring the primitive roots of so much that had been accepted as civilized behaviour.

Frye in his role of the academic moonlighting as the "public" critic is best seen in those occasional pieces on Canadian writing and painting that were gathered in *The Bush Garden*. Despite his acknowledged position as one of the great mandarins of Canadian letters, Frye has never written a formal work on the literature of his country. He has not even devoted to it any of those elaborately graceful lectures for which he is known and welcomed south of the border. What he has done in the intervals of building critical edifices like *Anatomy of Criticism* and of theorizing splendidly on Blake and Shakespeare and Milton, is to write a series of brilliant but more immediate and formally more fragmentary pieces on the literature of his own country, the writing with which he has been face to face in the sense that it had been produced in his own land, and usually in his own time, and often by people he knew. These circumstances made it inevitable that, when during the fifties Frye wrote his annual survey of current volumes of Canadian poetry for the *University of Toronto Quarterly*, when he did occasional reviews for the *Canadian Forum,* when he wrote the postscript to the *Literary History of Canada,* he should take on some of the attributes of the "public critic"—should study the writings of his neighbours pragmatically because he was living and creating the same culture as they were, and, in his role as a reviewer, would inevitably be affecting the way literature is "absorbed into a society."

It is worth noting that Frye's most schematic and academic works of criticism, in which he sets out to create or enter into a literary structure, are precisely those dealing with the literature of the past. The books in which he is most deliberately the critical architect are devoted either specifically to the great dead writers, or to enunciating principles drawn from the study of writers most of whom are not living; in *Anatomy of Criticism* I found references, which were usually unimportant, to only eleven poets who were living when the book was written, and all of these were poets whose reputations had been formed at least a generation before. In other words, the works by which Frye is best known outside Canada are those in which he is operating in the manner of the critical mandarin, who works always by afterthought, considering literature long after it has happened, as a substance already marmoreal, which can no longer grow of its own vital momentum and can therefore be used by the creative critic, as the temples of antiquity were used by mediaeval cathedral builders, to construct his own palaces and pleasure domes. But in Canada Frye has dealt mostly with work by living poets, and it is fascinating, in reading the series of yearly surveys republished in *The Bush Garden,* to see his view shifting and maturing in response to the development of the poets from year to year and constituting a perfect example of that pragmatic handling of literature which he relegates to the public critic.

There is a close resemblance here, I suggest, between Frye, who doubles as the academic critic concerned with creating edifices of eternal principle and the public critic following the actual year by year development of writers in the easy manner of a reviewer, and Frazer, in whom on the one hand there is the classical scholar attempting to discover the universal principles behind a group of antique rituals (themselves the source of literature over many centuries) and on the other the patient anthropological scholar who encourages his friends and disciples engaged in field

work among contemporary primitives and who even seeks to relate the surviving fertility customs of his own land and time to
those of the distant past. Just as Frazer realized that classical
scholarship was barren if divorced from the continuum of human
culture including the present, and shaped *The Golden Bough* with
that in view, so Frye has understood, even if he has not fully admitted it, that the most elaborate academic study of the writings
of dead men will have no meaning if it is not in some way related
to a growing contemporary literature, and this has made him
willy-nilly a Janus among critics, academic and "public" at the
same time.

When we come to the second point of resemblance — that between Frazer and Frye as disguised creative artists — we have to
consider the question of influence. Frye's own essay, "Sir James
Frazer," is not one of his better-known works; it was originally delivered as a CBC talk in a series by various speakers, "Architects
of Modern Thought," and was first published in 1959 in a collection bearing the same title.

The essay begins with a paragraph which curiously reminds
one of Proust's description of the books of the novelist Bergotte
standing in the shop window after his death and in a more than
symbolic way guaranteeing his continued existence.

If you spend much time in libraries, you will probably have seen long
rows of dark-green books with gold lettering, published by Macmillan
and bearing the name of Frazer. Fifteen of them have the running title of
The Golden Bough. Then there's *Folklore in the Old Testament,* three
volumes, *Totem and Exogamy,* four volumes. An edition of Pausanias, the
traveller, who wrote a description of Greece about A.D. 200, six
volumes. *The Worship of Nature,* two volumes. *The Fear of the Dead in Primitive Religion,* three volumes. *The Belief in Immortality,* three volumes.
These are the biggest lots, but there are many more; editions of
Addison's essays and Cowper's letters, two volumes each; editions of
several other classical authors; a book of extracts from the Bible; lectures,
essays, fugitive pieces. It would take a good many months of hard work,
without distractions, to read completely through Frazer.

The loving way Frye dwells on these titles suggests that he is
one who has indeed "read completely through Frazer," and that he
did so early in his scholastic career is suggested in his confession to
one interviewer (John Ayre, "The Mythological Universe of
Northrop Frye," *Saturday Night,* May 1973) that when he went to

theological school during the early 1930s, "theology for me was largely Frazer's *Golden Bough.*" When one takes into account another facet of his early reading which Frye admits in *The Critical Path* — that as a child one of his favourite books was *The Outline of History* by H.G. Wells — an interesting pattern is immediately created. For Wells, like Frazer, was an encyclopaedic writer who sought to discipline the chaotic facts of human existence into a strongly patterned framework, and in the end the form of his work became as important in imparting its message as the content.

Yet in terms of literary structure, it seems likely that Frazer's influence on Frye was stronger than that of Wells. For one of the reasons why *The Golden Bough* is still a book of repute and influence among writers, while anthropologists by and large ignore it, is that it goes far beyond its highly suggestive and stimulating body of content to present a literary edifice constructed with unusual artifice and imagination. In his recent and valuable study, *The Literary Impact of "The Golden Bough"* (1973), John B. Vickery points out that a strong case for Frazer's influence on the structure of much modern literature, as well as "a partial explanation of the attractions of *The Golden Bough,*" is to be found in its "nonchronological method of narration."

This method results in a work whose structure is shaped by most of the devices that characterize modern literature. Consider what we may call *The Golden Bough's* macroscopic form. Here is a work dealing with a vast subject which orders its material thematically; which juxtaposes conflicting evidence and scenes for dramatic purposes; which presents its point of view by indirect and obscure means; which sees human existence as a flow of recurring experiences; which employs repetition and restatement as both emotive and intellectual devices; which creates symbolic epitomes of human history out of apparently limited and simple actions; and which makes a unified whole out of an abundance of disparate scenes and topics by an intricate set of references backward and forward in the narrative. Without in the least denying the other contributory forces, we may legitimately suggest that *The Golden Bough* is also, in a very real measure, responsible for the form and shape of modern literature.

A very similar list might be prepared of the structural characteristics of Frye's *Anatomy of Criticism,* which also is a work of artifice as much as it is a work of argument, and if we assume that Frazer — and Wells to a less extent — anticipated and influenced Frye in his task of creating a literary structure which is much more than the sum of its contents (a task also followed in our age by such differing writers as Spengler, Toynbee, and Pound), then we are actually reinforcing Frye's view that art derives from art, the vital derivation being formal.

In posing such a theory Frye, of course, admits that content changes, and is dependent on the life and times of the artist. The lives and times of Frazer and Frye in fact overlapped, with Frazer playing a significant and central role in the modern movement in literature at least in the English-speaking countries, and Frye carrying over into the postmodern age the ideas that Frazer had first developed. And so, much of the content in Frazer is in fact transferred to Frye. How much one begins to understand in reading Frye's "Sir James Frazer."

Frye remarks that *The Golden Bough* is "more a book for literary critics than for anthropologists," which is true. He declares that it is "a kind of grammar of the human imagination," a description one could apply without any great distortion to *Anatomy of Criticism*. Then he proceeds to a passage which deserves extensive quotation:

Its value is in its central idea: every fact in it could be questioned or re-assessed without affecting that value. We don't have to assume that once upon a time everybody everywhere used to eat their kings, and then gradually evolved less repulsive customs. Frazer's ritual is to be thought of as something latent in the human imagination; it may have been acted out literally sometimes, but it is fundamentally a hypothesis which explains features in rituals, not necessarily the original ritual from which all the others have derived. *The Golden Bough* isn't really about what people did in a remote and savage past; it is about what the human imagination does when it tries to express itself about the greatest mysteries, the mysteries of life and death and after-life. It is a study, in other words, of unconscious symbolism on its social side . . . .

A ritual, in magic, is done for practical purposes, to make the crops grow, to baffle enemies, to bring rain or sunshine or children. In religion, a ritual expresses certain beliefs and hopes and theories about supernatural beings. The practical results of magic don't work out; religious beliefs disappear or change in the twilight of the gods. But when deprived of both faith and works, the ritual becomes what it really is, something made by the imagination, and a potential work of art. As that, it can grow into drama or romance or fiction or symbolic poetry. Poetry, said Aristotle, is an imitation of nature, and the structures of literature grow out of the patterns which the human mind sees in or imposes on nature, of which the most important are the rhythms of recurrence, the day, the month, the four seasons of the year. *Poets can get from Frazer a new sense of what their own images mean, and critics can learn more from him about how the human imagination has responded to nature than from any other modern writer.*

The italics are mine; I shall return to that key sentence. But before I do, there remain two brief passages of the essay that compel attention. There are only two mentions of *myth* therein, the first inconsiderable, but the second significant in terms of Frye's relationship to Frazer, and, indeed, his relationship to the theology he abandoned and the literature he embraced.

Up to Frazer's time, interest in religion was confined mainly to theology or to history, and myth was felt to be just something that wasn't true — something all the *other* religions had. But now we see how religion can appeal to the imagination as well as faith or reason.

And the essay ends with a summarizing passage that needs only slight changes to apply to Frye himself:

He was an old-fashioned agnostic who revolutionized our understanding of religion. He was a devotee of what he thought was a rigorous scientific method who profoundly affected the imagery of modern poetry. He was a believer in progress through reason who has told us more than any other man, except perhaps the Freud he disapproved of, about the symbolism of the unconscious. In a way he's not so much an architect of modern thought as of modern feeling and imagination. But one of the great discoveries of modern thought is that feeling and imagination are inseparably a part of thought, that logic is only one of many forms of symbolism. And that is a discovery Frazer helped to make.

If Frazer was an old-fashioned agnostic who revolutionized our understanding of religion, Frye might be described as an old-fashioned dissenting Christian who revolutionized — or helped to revolutionize — our view of literature. And if Frazer, out of a belief in rigorous scientific method and in progress through reason, led us into the realm of the unconscious and hence into that of imagination, Frye out of his faith in the imagination evolved a rigorous method of criticism and enclosed literature within a framework of reason. In this sense, Frye and Frazer complement each other, and demonstrate how, in our understanding of the great myths that subsume all cultures, the play of the imagination and the work of reason are equally necessary.

Yet what Frye takes from Frazer, apart from the structural influence that stems from *The Golden Bough* to *Anatomy of Criticism,* is only a part of his content. What doubtless seemed most important to Frazer — the mass of collected and arranged anthropological data — is dismissed as of secondary importance. It is Frazer's recognition of the evolution of magic and ritual into myths which profoundly affect the human imagination that Frye has appropriated and turned, of course, to quite other ends than those pursued by Frazer.

Now we come to the third reason for Frye's fame, and to his third similarity with Frazer: the fact that he began to write at a time when his theories coincided with current developments in the literature of his country and of the whole Anglo-Saxon world. No one — least of all Frye — has claimed that he invented mythopoeic criticism; writers like Robert Graves were charting that territory, as poets and novelists were exploring it, long before Frye began to write. What he did in *A Fearful Symmetry* and *Anatomy of Criticism,* and in many of his lectures and essays, was to give the approach a clear and well-organized expression just as academic criticism was freeing itself from the rigours and restrictions of the New Criticism.

In Canada, undoubtedly, Frye has wielded a profound and direct influence on a certain school of academic critics. Not only his approach through myth, but also his insistence on the need for the critic to "create or enter a literary structure," has obviously affected what younger critics have to say, so that *Butterfly on Rock* by D.G. Jones is almost a textbook example of Frye's method of analyzing and correlating the elements of literary criticism; it has also encouraged academic critics and even some critics on the verges of the grove to present their insights within highly organized schemes, like Margaret Atwood's *Survival* or — to give a more recent example — John G. Moss's *Patterns of Isolation.* (Both these titles almost literally describe the central concepts around which these two post-Frye Canadian critics erect their "literary structures.") Such books, as another Frye-influenced critic — Eli Mandel — has remarked, are in fact "mythic geographies."

Three at least of these critics, Jones, Atwood and Mandel, are also leading Canadian poets. Other poets of the same generation, such as Margaret Avison, James Reaney, Dennis Lee and Jay Macpherson, were Frye's pupils at Victoria College and most of them have remained his friends. There has been talk of poets moulded by Frye, but perhaps the most judicious remarks on the actual situation were made by one of the poets involved, Eli Mandel, in his introduction to *Contexts of Canadian Criticism*.

It is difficult if not impossible to know to what extent a critic moves poets, but, along with Frye's contribution to the "Letters in Canada" series of the *University of Toronto Quarterly* for a period of ten years, a mythopoeic poetry of some power, in fact, did develop; and without claiming them as Frye's disciples, one notices certain poets whose work takes shape around this time: Wilfred Watson, Douglas le Pan, James Reaney, Anne Wilkinson, and Jay Macpherson.

In fact, if one examines Frye's surveys in "Letters in Canada," no direct preaching for a particular way of creating poetry becomes evident. The criticism seems always to come *after* the poetry, when Frye explicates and praises the verse of the poets Mandel mentions. It seems as though Frye and the poets were *moving together* towards the conclusions that — towards the end of his work on "Letters in Canada" — Frye gave systematic form in *Anatomy of Criticism.* If Frye indeed wielded an influence over these poets (and I am not inclined entirely to deny it) it more probably came from his teaching and from that cultivation of the imagination which he incited in and out of the classroom. Here it is appropriate to quote again the sentence on Frazer which I earlier italicized:

Poets can get from Frazer a new sense of what their own images mean, and critics can learn from him about how the human imagination has responded to nature than from any other modern writer.

Unconsciously — or perhaps after all consciously — Frye was identifying with Frazer, and he described himself by describing his master. He did not create a school of poets; he did stimulate a generation of poets by clarifying their poems for them, and, to the extent that this happened, by liberating their imaginations for further efforts. But this he did, not because he had any power to inspire them, but rather because, sharing their vision, he shaped it in rational form and made logic a mirror for the imagination.

[1974]

McLuhan's Utopia

It has become a commonplace in discussing the effect of the media in modern society to point to the way in which reputations can be instantly made, and lost with equal rapidity. The situation is all the more piquant when this happens to a media figure like Marshall McLuhan. Remembering his career, one is tempted to adapt the slogan of a celebrated gasoline advertisement which for some reason he overlooked in compiling *The Mechanical Bride:* "That's McLuhan — that was."

It is true that, as a disturbing sport among academics, McLuhan has been in evidence for twenty years. But neither *The Mechanical Bride* (1951) nor *The Gutenberg Galaxy* (1962) marked the real beginning of his brief reign as a mod hero. That came with the publication of *Understanding Media* (1964), a thinly veiled celebration of the impending reign of the electronic media and the return to tribalism, now universalized. All the basic ideas of that book (and McLuhan really has few ideas, but repeats them constantly in varying forms) had in fact been sketched in *The Gutenberg Galaxy,* and the notion of swimming with the maelstrom had made its appearance in *The Mechanical Bride.* But in *Understanding Media* McLuhan translated his gospel from academic hieratic into Madison Avenue demotic, and stunned many apparently intelligent people into accepting a highly exaggerated view of the role of electronic communications in our lives.

None of the curious intermedial volumes in which, after *Understanding Media*, McLuhan tried to develop a mosaic of picture and aphorism (in a vain attempt to evade the charge that he used print to declare the end of print), made an impression like that of his earlier books, and their failure confirmed the implications of the continuing success of the paperback revolution in publishing: that under modern conditions people are in fact reading more than they did a generation ago, and that the Gutenberg dynasty remains in control of a very large territory in the Western consciousness. Since 1964, moreover, there is evidence that, like mosquitoes resisting DDT, the human mind is learning to absorb television without the extraordinary changes in consciousness McLuhan predicted. We have not yet become Global Village enough to diminish the passions of nationalism; indeed, to give an example very close to the bone when dealing with McLuhan, the spread of television in Canada, and particularly the prevalence of American shows, has been followed by an upsurge of national feeling, a strong reaction against the very influences that not long ago made it seem as though North America might become the prototype of the Global Village.

I do not know how far the evident failure of his teachings to work out in the short run has affected McLuhan's viewpoint; recently he has withdrawn into the academic fastness from which he emerged. But it is certain that during the past three or four years his influence has waned, and I doubt if there are many ardent McLuhanites left except among slightly unfashionable PR officers and belated Op artists. And now the burial beetles are at work on his reputation; interestingly, they are led by late disciples. The authors of two recent books, Jonathan Miller (*Marshall McLuhan,* 1971) and Donald F. Theall (*The Medium is the Rear View Mirror,* 1971) are former McLuhanites turning against the master, Miller in total opposition and Theall in that spirit of revisionism which to the faithful always seems worse than downright rejection.

Having held even at the height of general McLuhanacy the critical attitude of the working journalist, who knows that things are never as simple as aphorists and myth makers declare, I find it hard to resist the kind of I-told-you-so smugness which anarchists used to assume towards Trotskyists when they talked of Stalin. It is easy — all too easy — to say: How could you really believe McLuhan's nonsense about TV being *tactile*? How could you swallow those absurd assurances that an Eskimo lived in an *auditory* world when his very survival as a hunter depended on a visual sense that *reads* the landscape as accurately as any of us reads a page of print? How could you allow McLuhan the insolent claim that the front page of a newspaper, with its "instantaneous mosaic," is less rather than more visual than a page of print?

Yet McLuhan remains a phenomenon that has to be acknowledged. Even after his vogue has dissipated, some of his works will remain as curiosities in the history of Western culture. *The Gutenberg Galaxy,* for example, is likely to be read for the very feature that the later McLuhan would have dismissed as irrelevant — its content. It is, like Burton's *Anatomy of Melancholy* or Proudhon's *De la Justice,* one of those eccentric compendia of strange knowledge that omnivorous readers will find entertaining long after the argument has ceased to be topical. And even his earlier scholarly essays, recently collected in *The Interior Landscape,* plodding and murkily written though they may be, are interesting because of the traditionalist and elitist gloss which they provide on his latest work. "The Southern Quality" and "Edgar Poe's Tradition," neither of which McLuhan has repudiated, read like parodies on the myths of gentlemanly Dixie, while an anticipation of his later excesses in relation to the media appears when he seeks to show that the symbolist theory of analogies and correspondences originated in the front pages of newspapers, whose arbitrary juxtaposition of dissimilar incidents supposedly inspired Mallarmé and Rimbaud.

The study of this earlier McLuhan, the search for the roots of his later ideas in his Canadian origins, in his convert's Catholicism, in his admiration for Joyce, Eliot and Wyndham Lewis, provides the most interesting chapters in both Miller's *Marshall McLuhan* and Theall's *The Medium is the Rear View Mirror.*

Unfortunately Miller becomes so involved in tracing McLuhan's debt to Innis and Whorf and Giedion and the prairie Populists and the Sophist tradition that he leaves little room for what one had imagined to be the purpose of the Modern Masters series in which his book figures, the lucid exposition and criticism of the chosen writers. It seems obvious that a consciousness of space running out induced him to concentrate on the books up to *The Gutenberg Galaxy* and to say virtually nothing about *Understanding Media* or anything later. Yet it is in *Understanding Media* that McLuhan's most pernicious maxim, "The medium is the message," was worked out in such a way that the leaders of industrial and advertising corporations adopted him briefly as an instant guru. That monstrous half-truth, implying that content is irrelevant, seemed for a time to be accepted as a white flag of surrender offered on behalf of the whole intellectual community — offered not merely because McLuhan's growing determinism made him regard the triumph of the electronic media as inevitable, but also because he seemed to desire the re-creation of a community hostile to the intellect. It is in *Understanding Media* that McLuhan finally reveals himself in all his effrontery as the know-all know-nothing, a character worthy of the imagination of his master Wyndham Lewis.

There are of course good things in Miller's little book. As a doctor knowledgeable in neurology, he is able to pick apart very effectively McLuhan's assumptions regarding the co-ordination of the senses, and as a television man he can show how McLuhan's theories fail to work out in the practice of the media. But his general hostility to his subject weakens his case. One reacts with incredulity to the dismissal of all of McLuhan as "a gigantic system of lies." It is of course something far more insidious — a gigantic chaos of half-truths.

Here — as well as in his fuller treatment of his subject — Theall is more credible than Miller. While the most Miller will allow McLuhan is that he sets us thinking, Theall does him the justice of granting that, despite his monstrous exaggerations and his pedantic ways of shocking the pedants, McLuhan has spotted some genuine trends in our society. What Theall does not develop clearly is the process by which the trend-spotter became the trend-setter. I still think the book which McLuhan has since rejected as obsolete, *The Mechanical Bride,* is his most true and useful book, since here he is merely revealing, with some acuteness, the way in which advertising both reflects and moulds the attitudes of our world. It is when in his later books he himself takes a role in moulding attitudes, and does so by intellectually dubious means, that McLuhan becomes one of the great exemplars in our generation of *la trahison des clercs.*

I am always surprised that, except for a few rather slight hints in the essays Raymond Rosenthal collected some years ago in *McLuhan: Pro and Con* (still the best book on McLuhan), nobody — and that includes Miller and Theall — has examined seriously McLuhan's role as the leading Utopian fantasist since Huxley and Orwell, or how this role is related to the fact that his transformation into a prophet took place in Canada.

Seen as a great false metaphor for the ideal society, McLuhan's vision reflects in its form the discredit that in recent years has fallen on the conventional Utopia. As a detailed model of an ideal society, Utopia began to lose its appeal as soon as the first signs of the welfare state appeared, and the failure of Utopia in time present — i.e. Communist Russia — resulted in the inversion of Utopia in the future into a negative vision, pioneered by E.M. Forster and Zamiatin, developed by Huxley and Orwell. But the desire persisted for some kind of Utopian pattern in which human alienation could be shown ending in a culture that reunited man's nature as well as his society; it persisted especially among Catholic converts who fervently believed in their own kind of vanished golden age. Man came out of a tribal world, where the unity of the group protected him psychologically as well as physically from the hostility in the darkness around the tribal fire. Let him return to a worldwide tribalism, a global village, in which a balance of all the senses and a reconciliation of intellect and emotion would at last prove itself superior to nature and transform the earth into a vast artifact.

Once one considers it in this way, McLuhan's vision is seen to have a great deal in common with many Utopian novels, and here I am not merely talking about the incidental anticipations of electronic devices which one finds in books like Bellamy's *Looking Backward.* Much more impressive is the forecast in Forster's "The Machine Stops," written about sixty years ago, of a world where man's fate is actually determined by a technological structure he himself has created and which brilliantly anticipates the type of communications network McLuhan imagines as the arterial structure of world tribalism.

Even more interesting is the anti-intellectualism, the prejudice against a literary or even a literate culture, that pervades so many Utopias. Even in *Utopia* itself there is a strong suggestion that oral is superior to written discourse, and Swift's Utopians, the Houyhnhnms, like the inhabitants of Plato's golden age, have no writing and are the wiser and more moral for the lack; the same applies to the underground people in Herbert Read's *The Green Child.* In the anti-Utopias the attack on literacy becomes an attack on thought. Anything but the most elementary intellectual activity is forbidden in the worlds of *We* and *1984* and *Brave New World,* and in the last of these, technological advances are used, as McLuhan envisages, simply to cultivate and gratify all the senses.

In Huxley's novel there is also a kind of world tribalism, exemplified particularly in the ritual orgies of its people.

Though he acknowledges no debt to Huxley, what McLuhan poses as inevitable and therefore — by its Panglossian logic — desirable, is something very near to a realization of *Brave New World*. The flaw in the vision is that he does not take into account that serpent in the electronic Eden, the content in the message; man will still want to eat of the Tree of Knowledge, and from that reality McLuhan can escape no more than he now escapes the tyranny of print.

That a late-blooming Utopian vision should emerge in Canada is not surprising, particularly if one remembers the teachings of another and more reasonable Canadian guru of world fame, Northrop Frye. Writing on Canadian literature, Frye has developed the thesis that traditionally Canada was a garrison society, a society of pioneers whose situation until the recent wave of urbanization was analogous to that of a tribal people, with the northern Wilderness fulfilling the same role of circumambient enmity as the African forest. One can go beyond Frye to remark that, since a common fear creates unity in tribal and garrison communities alike, they have no need of Utopian visions. It is when human societies loosen out into civilizations, and the sense of community dissipates, that the dream of ideal worlds in past or future emerges. The Homeric Greeks, if one is to believe the epics, had no thought of either a lost golden age or an ideal Platonic republic. Similarly, one of the striking features of Canadian literature until recently was the almost complete absence of Utopias or anti-Utopias; keeping the watch in the garrison was the important task. But now, in a mere generation, Canada has passed out of the pioneer phase, Canadian critics like Frye himself have begun to study Utopian myths, and Canadian *poètes manqués* like McLuhan have begun to create Utopian visions. The fact that what to Forster and Huxley was anti-Utopia should have become Utopia to McLuhan may be an alarming symptom of the degree of alienation in the collective Canadian psyche, struggling towards self-recognition, yet plagued by dissension. It may also be merely an externalization of McLuhan's own plight, of a longing for the return, at any cost to human dignity, to the great warm womb of the tribal unconscious.

[1971]

Poetry of Time
and Place: Recent
Canadian Trends

MORE THAN SIXTY years ago the British poet and critic, T.E. Hulme, gave a series of lectures on "Modern Poetry," in which he made a remark that in recent years has seemed to me in its essence prophetic. "Speaking of personal matters," said Hulme, "the first time I ever felt the necessity or inevitableness of verse, was in the desire to reproduce the peculiar quality of feeling which is induced by the flat spaces and wide horizons of the virgin prairie of western Canada."

Hulme went to Canada in July 1906 and spent about eight months there, working as a farm labourer and in some of the more menial tasks which the lumber camps offered. Hulme, of course, was to become one of the Imagists, and if he began to write the scanty body of rarely anthologized poetry through which we know him while he was still on the Canadian prairies, then he must indeed have been not only an Imagist, but the first Imagist. And that may justify one in seeing the great plains of western Canada, where the images of grain elevator and red barn, of golden field and winter whiteness, of endless straight roads and vast flocks of migratory birds and storm-swept curtains of rain surging in from boundless horizons, are so sharp that they indeed stay long and clear in one's mind, as one of the birthplaces of the modern movement in English-language poetry.

But there is no actual continuity between that point in literary history and the present time, when the west of Canada is producing a surprising number of poets who are affected — like Hulme — by "the peculiar quality of feeling" induced not only by the "flat spaces and wide horizons of the virgin prairies," but also by the different vastnesses of the Rockies beyond them and the intricate Pacific coastline into which the great rain forests spill from the tall coastal ranges. There is a kind of Canadian imagist tradition, indeed, but that began in eastern Canada during the early 1920s, after the historic Imagist movement had already ended, in the early work of W.W.E. Ross, and it found its way mainly through his poetry and that of the Toronto poet Raymond Souster into the wider Canadian movements of the post-World War II era.

Yet what has happened in recent years in western Canada is really an exemplification of the original Imagist perceptions that came to Hulme in western Canada. Hulme anticipated modern Canadian poets by about a quarter of a century when, in 1906, he realized that it was not enough to recognize the special character of the Canadian terrain, where even history followed courses different from the history of western Europe. The so-called Confederation poets, and especially Roberts and Lampman and Duncan Campbell Scott, had made that recognition, and as a result had written Canada's first poetry of independent perception, but the way they rendered their insights was marred by the artificial language and the stereotyped metaphors that they took over from the later romantic trends of the Victorian age in Britain. Hulme saw that, as Barry Callaghan remarked in his introduction to *Shapes and Sounds* (1968), a posthumous collection of W.W.E. Ross's poems: "What was needed to capture a landscape so raw was direct poetic statement, a language that was clear and hard, images that would convey immediately the incomprehensible prairies and northland."

It is strange that the poets in fact waited so long, in both the prairie provinces and in British Columbia, before they found the kinds of language and imagery that allowed them to write powerfully of the Canadian west. It was the novelists and the painters who first mastered the rendering of these regions in terms of their respective arts. Paul Kane and William G.R. Hind in their sketches, Lucius O'Brien and F.H. Varley and Emily Carr in their paintings, were catching the visual essence of the west long before writers like Earle Birney began to do so in verse during the late 1930s, and in the early twentieth century the novelists found such congenial elements in the vast landscapes and in the strong passions aroused by isolation in this environment that an authentic Canadian realism appeared in prairie fiction before it appeared elsewhere. Canadians began to feel that only in the leisurely expanses of novels could the physical breadth of the land and the psychological narrowness of human life there be truly rendered. Fictional small towns like Sinclair Ross's Horizon in *As for Me and My House* and Margaret Laurence's Manawaka in *The Stone Angel* and *A Jest of God,* and the climate-isolated pioneer farms of F.P. Grove's dark and imperfect novels, seemed to embrace the whole truth about prairie life, and that truth appeared to be delimited when Heather Robertson's memorable reportage, *Grass Roots* — nonfiction but also prose — finally revealed that towns which were founded no more than two generations ago and perhaps had never learnt to live had an astonishing tendency to die. Until the 1960s it was very hard to think of prairie poets other than the ladies who resolutely published from small-town printing presses their exiled imitations of Bliss Carman and Felicia Hemans; Charles Mair alone sprang to mind — and was easily forgotten.

But in very recent years there has emerged an identifiable school of prairie poets, identifiable not merely because of the places where they live, but because they have at last brought into effective poetry not only the great plains as visible facts but also the feeling of living among them. John Newlove was perhaps the first of this school of modern prairie poets, but Gary Geddes, Andrew Suknaski, and above all Dale Zieroth belong among them, and related are the poets of the mountains and the coast like Sid Marty and Pat Lane and Peter Trower, whose recent *Ragged Horizons* (to which I shall return) set me on this line of thought.

What strikes one about the prairie poets, as distinct from the mountain and coast poets farther west, is that they are not only the first of their kind; they may also be the last — a brief yet brilliant generation. They elegize, as Heather Robertson did in prose (and Margaret Laurence in *The Diviners*), a passing and largely past way of life. The pioneers — and prairie pioneering took place so recently that my father was one of them — were too deeply immersed in the immediacy of elemental experience to reflect on it. Dale Zieroth's grandfather, as he describes him in *Clearing,* is an example.

> In winter everything
> went white as buffalo bones and
> the underwear froze on the line
> like corpses. Often the youngest

> was sick. Still he never thought
> of leaving. Spring was always greener
> than he'd known and summer had
> kid-high grass with sunsets big
> as God. The wheat was thick,
> the log house chinked and warm.

Yet that pristine experience, hard and beautiful, did not last. In a sense history killed geography. The buffalo grass went the way of the buffalo; the delight in high skies and rich crops gave way to the nightmare of low prices and drought. And the later generations found that the land had turned unwelcoming, so that in Zieroth's Lansdowne,

> Now only the old men from north of town
> want to stay and die . . .

and his Glenella is full of young men

> who know that Winnipeg
> (200 miles south and not big enough
> for a place on the map of the world
> in the post office), that Winnipeg
> is where the world begins.

The prairie poets themselves write mostly poems of memory and absence. John Newlove's best prairie poem remembers his childhood in the Doukhobor village of Verigin:

> all sights and temperatures
> and remembrances, as
> a lost gull screams now
> outside my window,
> a 9-year-old's year-long
> night and day in tiny
> magnificent prairie Verigin

Zieroth is already looking from outside as a chronicler when he devotes one of his best poems of time and place to Manitoba.

> Summer comes in from Saskatchewan on
> a hot and rolling wind. Faces
> burnt and forearms burnt, the men seed
> their separate earths and listen to the CBC
> for any new report of rain. Each day now
> the sun is bigger and from the kitchen
> window, it sets a mere hundred feet behind
> the barn, where a rainbow once came down.

Yet he opens *Clearing* with a poem of personal recollection—
visiting the deserted prairie school of his childhood—and he ends
it with a poem celebrating his flight by "the trail to the top of the
world," to the valleys beyond the Divide where he finds that

> still I will inhabit
> the bitter geography of my own making....

Sid Marty is a poet of the mountains over which Zieroth
crossed into British Columbia. His poems are less those of a dying
society than of an enduring wilderness that man's intrusion has
left, up to now, essentially unchanged. One of the poems in his
first book, *Headwaters,* begins:

> Each mountain
> its own country
> in the way a country
> must be
> a state of mind

And another poem in the same volume ends with the lines:

> But I am reminded
> I am not at home
> here where I live
> only at hazard
>
> There is a darkness along the bright petals

Between them, it seems to me, these fragments bound a territory
that recent poets of the western Canadian mountains and coast
have made peculiarly their own. The geography of the land extends the geography of the mind, yet in the very act of extension it
takes us, perhaps not into enemy territory, but into country where
we are exposed beyond the benefit of certainty.

Sid Marty's poems have a telling directness when they describe
the incidents of his life as a park warden in the Rockies, drawing
the reader close to the mountain faces, to the guarded encounters
with nature personified by a grumpy grizzly, to the companion-
ship that grows up between men and their horses, to the uncertain
line between human mind and animal mind created by the
coyote's cleverness.

Ever since the mid-1950s, the British Columbian coast has been
a poet's haunt and poet's destination, and two anthologies of the
late 1970s give an idea of the number and quality of the poets

working in the area. *New West Coast,* edited by Fred Candelaria, is
a thick collection containing work by seventy-two poets, with personal comments on their poetic attitudes. And the first issue of
Malahat Review (edited by Robin Skelton in Victoria) for 1978 is a
special issue of 353 pages which contains stories and critical
articles but of which the greater part comprises the work of forty
poets; by no means all of them appear in *New West Coast,* so that
in the two collections we are looking at the work of about a hundred active poets.

Taken together, the two anthologies present an excellent cross
section of what Pacific Coast poets in Canada are creating in the
later 1970s. Nothing like a regional school is evident, but, perhaps
more important, one becomes aware of a regional cast of mind,
very much influenced by a kind of animism perhaps not derived
from but certainly empathetic to that of the Coast Indians, whose
songs and legends have influenced local poets like Susan Mus-
grave and Sean Virgo in the same way as they influenced painters
like Emily Carr and Jack Shadbolt.

It is always rather difficult to discuss anthologies, since there
are so many different levels of achievement, so many personal
attitudes — unless of course it is the anthology of a special school
with a unified view of the purpose of poetry. But one can say of
both these collections that they are reasonably representative, that
they effectively complement each other, that anyone who reads
them will get a fair idea of the poetic climate in British Columbia,
and that a handful of figures emerge as poetically powerful. In
this connection I would mention the long philosophic poem —
"Deathwatch on Skidegate Narrows" — by Sean Virgo which
appears in the *Malahat* collection, some interesting posthumously
published poems about the Interior by Eric Ivan Berg (who died
young in a logging accident) in *New West Coast,* and splendid
landscape poems — again in the *Malahat* collection — by R.W.
Stedingh, Ken Cathers and Patrick Lane. There is an almost pure
imagism in Cathers's "Blue Heron":

> thin boned thing
> from the grey world
> I grew out of
>
> poised
> in some dark
> part of me

And the single-mindedness of nature poetry at its best appears in Pat Lane's "Day after day the sun":

> Day after day the sun hurts these hills into summer
> as the green returns to yellow in filaments as hard as
>   stone.
> Everywhere the old mortality sings.
>
> Sagebrush breaks the bodies of the small.
> Dessicated bits of fur huddle in the arroyos
> as the land drifts away, melted by the wind.

Not merely is the imagery moonlight sharp in Lane's verse, and the language direct yet sufficiently allusive, but there is a remarkable rhythmic control in the longish lines which few poets gain without imposing some kind of metrical regularity.

I do not know why, but neither of these collections contains any poems by Peter Trower, whose work has been interesting other poets (not only British Columbian ones) for some years, and whose first book to be published by a major house (McClelland & Stewart) has just appeared. It is *Ragged Horizons* (1978); it follows three collections published by small presses in British Columbia, *Moving through the Mystery, Between the Sky and the Splinters* and *The Alders and Others*. Certainly, even if local anthologists neglect him, Trower is one of the most interesting poets to emerge recently in western Canada, and a poet intensely conscious of the landscape, the townscape, the total environment of the Coast.

Al Purdy, who wrote an introduction to *Ragged Horizons,* describes Trower as "a poet of mean streets, logging camps, pubs, and the immense blue and green sprawl of British Columbia," and that does give some idea of the breadth with which Trower has rendered the experience of British Columbian life in his poetry. Autobiographically, *Ragged Horizons* sketches out Trower's life and background: his English childhood, coming to Canada as a boy in World War II, adolescence in Vancouver, and then the logging camps as work places and the "mean streets" as haunts of choice.

There is in Trower a fortunate combination of plain speaking and artifice. He can draw out in bald language the grim pathos of a courtroom scene where, on a drunk charge, he sees old junky acquaintances

> grown so much older so suddenly
> nodding vaguely, ironically at me

and concludes

> Me with my dumb drunk charge
> who'll get nothing more than a slap on the wrist
> or a ten-dollar fine.
> For damnsure I'm glad I'm not them
> and yet in some dim, perverse way
> I feel like a piker.

And at the same time he can use a traditionally lyrical diction to capture the feeling of something beyond what the eyes see which one senses walking along old roads in the summer rain forests where "slugs move like severed yellow fingers."

> In the green tunnels
> there is a universe of reaffirmation
> desperation fades —
> this is the underbelly, these the curious veins —
> time sings like a minstrel
> in the harped forgotten forest
> and I am one with the secret places
> though summer floods down through the lattice at last.
>
> Only along lorn roads
> where buds burst more cleverly than minds
> can I walk through witched green twilight
> in suspicions of truth —
> rain comes, rain goes in these aisles
>
> in this trenched incredible quiet
> I am one below summer
> burning in the neutral wood.

"Minstrel," "harped," "lattice," "lorn," "witched" — the Keatsisms are thick, and yet so adroitly woven into the fabric of a poem of direct perception that their allusiveness enhances the sheer visuality of the poem, deepens it into mood, suggests the presences beyond the mirror. Imagism, we have long since learnt, was not enough.

The poet who can write with the bleak directness of "Outside the Courtroom" and the poet who can evoke with such rich allusiveness the ambient atmosphere of a place in "Along Green Tunnels," perhaps come together most happily in the Trower who is the work-poet, the recollecting logger of pieces like "The

Last Handfallers" and "The Last Spar-Tree on Elphinstone Mountain." In some of these poems, like "Bullpuncher," all the drudgery of work in the woods is portrayed, and yet, in a piece like "The Last Spar-Tree," while the danger and discomfort are still there, one encounters also the joy that comes from shared work and shared perils:

> I'm getting melodramatic again but it's hard not to be.
> Logging's larger than life. Keep your sailors and
>   cowboys!
> I'm always stressing the sombre side
> but there was much comradeship and laughter—
> great yarns beside noon donkeys, hillhumour between
>   turns,
> excellent shits behind stumps with the wind fanning the
>   stink away,
> sweat smelling good and cigarette smoke celestial.
>
> Dream on in peace old tree—
> perhaps you're a truer monument to man
> than any rocktop crucifix in Rio de Janeiro.

To know one's world, to express it in direct and memorable honesty, and yet to know where artifice must shape experience into poetry; these seem to me the attributes of a poet who speaks for his region, for the *patria chica* which is in the heart as well as in the eye, and Peter Trower possesses them.

[1978]

Beyond the Divide:
Notes on Recent Poetry
in British Columbia

POETRY IN THE present time has been a great deal more than just writing verse, a great deal more even than self-expression. Its great upsurge and its immense democratization over the past decade or so has been an authentic and necessary part of the alternative culture, linked with the challenges to conventional mores and political forms, linked with the environmental movements and with the struggles of submerged minorities to establish their places in the sunlight. And though the aims and the impetus of the alternative movement in general seem to have changed as the 1960s have given way to the 1970s, the impetus towards poetry has remained the same while, in general, the kind of poetry being written has become more varied in its sensitivity to the forms of liberation which the present offers and also to the kind of threats the future may contain.

I can envisage a time not very far ahead — perhaps even *before* 1984 — when censorship and general repression may force resistance and radical ways of thinking to find expression largely through poetry, as they found expression through fiction during the governmental terror imposed by the Tsarist autocracy in nineteenth-century Russia. Therefore, it seems to me, the present vigour of poetry should be cherished and encouraged by anyone who is concerned to keep what freedom we have and to achieve, in spite of all the omens to the contrary, a libertarian society which acknowledges the ecological alternatives. A rebel poet of another age, Percy Bysshe Shelley, claimed that "poets are the unacknowledged legislators of the world." Quite obviously they are not, especially in an age of multinational corporations and monolithic bureaucracies, and power being the corrupting thing it is, I doubt if poets would be any better than other men if they fancied themselves as legislators; with all due respect to Ezra Pound's *poetics*, imagine the kind of legislation that would have emerged from his pro-Fascist *politics!* But poets as spokesmen — which is their real role — is another question: we need them to reveal the secret motions of the heart and blood, which also have their political relevance; to say obliquely what may not always be sayable with prose directness; to use the ambiguities of language to expose the ambiguities of politics; and to record the merging of individual agonies into a collective consciousness. When the poets survive and are active, there is still hope; this is why the totalitarians have always regarded them as enemies, why the Nazis murdered Muehsam and the Francoists slaughtered Lorca, and the Bolsheviks drove Yesenin and Mayakovsky to despair and suicide.

The poetic upsurge of the last decade has probably been more marked in Canada west of the Rockies than in any other part of North America — marked, that is, in proportion to the population. Recently the library of Dalhousie University published a *Checklist of Canadian Small Presses*, edited by Grace Tratt and devoted mainly to noncommercial presses run by individuals or small groups unconcerned with turning a profit from literature. British Columbia came second only to Ontario, with sixty presses listed, mainly devoted to the publication of poetry — and the list was not complete. Some of the presses that were listed have survived only long enough to publish one book, but there were others with an impressive record, like Talonbooks of Vancouver which has published more than eighty books, mainly of poetry and drama, over the past eight years. Altogether this means that during the past decade several hundred books of verse have been written by poets in British Columbia and have been produced and distributed mainly outside the commercial book world; usually the publishers and often the printers have been poets themselves. Also, in keeping with the tendency of the alternative society to decentralize and to establish new centres of vitality in small places, poetry publishing in British Columbia has largely moved out of the two main urban centres, and a random batch of fifteen recent books which I have just looked through included titles emanating from Prince George, Delta, Nanaimo, Burnaby, as well as Vancouver and Victoria; it is not so long ago, after all, that Sono Nis Press was located in the Queen Charlottes, and Oolichan Press still operates from Lantzville on Vancouver Island. All this activity in many British Columbian centres is quite apart from a fair number of books by British Columbian poets—ranging from Earle Birney and P.K. Page to Bill Bissett and Tom Wayman —that have been published by Toronto houses like McClelland & Stewart, Macmillan and House of Anansi, and by the dedicated Ottawa publisher, Michael Macklem, whose Oberon Press—like House of Anansi—hovers somewhere between the small press and the commercial house, using orthodox publishing methods but gaining more pleasure than profit from the operation.

In this essay I am leaving out the books by local poets published in eastern Canada, since most of these tend to be reviewed in national periodicals, and even in British Columbia they are more likely to be available in bookshops and in public libraries than are the books produced by local small presses. But the undergrowth of contemporary poetry is rich, and obviously contains some saplings that will grow to full height; the problem at present is to see the potential trees for the wood.

Why there should have been such a great upsurge of poetry writing and publication west of the Rockies is an interesting question, to which the critic Warren Tallman attempted recently to give an answer in a long and vigorously written essay entitled "Wonder Merchants: Modernist Poetry in Vancouver during the 1960s," which he published in an American magazine, *Boundary 2*. The thesis Tallman puts forward is that the whole phenomenon was really set going by the visits to Vancouver in the early 1960s by a number of American poets, whom he classes as "Modernists," including Robert Duncan, James Creeley, Denise Levertov, and the mystic showman, Allen Ginsberg. According to Tallman's thesis, there was a kind of pentecostal experience, in which the visitors from outer poetic space revealed the gospel of the "Modernist" movement, and a group of young University of British Columbia undergraduate poets, including George Bowering, Frank Davey, Lionel Kearns and Fred Wah, received the esoteric fire and became the local apostles, founding a magazine called, anagrammatically, *Tish* and operating as a school of poets who shared theories about the proper writing and speaking of verse.

There are a number of flaws in that scenario which, I suspect, are due to the limitations of Tallman's viewing stance. I respect Tallman as an acute critic of any book that is actually placed before him; I esteem him as a friend; but I nevertheless believe that his loyalties to the American literary world of the best age (his own youth), and his preoccupation with writers of that time and place like Kerouac and Ginsberg and Duncan, have inclined him to view literary movements in continentalist terms, a view hardly justified by the real pattern of events on the West Coast.

To begin, there is the question of just what is meant by modernism. Classic modernism was the movement of dissociation from earlier beliefs in art as mimesis that began on the continent of Europe early in the present century and spread later to Britain and the United States. It affected all the arts; in literature it was especially characterized by an emphasis on language as the equivocal dominating factor in literature, though the emphasis was rarely applied purely, since the modernists were opinionated men and many of them were deeply conscious that in imaginative literature language was complemented and even subverted by the element of myth, which crosses all languages, all cultures. In any case, classic modernism flowed away into the sands of the thirties, and to apply the title to any living American or Canadian poet creates identifications—with writers like Pound and Eliot and Wyndham Lewis and William Carlos Williams and Gertrude Stein—that historically are invalid.

Even in its classic period, modernism in English-speaking countries was never the kind of movement that—like its offshoots such as Dada and Surrealism—it became in Europe and notably in France. Neither the English nor the Americans nor the Canadians have been strong in "schools" of writers dominated by theoretical disciplines (which in France became so strong that André Breton—as the pope of Surrealism—would actually expel artists from the group for aesthetic heresies). This, I believe, derives from the nature of all varieties of the English language, so much of whose poetic quality stems from its double roots, from the fact that it has always existed in the interface between its Anglo-Saxon and its French origins, so that almost every English word with a Germanic root has its subtly differing counterpart with a Latin root. The result is an essential ambiguity which does not exist in other European languages; the presence of that ambiguity explains why the English language has been so well adapted to poetry, which lives by suggestion rather than statement, and also why poets writing in English shy away from the kind of group disciplines that French poets often accept. The writing of English poetry is essentially a romantic exercise, depending on intuition and feeling, on catching the suggestive alternations of words, far more than it does on intellectual construction.

All this applies not only to the modernists of the past, but also to Canadian groups like that which gathered around *Tish*. Much more important than the mythical existence of the group as a neo-modernist mafia was the fact that it did publish a magazine where young British Columbian poets got into print. Significantly, many of the contributions to *Tish* failed to subscribe to any kind of modernist dogma. To the chagrin of literary historians and of academics who like to arrange poets neatly into schools, even the original members of the *Tish* group have since gone their own ways, and the two most interesting of them, George Bowering and Frank Davey, have shown themselves to be very individual poets. Davey has left Vancouver, probably for good, though he maintains an important link with his base here, since his poems are still published by Talonbooks. He has become a rigorous poetic technician, almost classicist in the spareness and starkness and ceremonialism of his poetry. George Bowering, who is certainly the most appealing and perhaps the best of the *Tish* poets, has returned to Vancouver, where he teaches at Simon Fraser University, and writes prolifically, with a great sense of the environment which in another age would have led to his being labelled a romantic.

That matter of the environment brings me back to the whole question of the origins of the British Columbian poetic upsurge. Tallman's attempt to place its beginning in the early 1960s is viable only if one ignores what went on here before that time. In fact, British Columbia has been unusually active in poetic terms since the 1940s, if not before. When I reached the Coast in 1949, *Contemporary Verse* was being published in Victoria, one of the two poetry magazines then existing in Canada. Earle Birney, Dorothy Livesay, Floris McLaren, Anne Marriott and many younger poets, like Marya Fiamengo, Daryl Hine and Gwladys Downes, were living and writing here. Later, during the 1950s and the early 1960s, poets like Al Purdy, Milton Acorn and John Newlove, lacking in academic backgrounds or connections, lived and wrote in Vancouver, and much of the current poetic life of British Columbia, exemplified in the work of poets like Patrick Lane and Red Lane, Peter Trower and Ken Belford, has followed the plebeian line they established, reinforcing it with experience.

This lineage in fact involved an experiential return to the environment, which is of course the phenomenon of post-pioneerism. Pioneers create a new world, reacting hostilely against the given environment. But one may return to the world of the pioneers as many British Columbian poets have done in recent years, farming again the decayed homesteads, living as loggers and fishermen, but seeing the same world anew, with acceptance instead of hostility. This sense of approaching the native environment in a fresh way has — in my view — become one of the strong forces behind the upsurge of British Columbian poetry during the last decade or more. Of course, there have been other causes: the fact that everywhere in Canada poetry was in an ascendant mood, and the fact that, for the time being at least, new printing techniques made the development of little presses far more viable than it has ever been in the past.

The extraordinary sensitivity to the setting, historically as well as topographically, is the element I find distinguishing British Columbian poets of all kinds, whether they are conscious for-malists, like some of the writers favoured by Sono Nis Press, or apparent antiformalists and anti-intellectuals like those who seem to be favoured by the extreme radicals of Pulp Press. Obviously it is impossible to discuss with anything approaching justice all or even many of the interesting poets who in recent years have been published in British Columbia. Some I have mentioned and necessarily passed on. Others, like Bill Bissett and Judith Copi-thorne are probably enough known to poetry readers and at-tenders at poetic events for it to be unnecessary for me to enlarge on the mantric experiments of the first and the excursions of the second into the region where the visual and the poetic meet. I accept the integrity of both, but I am temperamentally in tune with neither.

Perhaps I can best spend my remaining space on a few poets to whose work I do respond directly and who — among the lesser-known writers — represent for me the best that is being done in British Columbia. I approach them through the local small presses who publish them, and begin with Talonbooks. The Talonbooks list is long and the house has received considerable support from the Canada Council and other official funding agencies. At the same time, Talonbooks seems to be carried on in a basically libertarian way, by an affinity group whose members are willing to accept a fraction of average printing trade union rates to publish beautifully produced books by good writers. Their drama list is unrivalled in Canada; their poetry list is good, though in the last two or three years it has tended to become rather heavy with familiar names. Still, good and original things continue to come from Talonbooks, and the one I would mention now is a visual-poetic documentary, with an epigraph from James Agee, called *Steveston*; it consists of photographs by Robert Minden and poetry — one cannot call it verse since it is strictly prose poetry — by Daphne Marlatt.

Steveston is a name likely to arouse emotional responses in any-one familiar with that dejected farthest margin of the island in the Fraser River delta named after the gold rush actress Lulu Sweet. I see Steveston as almost the last beachhead of an earlier, more natural way of life on an island which was still a place of market gardeners and fishermen only twenty years ago when I first saw it and has since been consumed by the developers. Others think of earlier Stevestons — the old Steves farm in the marshland on the edge of the Fraser before the canneries came, and later the "salmon capital of the world," smelly boomtown where two thousand Japanese worked as serfs to "the company," until after Pearl Harbour they were shipped like cattle into the dry valleys of the Interior. It is this whole sweep of Steveston history, caught in the memories of the old, in the impatiences of the young, that Daphne Marlatt recorded in patient notebook pages as she wandered about Steveston, and then turned into a series of nota-tions on experience remembered, on the relentless passage of change, on the sadness permeating most human lives and deter-mining most human fates as instinctual patterns determine the "Life Cycle" (a title of one of the poems) of the salmon.

> Safe against that river cresting at
> over 20 feet. Safe again, forgetting she's a way in, to
> return, in time, the stream. Against all odds they home
> in, to the source that's marked their scales first birth
> place: environing:

> It rings us
> where we are (turn & turn about), however the
> depth   its cool waters glide (over us), erase, with
> vast space elide the code we've managed to forget: this

> urge to return, & returning, thresh, in those shallows,
> death, leaving what slips by, the spore, the spawn,
> the mark that carries on . . . like a germ, like violence
> in the flesh

That is one kind of British Columbian poetry, still closely bound to experience, yet searching beyond it for the vital correspondences (man's life and salmon's) and permeated with the strange bittersweet aura that envelops the mind when we talk of some cycle ended, whether it is a fish's life or a human community, which in Canada can be so swiftly consummated, passing from birth to death in less than a man's normal life.

Blackfish Press, for which Alan Safarik seems to do most of the editorial work in Burnaby and Brian Brett most of the printing in White Rock, is a different kind of enterprise from Talonbooks, a more personal one and in scale more modest. It began with a little magazine, *Blackfish,* which published works by many established poets, Birney, Atwood, Page, Purdy, Acorn, Mayne, Livesay, but also work by interesting younger writers, including Susan Landell, Jim Green, Pat Lowther, and Brett and Safarik themselves, the first inclined to neo-Wordsworthian contemplations of the landscape, the latter to a kind of imagism sometimes expressed in "translations" from Japanese poets who may, rumour suggests, be creations of Safarik's imagination; that, of course, is of no great consequence, since the poems are extraordinarily evocative in themselves (Safarik has just published a whole book of them under the title *Okira*) and, if they are imitations and not translations, are splendid inventions in their own right.

Blackfish Press went on to print broadsheets by various poets, each containing several examples of the poet's work, preferably arranged in a cycle. They include *Disasters of the Sun* by Dorothy Livesay, *Face* by Seymour Mayne, and *The Age of the Bird* by Pat Lowther. Blackfish's more ambitious productions are a long reflective poem by Al Purdy, who keeps his West Coast links reasonably warm, entitled *On the Bearpaw Sea* and, most recently, Jim Green's *North Book.* Alan Safarik proudly announces that none of the Blackfish books receives "government funding"; since the demonstrative far-outers of Pulp Press and Intermedia work with Canada Council subsidies, this is something worth recording.

Pat Lowther and Jim Green are the lesser-known Blackfish poets whom I found most interesting. Lowther's *Age of the Bird*, a cycle suggested by the death of Che Guevara (garnished, one suspects, by memories of reading W.H. Hudson's *Green Mansions*), is easily the best of the Blackfish Press series of broadsheets. Some of her other poems appeared in the issues of *Blackfish* and, taken with *The Age of the Bird*, they present a poet of versatility, of an impeccable verbal appropriateness, of the ability to write discursively or densely, to trace a taut narrative through a series of poems leading to a muted climax, or to catch a complex binary image in a brief poem like "Vision":

> The Woman looks out of the whale's bone
> her eyes eroded
> sinking
> into the marrow
> the source of vision.
> The whale cutting
> the water
> sings like a huge machine.
> All his bones
> have eyes.

Jim Green is a less reliable poet than Pat Lowther: a divided man. He can write straight evocative poems of the northern wilderness, sharp facets of impression that lodge in the mind like glass splinters, but he is just as capable of presenting a tedious diary in verse, and he has too frequent a predilection for the kind of fake-tough vernacular which nobody actually speaks, even in the bush. This kind of talk quickly becomes boring, mainly because the jargon is so limited, just as words once considered obscene lose their effect once they are used habitually.

However, in *North Book*, which emanates from the experiences of a period in the Arctic, Jim Green seems largely to have resolved his contradictions, at the same time as he has avoided merely imitating Purdy's *North of Summer*. Purdy was the quick visitor; Green went there long enough to know that he could never be more than an outsider, even if a sensitive and observant one, and in spite of the fine bravura effects of some of Purdy's Arctic poems, I think that Green's *North Book* is perhaps the best book of non-Eskimo poetry to come out of the North. His message, insofar as it is a didactic one, is contained in three lines from his "Postscript":

> We must learn to understand ways other than our own.
> We must learn to love.
> We must learn to accept our limited role in this life.

And no one who has actually been to the Arctic will fail to respond to the sheer lyrical authenticity of Green's last poem, "Silence":

> a white arctic owl
> slow stroking by
> a backdrop of snow
> half a mile away
>
> head of a dog
> on blue sea ice
> small drift between it
> frozen snow fingers
>
> small tent ring
> on ridge crest
> bones
> of small birds
> under stones

There is an undemonstrative excellence about many of the poems Blackfish produces, and a muted elegance about the production. Sono Nis Press is louder and more obvious. The production is mandarin in its superbness: the best work of Charles Morriss, the Victoria printer, and that is as good as can be got west of the Cambrian Shield. Any of the three volumes published most recently as I write — Rona Murray's *Selected Poems,* Derk Wynand's *Snowscapes* and J. Michael Yates's *Breath of the Snow Leopard* — would stand a good chance of winning a prize in a typography competition. And J. Michael Yates, who runs Sono Nis, is in no way modest in his claims. We are told twice and with italics on the dust cover of *Selected Poems* that *Rona Murray is a major poet,* and on his own book Yates quotes as serious what one can only assume was a jest by another poet: "If the other Yeats had read the poetry of this Yates, he'd have put down his pen and gone to bed early." J. Michael is a clever fellow, but a pygmy compared to William Butler!

In any case, I'm inclined to resent being told too emphatically before I've even opened it what I should think about a book. Still, I don't think that has affected my admiration for J. Michael Yates's sheer verbal skill and his power of intellectual prestidigitation. Yet I am not inwardly moved by him, whereas I am moved, and kept perpetually attentive, by both Derk Wynand and Rona Murray; she may not be a *major* poet (who cares?) but is a very genuine and warm poet, powerful with words, and a poet whose progress from a kind of universal mythology into the moving poems of the last section of her book, "Ootischenie," named after the old Doukhobor settlement in the Kootenays where it is set, duplicates the postpioneer urge back to the terrain that so many of the British Columbian poets I have mentioned display.

Derk Wynand's *Snowscapes* goes to the terrain also, but in a different way, for he constructs a cycle, with a kind of tenuous story and a shimmering variety of points of view, but all linked by the nature of snow. Snow, he is telling us, masks the shape of actuality (hence "snowjob"), but it creates its own reality, and in its special silence sounds assume a preternatural clarity and meaning, and so do human actions. In fact snow forms a kind of judgement by the earth of its inhabitants, devastatingly revealing, capriciously concealing, so that most of the time we see its effects and not its true nature, which is, after all:

> The real snowscape.
> A little bit of snow, just like this.
> Real snow in a genuine wind.

Derk Wynand has been writing interesting poems for a number of years, and his *Snowscapes* establishes him as one of the good poets of the time. A *good* poet, like Rona Murray! And what more can you want? To be a major poet? Wordsworth, I'm told, was a major poet.

[1975]

On the Poetry
of Al Purdy

AL PURDY'S WRITING fits Canada like a glove; you can feel the
fingers of the land working through his poems. I suppose that is
why, the deeper I have gone in understanding the country and the
more I have found myself a surprised patriot, the closer I have felt
to Purdy as man and poet.

But this is not the reason why I first became interested in him.
Writers who are contemporaries often come together in the beginning for odd, inconsequential reasons. Twelve years ago—or
perhaps only eleven—I wrote a play, *Maskerman,* which the CBC
produced, and out of the northern wilds of British Columbia, up
near Hazelton, came a postcard in an unknown hand compli-
menting me on a fine *decadent* piece of work, which was precisely
the effect I had been seeking. I was further disposed towards
Purdy when I learnt that he had spent the war at the only place on
earth that bears my name—the minute whistlestop hamlet of
Woodcock somewhere in the lost lands between Prince George
and Prince Rupert.

This was enough to set me reading Purdy, still, in the early
sixties, awaiting his sudden and splendid arrival as a major contemporary poet. I met him shortly afterwards, and realized we
shared a total absence of any original connection with academe
and all it meant. We were both autodidacts, omnivorous readers,
furious generalists, restless travellers, maverick radicals, gluttons
for variety of experience, interested in the assemblage of every
kind of apparent irrelevancy. We were amateur historians, back-
yard philosophers, jacks-of-many-trades who had built houses
with our own hands and learnt what we knew by our own efforts.
Rare types a decade ago when every poet in the grove except

262

Milton Acorn seemed to sport at least an M.A., for those were the days before the Great Dropout began.

The matter at hand is Purdy's poetry, not his persona, but I think what I have said is relevant because it illustrates two facts that are necessary to an appreciation of Purdy as poet; he *is* the kind of poet with whom one's first contact can be a postcard sent from among the totem poles in decayed Indian villages far to the north, and he is also a man of vast and miscellaneous knowledge which constantly flows in and out of the open ends of his poetry.

I began by talking of the glovelike closeness of Purdy's poetry to the Canada of one's experience, and there is no doubt of his deep intuitive grasp of the nature of the land, of the character of its history, though to claim him as a purely Canadian poet would be to do him an immense injustice. But Canada—and Loyalist Ontario in particular—is indeed the heart of his world, of which he can say:

> and if I must commit myself to love
> of any one thing
> it will be here in the red glow
> where failed farms sink back into earth
> the clearings join and fences no longer divide
> where the running animals gather their bodies together
> and pour themselves upward
> into the tips of falling leaves
> with mindless faith that presumes a future

Out of that land where the wilderness seeps back over the labours of a past generation, Purdy's poetic eye journeys eastward to Newfoundland, with its lost memories of the Vikings (curiously skipping Quebec as he also skips the prairies), westward to British Columbia, which he knew in the thirties long before it became a special haven of poets, northward to the Arctic. These extremities of the land are the poles between which he suspends his vision of Canada, a vision that interprets geography and history as interpenetrating versions of each other. To further narrow his vision, it is essentially a rural one, which hardly recognizes a city except Vancouver (deurbanized by the penetrating sea), and it is based on the knowledge, which most Canadians are curiously anxious to avoid, that this is, even in human terms, an ancient and not a new land, a land already beginning to decay into maturity.

The very spinning point of his world, its watery omphalos

which in Canadian eyes may some day become the equivalent of
Walden Pond, is Roblin Lake near the lost Loyalist hamlet of
Ameliasburgh ("named after a German dumpling named
Amelia"), where Purdy built his house among the larruping frogs
and above the silent pike, and about which so many of his poems
are written. Perhaps one can take these Roblin Lake poems, like
Roblin Lake itself, as master fragments in the mosaic of Purdy's
vision. What they are about is place and change and continuity.
Some of them are elegies for those who built the stone mills of old
Upper Canada, most of them now more vanished than the Breton
megaliths:

> The black millpond
>   holds them
> movings and reachings and fragments
> the gear and tackle of living
> under the water eye
> all things laid aside
>   discarded
>   forgotten
> but they had their being once
> and left a place to stand on

Yet it is not ghosts only that appear in Purdy's eye, nor merely old
men like his grandfather talking long ago of a day when there was

> nothin but moonlight boy
> nothin but woods

For what makes him a real rural poet, as distinct from a country
sentimentalist, is his concreteness of view, an awareness as clear
as an imagist's of the brilliant surface of the earth, and yet at the
same time a sense of depths and heights, of super-real dimensions, so that common things can suddenly become irradiated and
the world swing into ecstasy.

But not too far into ecstasy for the existential relations to continue and the vision of place to be poised between tradition and
change, as in "Wilderness Gothic," one of his most completely
successful poems, where he is watching a man across Roblin Lake
repairing a church spire, working his way up towards its
vanishing point, as if his faith were pushing him beyond it. It is
one of the poems in which Purdy deftly juxtaposes the different
elements of his world, for as the man works at patching the edifice

264

of a dying religion, the life of nature goes on in its old merciless
way.

> Fields around are yellowing into harvest,
> nestling and fingerling are sky and water borne,
> death is yodelling quiet in green woodlots,
> and bodies of three young birds have disappeared
> in the sub-surface of the new county highway

But the picture, as Purdy says, "is incomplete" without the "gothic
ancestors" the church suggests, and at the thought of their disappearance, together with many generations since, an ominous tone
vibrates in the whole scene.

> An age and a faith moving into transition,
> the dinner cold and new-baked bread a failure,
> deep woods shiver and water drops hang pendant,
> double yolked eggs and the house creaks a little —
> Something is about to happen. Leaves are still.
> Two shores away, a man hammering in the sky.
> Perhaps he will fall.

It is indeed a shadowed world that Purdy often presents, a
world in which

> We have set traps,
> and must always remember
> to avoid them ourselves.

We forget our forebears and yet in ways we do not recognize we
share their predicament. In "The Road to Newfoundland," Purdy
applies to driving a car what at first seems a far-fetched metaphor:

> My foot has pushed a fire ahead of me
> for a thousand miles

But as the poem continues we realize that he is reading time back
depth by depth to the primal human dependence on fire:

> A long time's way here since stone
> age man carried the fire-germ
> in a moss-lined basket
> from camp to camp
> and prayed to it

And when he comes to talk later in the poem of his flesh "captive
to a steel extension of myself," we realize he is saying that it is the

general condition of man, who owes his civilization to his tools, to
be enslaved by his technology. But the situation is reciprocal; the
technology is captive too, and this is a paradox without end as
Purdy suggests when, at poem's close, he imagines himself driving

> steadily north
> with the captive fire
> in cool evening
> towards the next camp

North, like West, is a cardinal direction for Purdy (as South
over the border most certainly is not), and it is in some of his
Arctic poems that he becomes most purely the poet of place,
though even here it is often still the kind of dialogue between the
man and his environment with its finned and feathered and
flowered inhabitants which is almost incessant at Roblin Lake,
going on in other ways. In "Trees at the Arctic Circle," he sets off
in a kind of parody of Lawrence's *Birds, Beasts and Flowers*, re-
proaching the dwarf willows for their cowardice in crawling under
rocks and grovelling among lichens; trees should be proud like
Douglas-firs or "oaks like gods in autumn gold." And yet, he tells
himself, they are going about their business of making sure in the
only way they can that the species does not die out, and he brings
himself to a statement that might be taken as a summary of his
sense of the brotherhood of life:

> To take away the dignity
> of any living thing
> even tho it cannot understand
> the scornful words
> is to make life itself trivial

And the next poem is in fact a pure lyrical celebration of the
beauty of the rapid springtime florescence of the North, "Arctic
Rhododendrons."

Yet even from the Arctic the best poem Purdy brought back
was that grave and beautiful meditation on the fate of man and
the nature of art, "Lament for the Dorsets," those massive early
Eskimos who appear to have been made extinct five or six hundred years ago by the competition of smaller men whose dog-
drawn sleighs were more effective than those the Dorsets dragged
by hand. He wonders if the Dorsets really knew what was
happening to them, and behind that thought whispers the hint

that modern man, so different from them in every other way, may share the same ignorance. Yet at the end the poem comes round to dwelling on the chance that, if the last of the Dorsets spent his last hours carving "for a dead grand-daughter" one of the little ivory swans that come down to us from his people, he may have left us a thought turned into ivory and so made enduring as long as man survives to see and interpret it. As Malraux argued more elaborately, there is a way in which through art man can evade the extinction that overtakes his body and mind.

> After 600 years
> the ivory thought
> is still warm

His dream of history, and his constant transfiguration of thing into myth, does not mean that Purdy's grasp is circumscribed by Canadian frontiers of time or space. Indeed, he shows the maturity of his vision by allowing it to flow freely beyond the passionate nucleus, and so, when he crosses the Divide (and he is perhaps the only eastern Canadian poet to live as comfortably on one side as on the other) and sees the cowboys riding into a little Cariboo town and their horses hitched outside the taverns, he recognizes them for what they in fact are:

> only horse and rider
> .   .   .   .   .
> clopping in silence under the toy mountains
> dropping sometimes and
> lost in the dry grass
> golden oranges of dung

But the horses have already set him meditating on the past of the region, the Indian past, and then he remembers the horses of history, of mythology, sweeping over a lost ancient world, and sees in fine Spenderian phrases

> the ghosts of horses battering thru the wind
> whose names were the wind's common usage
> whose life was the sun's

And though the poem ends in the anticlimax—the slump into existential reality—that Purdy often practises, with the thought of the Cariboo horses waiting outside the grocer's in the stink of gasoline, he has left in our minds an ineradicable image of the horse as the symbol of wild freedom in a world that man is fatally subduing and destroying.

Perhaps the most developed treatment of history as process, of man's fate to shape and be shaped, of his dual role as victor and victim, appears in Purdy's poems on Cuba, which he visited in 1964 and which filled his mind with ambivalent perturbations. It is too facile to class Purdy, as some writers have done, as merely an admirer of Castro and of Che Guevara. He admires them as men, yes, as enthusiasts fired by visions that raised them above ordinary humanity and led them to perform extraordinary tasks. But he sees clearly the trap action led them into. Castro delivers the kind of oration any other dictator might deliver; Che has a politician's handshake; and when Purdy talks in a Havana bar with Red Chinese sailors he sees the whole Cuban setting as a kind of unreal Graham Greene-ish world whose strangeness is emphasized by the inconsequential memories of an Ontario childhood which come into his mind as he stands there. Yet tragedy, he insists, restores such men to humanity, and even if we cannot know the final consequences of "Che's enormous dream," the poet, thinking of his death, of his fingers cut off to identify the prints, can

> remember his quick hard handshake
> in Havana among the tiny Vietnamese ladies
> and seem to hold ghostlike in my own hand
> five bloody fingers
> of Che Guevara

Anyone who has followed Purdy's writing for a long time will be aware that he is not only wide-ranging in thought and subtle in vision, but also extremely versatile as a poetic craftsman who has worked his way through the forms and styles to his present open manner. Poets nowadays seem to be divided into the short-liners and the long-liners, the halting and the fluent, roughly corresponding to the discontinuous thinkers (who are usually the eternal-moment men) and the linear thinkers who, as Purdy does, tend also to be the historical poets. In his manipulation of the long line to create a variety of moods Purdy has shown his growing power to fit the form exactly to the thought and thing, which is the sign of ultimate poetic craftsmanship. This is not to say his poems are entirely linear in their overall structure, for often the juxtaposition of jarring or contrasting elements is an essential part of the effect he is seeking, and there are times when he uses the moderately short line very successfully.

> tho we keep on running
> past the Land of Flat Stones
> over the Marvel-Strands
> beyond the country of great trees. . .
> Tho we ran to the edge of the world,
> our masters would track us down

But he is never one of your gasping, grunting, three-or-four-syllable-a-line men. No discursive, philosophic, historic, didactic poet — and Purdy is all these — ever can be.

Yet for all its didacticism, there is much in Purdy's poetry that has the effortless, gratuitous magic which has been the sign of a good poet in any age — lines like

> we live with death but it's life we die with
> in the blossoming earth where springs the rose

or the whole of "Necropsy of Love," whose last lines have the kind of hypnotic midnight power of some of Keats or some Decadent poetry (compliment returned!):

> If death shall strip our bones of all but bones,
> then here's the flesh, and flesh that's drunken-sweet
> as wine cups in deceptive lunar light:
> reach up your hand and turn the moonlight off,
> and maybe it was never there at all,
> so never promise anything to me:
> but reach across the darkness with your hand,
> reach across the distance of tonight,
> and touch the moving moment once again
> before you fall asleep

There is not enough time and space here to consider the various poetic devices to which, having abandoned rhyme and ordinary metre, Purdy has recourse on the appropriate occasion: it is enough to point out, and leave the reader to find his own examples, the use of alliteration and repetition, the presence at times of regular syllabic patterns, the occasional resort to galloping trochaic rhythms, and, as a matter of rhythm as well as language, his superb colloquial ear.

Finally, after having said so much about Purdy as the history-conscious poet, the philosophizer on the human condition, the geographer of the imagination, one is suddenly aware of a noisy fellow dragging at one's legs under the impression they are wild-grape vines, and Purdy pulls one down to the earth on which, however high his head and wide his scope, his feet are surely set. For he is also the poet of comedy: picture postcard domestic comedy with nagging wives and blundering husbands; high low comedy as when the poet makes a mock epic out of trying to defecate in the presence of Eskimo huskies hungry for human excrement; original Dionysiac comedy in that wild drunken poem, "The Winemaker's Beat-Etude." It is comedy that easily runs black, for it is based on a totally realistic sense of what individual man's fate is in a world where grandeur is a feat of the imagination; where man grows old though his lusts stay young; where his actions are contemptible though his thoughts are high; where his attempts to reconcile the animal and the human within him always end in comic absurdity. The decay and death that finally await him Purdy portrays with realistic horror, yet with compassion for the defeated, and with admiration for those who cry out in rage against the destiny that makes an old woman die, as in the grim poem "Evergreen Cemetery," stuffing her false teeth up her rectum. "Old Alex," an elegy on a venomous old man, is by way of an antidote to some of the nobler thoughts Purdy has dwelt on, yet it is also a sign of the universality of his sympathy, since what in the end it communicates is the paradox of sublimity realized in meanness:

> I don't mourn. Nobody does. Like mourning an ulcer.
> Why commemorate disease in a poem then?
> I don't know. But his hate was lovely,
> given freely and without stint. His smallness
> had the quality of making everyone else feel noble,
> and thus fools. I search desperately
> for good qualities, and end up crawling
> inside that decaying head and wattled throat
> to scream obscenities like papal blessings,
> knowing now and again I'm at least God.
> Well, who remembers a small purple and yellow bruise
>   long?
> But when he was here he was a sunset!

[1972]

Note: The poems quoted in this piece are all included in *Selected Poems* (1972) to which it served as an Introduction.

On A.M. Klein:
A Tentative Note

I HAVE HESITATED in the past to write on A.M. Klein, for a number of reasons. To begin, I never knew him, though I always felt attracted to the personality his poems seemed to project, and when after his death I talked to people who had known him, like P.K. Page and Irving Layton, I knew that my feeling had been correct, that he was in fact as Louis Dudek described him almost a quarter of a century ago:

There is a shyness about him and a simplicity which he makes an effort to conceal; something, one feels, that might be easily bruised. But he has learned to live in the world; he is an active and successful man of affairs. In private, he is a great talker, humorous and always stimulating. He glows with sympathy and with every kind of enthusiasm. And in his best nature, he would not hurt a fly.

Except for a persistent doubt that Klein really was a "successful man of affairs" or wanted to be such, I am convinced, on the evidence of his written work, that Dudek's assessment was correct.

Yet my knowledge of Klein's written work, when I was first asked to write this essay, was almost as unsatisfactory as my knowledge of the man himself. I had never made a close study of his poetry. True, at intervals over the years, getting them out of libraries, I had read all the volumes he published, but the lack of easily available editions of any of them, apart from his prose fantasy *The Second Scroll,* had made my reading of him uneven. Some poems I had read once or twice in twenty years. A few, because they had appeared so often in anthologies, I was probably excessively familiar with, but I imagine that is the situation of most literate Canadians. Klein has in recent years been a poet more praised than read, and more read than known.

Finally, when I did read Klein again, and began to glance at what other people had written about him, I was disturbed by the heroic aura that had begun to build around him even before the breakdown which withdrew him so absolutely from the world. As long ago as 1940, Ludwig Lewisohn made the claim that he was "the first Jew to contribute authentic poetry to the literature of English speech," and thirty years later, when Klein lived among us as no more than his legend and the poems in anthologies, Tom Marshall spoke of him as "the man who has come closer than any other Canadian poet to greatness."

I felt uneasy moving into an area where this kind of mythological pattern was emerging. I felt that Klein was ossifying in the minds of Canadian litterateurs into a kind of tragic cliché, into a biographical problem, into a cultural phenomenon; I felt he was becoming, like his own character Melech Davidson in *The Second Scroll,* "a double, multiple exposure." What I wanted to see was a poet, and a poet is what I hope I refound when I went back to reading him.

I think particularly of one sentence from *The Second Scroll.* "In quiet tones, as if they were talking of their own souls, they spoke of Uncle Melech and of how he had become a kind of mirror, an *aspaklaria,* of the events of our time." This, I suspect, was in a way how Klein saw himself, not as a man, for he was clearly too humble and sensible for that, but as a poet. And it is possible to present this case very convincingly. He was at the same time, with great awareness, a Jew and a Canadian and a citizen of the world. He wrote with some bitterness and an even deeper sadness on the political events of our time, exemplified so devastatingly in the tragedy of his own people, and a poem like "Gloss Beth" in *The Second Scroll,* which one reads with pain, was obviously composed in an extraordinary tension between inner agony and the demands of the poetic craft. Yet, as Margaret Avison remarked, he could also "speak of Canada and sound the note that makes vibrations through all times and places."

There are some poets whose function is to gather in and recapitulate, to make what Klein himself has called "the poetry of the recaptured time." Klein used that phrase in a very specific way, to refer to the spirit of the new life in Israel, yet it can be used to describe an aspect of his own work, for in his poetry he recaptured — and recapitulated also — two traditions, that of Jewish religion and that of English poetry, and he celebrated a third too new for recapturing—that of the Canada he described as one of "God's apolitical zones of temperature."

It is this essentially recapitulative element in Klein's poetry that we have always to remember in criticizing him. Tom Marshall has suggested correctly that Klein sought to *enrich* poetry, not to *purify* it. With the bare, republican, American tradition he has little empathy; his axis of inspiration spans Europe and Canada. Europe gave him the literature, the cultural traditions, that shaped his speech and symbolism. Canada and the wider world of his time gave him the themes and the images for his more mature and more satisfying poetry.

There is much in Klein that is deliberately archaic; for example, the Elizabethan diction and tone of *Hath Not a Jew*. That remarkably fine poem, "In Re Solomon Warshawer," could hardly have been written if Browning had not lived. And critics, even friendly ones, have been liberal in their accusations of derivations from more modern writers, from Eliot (and again one cannot deny the Prufrockery that Pratt found in "Soirée of Velvel Kleinberger"), from Auden and Thomas (though here I feel John Sutherland in his very outspoken study of Klein's defects was being excessively accusatory), and even from his Montreal contemporaries, Patrick Anderson and P.K. Page.

But before we begin condemning on such grounds, we have to define derivativeness. Since literary forms tend to be continuous if changing, and since much of the apparatus of symbolism seems to be firmly lodged in that common ground of inspiration from which we all draw our literary strength, there is a large area of creation that appears to begin precisely by writing feeding on writing. In that sense, we are all derivers, conditioned by what has been written before and sometimes by books or poems we have not even read. It is surely less the derivation than how we spend the inheritance that really counts. The Elizabethan derivations of Heavysege, for example, led to very different results from those of Klein, who assimilated them, as he assimilated the Talmud and Pope and *The Waste Land* and *New Signatures* and *Preview,* and came out in the end with a handful of poems as good as the best any Canadian poet has written. I don't know about Klein's greatness, and I don't think greatness matters in poetry. But I do think it matters to have written a good work of symbolic fiction and a few poems that are excellent, and to have given a renewed expression in doing so to the traditions to which one belongs, as Klein did for the Jewish tradition, in *The Second Scroll* especially, and for the Canadian tradition, meagre as it is, in poems like "The Grain Elevator," "Political Meeting," and "Montreal."

To say that Klein was a traditional poet in the best sense, in Marshall's sense of enrichment, is not to deny a concern for innovation. Klein himself describes with befitting irony the unsuccessful search that the narrator of *The Second Scroll* carried on for "the completely underivative poet. . . bard without antecedents or influences," and one feels—without discovering any explicit statements—that he would have found the more extreme imitators of William Carlos Williams as insipid, in their search for poetic purification, as distilled water. But he followed poetic developments in his time very closely, and it is obvious that there was little significant new poetry appearing during his time in the world that he did not read with a careful eye. He moved, after all, from an archaic to a modern mode, and the modern mode was his own.

The enrichment that was Klein's temperamental inclination led to faults which have at times troubled many of his readers. The richness moves out of language, invading imagery and tone; it can produce an exciting colourfulness, and when Klein is in the mood he can luxuriate in the exotic as lushly as Oscar Wilde or any of the other Decadents ever did. Consider, for example, the introductory description of Casablanca in *The Second Scroll*.

Everything was fascinating, rich, crayoned. After the drabness and austerity of the Italian camp, after the wan bleached faces among whom I had spent my life up to now, this was cornucopia and these people an arc of the rainbow of race. I lingered in markets and souks, my eyes luxuriating upon each opulent still life displayed on barrow or heaped up behind the windows of the cool marble-slabbed arcades—the golden oranges of Tetuan, pyramided; navelled the pomegranates of Marrakesh; Meknes quinces; the sun sweet inside their little globes, and upon their skins the mist of unforgotten dawn, the royal grapes of Rabat. Even the sheathed onions, mauve, violet, pink, poll-tufted like the warriors of Atlas, seemed fruit I had never seen before. And dominating—whether in the cool smooth round or, sliced, as crimson little scimitars adorning the Negro smile—were watermelons, miniature Africas, jungle-green without, and within peopled by pygmy blacks set sweetly in their world of flesh.

Very pleasing if one likes this kind of writing in small portions, which is what Klein is wise enough to give one, but decorative, inessential in a basic narrative. A purist would have left it out; Klein, fortunately in my view, did not, and by including it illuminated the complexity of his narrator, not of his narrative.

More serious than this kind of playfulness is Klein's inclination to a type of rhetoric that tends to force feeling rather artificially, with a resulting sentimentalization of vision. This to me is what mars an otherwise vivid poem like "Gloss Aleph" in *The Second Scroll*. The break from true feeling into forced feeling on the edge of falseness ruins the final verse as the poet moves from two lines of fine mythic statement:

> It is a fabled city that I seek;
> It stands in Space's vapours and Time's haze

to an ending which dissolves into softness:

> Thence comes my sadness in remembered joy
> Constrictive of the throat;
> Thence do I hear, as heard by a Jewboy,
> The Hebrew violins,
> Delighting in the sobbed Oriental note.

Not merely softness, but *contrived* softness in that phrase "constrictive of the throat"!

Many of Klein's poems attract one by a sheer charm that was obviously an attribute of the man himself, and this appears especially in genre poems like "Snowshoers," which A.J.M. Smith once praised for its resemblance to a Krieghoff painting. The likeness is there indeed, and particularly in the opening lines:

> The jolly icicles ringing in their throats,
> their mouths meerschaums of vapour,
> from the saints' parishes they come, like snowmen
> spangled, with spectrum colour

But the bright, varnished picture surface is not all; the poem moves forward to an ending liberated into motion, and the motion takes us into the white heart of the Canadian world, which Klein, a city man of European background, made eventually his own.

> And now, clomping the packed-down snow of the street
> they walk on sinews
> gingerly, as if their feet were really swollen,
> eager for release

from the blinders of the buildings; suddenly they cut
a corner, and—the water they will walk!
Surf of the sun!
World of white wealth! Wind's tilth! Waves
of dazzling dominion
on which their coloured sails will billow and rock!

In less dazzling, romantic poems Klein himself moved on into the Canadian land, and in "Grain Elevator" and "Filling Station" I see him as the pioneer of those poems of the road that in the generation following his were to become so expressive of the Canadian sensibility.

Yet it is back to his native town, his many-tongued Montreal, that one returns for Klein's best poems. His eye for the wider land was exceptional in such an urban man, yet a citizen in the literal sense he remained, despite his poetic journeys beyond the metropolitan island. For once the anthologists have done well, for Klein's most collected poems are among his best: poems like "Political Meeting" and "Monsieur Gaston" and, of course, "Montreal," in all of which one gets the sense of a penetrative knowledge of urban relationships, of an extraordinary empathy translating itself almost directly into the dense texture that is original because of its total rightness of feeling. No one, not even any francophone Québecois, has presented the depth of French-Canadian feeling so potently as Klein in the last phrases of his portrait of Camillien Houde in action which ends "Political Meeting."

Calmly, therefore, he begins to speak of war,

praises the virtue of being *Canadien*,
of being at peace, of faith, of family,
and suddenly his other voice: *Where are your sons?*

He is tearful, choking tears; but not he
would blame the clever English; in their place
he'd do the same; maybe.

Where *are* your sons?
The whole street wears one face,
shadowed and grim; and in the darkness rises
the body-odour of race.

That, for me, is remarkably fine poetry; if the definition means anything, perhaps it does approach greatness. But, being of Lord

Acton's opinion that "all great men are bad," I feel the definition does not fit Klein. He was patently a good man and, something that does not always follow, at his best a good poet, as much praise as any man needs.

[1973]

Private and Public Images: The Poetry of Pat Lowther

> I am an eye in the forest,
> jewelled and spittled
> with dew
> I am the underside of a leaf,
> a bird moving
> in my own brain.

THAT STANZA FROM a fairly early poem entitled "Notes from a far suburb," expresses one side of Pat Lowther—the concern for ecology, the fascination with the theme of evolution, the search for a sense of empathetic unity with the world of nature, so that the birds which play an extraordinary role in her imagery (one of her collections of verse is actually called *The Age of the Bird*) enter into a relation of symbiotic identity with the intuitions that inspire her writing. To introduce another dimension entirely, let me quote a verse from *The Age of the Bird* (published in 1972):

> Often now I forget
> how to make love
> but I think I am ready
> to learn politics.

It is in the tense and perpetually threatened equilibrium between the passive receptor of the first quotation and the admirer of political activism who speaks in the second quotation that the special quality of Pat Lowther's poetry can be found. I suspect that she understood more than most poets—but perhaps subliminally—the fact that the confrontation of the personal and the political which occurs in every writer wishing to change the human world is undoubtedly a dilemma but may also be a source of poetic energy. Orwell and Malraux and Camus understood this in prose; none of the famous socially conscious poets of the thirties, except perhaps Roy Fuller, showed any real sign of having understood it in verse.

I never met Pat Lowther face to face, though we lived in the same city; our closest contact consisted of a few telephone conversations regarding the business of the League of Canadian Poets, in which she was active during the months preceding her death. I remember her personal voice as flat in tone, with ripples of hesitant friendliness; I recognized a fellow solitary.

I wrote about her once when she was alive, and looking back at what I said—it was only two paragraphs in a long review in *Canadian Literature*—I am glad I saw then that she was, as I said, "writing verse on a level with poets who are much better known in Canada," and that I knew her as—to quote the same review—"a poet of versatility; of an impeccable verbal appropriateness; of the ability to write discursively or densely, to trace a tense narrative through a series of poems leading to a muted climax, or to catch a complex binary image" in a brief poem like "Vision":

> The Woman looks out of the whale's bone
> her eyes eroded
> sinking
> into the marrow
> the source of vision.
> The whale cutting
> the water
> sings like a huge machine.
> All his bones
> have eyes.

"Vision" was one of Pat Lowther's later works, and none of us understood (though she with her great intuitive sensitivity may have done so) how far the identification of Woman and Whale was to work in her life. For she herself was as endangered as the whale or any other wild species, and died as brutal and gratuitous a death.

I have come to the point where the biographical and the critical meet in uneasy tension. If a writer becomes the victim of a sensational tragedy, his/her works are likely to be read far more widely than they ever were before, or, if she/he happens to be already a well-known writer, we find that consternation, anger, pity, all the emotions aroused by the poet's fate affect our ability to judge the work objectively. It is doubtful, for example, whether we shall ever be able to read the writings of Oscar Wilde independently of our feelings about the cruelty of his persecution and imprisonment for acts which now, in Canadian as well as in British law, are regarded as matters of personal choice. And Pat Lowther certainly became more widely known as the victim of a murder than she ever was as a writer of poems.

So be it. We have to accept the irony of the situation that destiny has presented. For in Pat Lowther's case her death actually brought her the degree of attention which she deserved but which she never received while she was alive. It is sad (but unfortunately not out of keeping with the Canadian inclination to reject any cultural manifestations less obviously commercialized than the tedious self-glorifications of Pierre Berton, Farley Mowat and Peter Newman) that while she was alive and writing poems of true quality, Pat Lowther should have received very little recognition. None of the leading Canadian publishers was then willing to bring out a book of her poems; they were always published by little presses like Very Stone House (which brought out her first book, *This Difficult Flowering,* in 1968), Blackfish (which brought out *The Age of the Bird*), and Borealis Press (which published *Milkstone* in 1974). She was unpublished in any of the general anthologies of modern Canadian poetry put out in recent years by Toronto publishers, though Gary Geddes did include three fine poems in his Oxford collection of writings of the Canadian far west, *Skookum Wawa* (1975); even in the otherwise rather comprehensive *Contemporary Poetry of British Columbia*, edited by J. Michael Yates and published in 1970, Pat Lowther's achievement and promise were underestimated to the extent that only one of her poems was included. Now, thanks to the accident of her death by murder, Pat Lowther is likely to receive the attention which her work on its own never received. Perhaps even one of the mandarins of the Toronto publishing industry will at last be moved to publish her collected poems.[1]

When they are published (for I feel there is no *if* about this happening eventually) a poet of remarkable verbal wit and of classic control will be revealed, but at the same time a poet who in

1. Since I wrote this essay, Oxford University Press has published a posthumous volume of Pat Lowther's poems, *A Stone Diary* (1977).

the range of her preoccupations, and in the power with which she involves us in them, projects the kind of world view that combines a deeply empathetic understanding of external nature with the desire to see her own personal predicament as a woman placed within a social continuum where women are only one of many groups seeking liberation and often doing so by means that threaten their objective.

Let me begin the examination of Lowther's complex sensibility by quoting entire a fine nature poem entitled "Octopus":

> The octopus is as beautifully
> functional as an umbrella;
> at rest a bag of rucked skin
> sags like an empty scrotum
> his jellied eyes sad and bored
> but taking flight: look
> how lovely purposeful
> in every part:
> the jet vent smooth
> as modern plumbing
> the webbed pinwheel of tentacles
> moving in perfect accord
> like a machine dreamed
> by Leonardo

Here are all the qualities of Lowther at her best: the skill in choosing utterly right words; the poised balance of structure; the sense of an inherent economy of form in nature which is related to perfection in human creation and by implication to the artifice of the poem itself; and beneath all this a unique combination of cool observation and empathy for the thing observed.

Or there are Pat Lowther's elegiac poems for the landscape of the Pacific Coast, which she loved as deeply as do all of us who have resisted the financial temptations of Toronto and Montreal and stayed among the mountains and the rain forests and the deep fjords. One of these is "Elegy for the South Valley," the story of a dam whose building scarred the countryside but which was already silting up. "We have no centuries/here a few generations/ do for antiquity," the poet sardonically remarks, and goes on to tell how

> The gravel pit is eating
> South Valley, the way you'd

> eat a stalk of asparagus
> end to end, saving the tender
> tip for last

She ends with the vision of nature and time taking their eventual revenge.

> Each year the tooth marks
> go deeper into the green
> overhanging falls and terraces
> of water, shearing toward
> the head of the south fork
> where the dam leans
> between time's jaws
> waiting for either
> the weight of its past
> or the hard bite of the future
> to bring it down unmade
> and original gravel
> bury its shards at last.

Such poems of nature ravaged by humankind must be posed against Pat Lowther's poems of humankind (and especially womankind) in the thrall of nature, such as "Two Babies in Two Years," which begins with the ironic opening verse (ironic in relation to the poet's intellectualist pretensions):

> Now I am one with those wide-wombed
> mediterranean women
> who pour forth litters of children,
> mouthfuls of kisses and shrieks,
> their hands always wet and full
> in motion. . . .

It ends with a laconic and at the same time curiously moving description of her own condition that seems to place the process to which she has become subject not only within the succession of human generations but also within the whole frame of animal living and experience to which man and woman by their nature irrevocably belong.

> Now that the late
> summer stays
> the child hangs in
> the webbing of my flesh

> and last year's baby, poised
> on the lip of the spinning
> kitchen, bedroom,
> vacuum, living
> room, clings to the crod
> of my skirt, afraid yet
> of her first step.

For me the most sustainedly satisfying work by Pat Lowther is the poem sequence entitled *The Age of the Bird*, which is based on the failure of Che Guevara's guerilla campaign and his death in the Bolivian jungle. It begins with the exhibiting of Che's body in the shed at Vallegrande, described with stark economy:

> outside, a shirt slung
> over a wire
> a wheelbarrow empty
> on scuffed ground
>
> inside, the body
> its eyes open
> the head propped
> in a tense posture

Like all good political poetry, *The Age of the Bird* deals with the ambivalences of political action, and the way dogmatic ideologies can negate deeds. Essentially, insofar as it has a message, what *The Age of the Bird* records is the fact that Che, moving among the peasants of the Bolivian *montaña,* neglected Mao's instructions that the guerilla must move among the people like a fish through water. The water of Che's Bolivia was still a peasant society suspicious of strangers and dominated by the ancient myths of the Quechuas. Partly by using passages adapted from the diaries of Che and his associates and partly by evoking the expectations which superstitious Indian farmers had evolved regarding liberating heroes, the poem shows how inevitable the mission's failure and Che's death actually were.

> Dead man you didn't dream
> deeply enough
> you were not romantic
>
> you didn't believe
> legends matter
> or language

she says, and, juxtaposing the revolutionary's stark recording with Quechua imaginings, she continues,

> The peasant base
> has not yet been developed.
> through planned terror
> we can neutralize.
> support will come later.
>
> You should have put on
> a mantle of mirrors.
> you should have worn
> gold and feather
> flashing upon
> the tallest mountain.

All this is as accurate as history. But there is an essential difference between history and poetry. "History to the defeated," said W.H. Auden, "may say Alas but cannot help or pardon." Poetry cannot help, but it can pardon, and it can suggest the hope that lies in defeat, even the defeat of a guerilla laid out in a laundry shed with his fingers cut off. *The Age of the Bird* ends with a passage dedicated to the great Chilean poet, Pablo Neruda, as the man of vision who may possess the dream that relates ideology with actuality. Neruda's vision one can grant, though whether even he had found a way to reconcile poetry and politics in practice one may doubt. But in poetic terms, in terms of verse that combines mastery of words and images with a tension between realism and compassion, *The Age of the Bird* stands as one of the few successful poems *about* politics ever written in Canada. A political poem in the sense of propaganda it is not; Pat Lowther never compromised in such a way her integrity as a writer, and she could well have said, as William Hazlitt did before he died: "I never wrote a line that licked the dust."

[1976]

The Wanderer: Earle
Birney as Poet
and Novelist

THERE IS A SENSE in which the Old English poets set a pattern
for the use of the journey in English literature. In poems like *The
Wanderer* and *The Seafarer* they established not merely the experience of earthly journeying as a metaphor for the inner journey
"down to Gehenna or up to the throne," as Kipling put it, but also
what we now tend to see as the romantic linking of scenes of
earthly desolation with the condition of man considered merely as
a being of earth. I am not suggesting that these early English
poets actually invented either of these connections between the
mundane and the spiritual, for they exist in *The Odyssey* and in the
Mahabharata, in *Exodus* and even in the *Epic of Gilgamesh* which
antedates all these works; almost certainly the first tales of wandering whose real goal was more than a worldly destination must
have been the oral epics and tales of nomadic, preliterate peoples
to whom the settled existence was unknown and all life was in
literal as well as figurative ways a journey.

The journey with its dual intent and double destination, the
journey that tests and initiates, has remained a constant of
European literature even down to the present age of futuristic fantasies like those of Ursula Le Guin, but in its recurrent manifestations it has tended to relate closely in content to the life of its
special time, even when formal elements have maintained a considerable constancy despite the lack of evident continuity in
traditions. There is little likelihood that the scops who composed
The Seafarer and *The Wanderer* knew *The Odyssey* and certainly they
were ignorant of the Hindu and Babylonian epics I have
mentioned; at most they knew *Exodus,* but the life of a desert
wanderer was foreign to their experience, and so they developed

themes that seem to echo late Judaic and early Christian concepts in the context of a wandering life proper to Anglo-Saxon times, the life of perilous sea voyages and of unstable realms.

We can imagine ourselves back among the warring kinglets and theyns of the Heptarchy when the author of *The Wanderer* tells how

> in many a spot through this middle earth
> the wind-blown walls stand waste, befrosted,
> the abodes of men lie buried in snow,
> the wine-halls are dust in the wind, the rulers
> dead, stripped of glee. . . .

Similarly in *The Seafarer* the chances of the seaman's life are contrasted with the delusive certainties of the complacent landsman's life, the life of unawareness:

> this life that is dead
> in a land that passes; I believe no whit
> that earthly weal is everlasting.

But the seafarer, like the wanderer, is saved from earthly weal precisely by

> the mood that drives my soul
> to fare from home, that, far away,
> I may find the stead where strangers dwell.

And in this faring, the man who journeys finds a liberty even more of the spirit than of the flesh and the mind.

> So, now, my soul soars from my bosom,
> the mood of my mind moves with the sea-flood,
> over the home of the whale, high flies and wide
> to the ends of the earth; after, back to me
> comes the lonely flier, lustful and greedy,
> whets me to the whale-way, whelms me with his
> bidding
> over deep waters. Dearer, then, to me
> the boons of the Lord. . . .[1]

From the life of toil and privation and nearness to peril which the seaman endures, rather than from the illusory ease of the landsman, come "the boons of the Lord," and so the hard voyage

1. The extracts from *The Wanderer* and *The Seafarer* were rendered into Modern English by K. Malone in *Ten Old English Poems*, 1941.

leads to a self-discovery that is a drowning of worldly pretensions in the harbour of enlightenment.

While there is not a continuing link between English literature and the literature of the ancient world, except that of Jewish antiquity, there is a succession from Old English poetry which is thematic even more than formal, and elements which we find in the poetry of the Anglo-Saxon era tend to re-emerge with a special emphasis when modern or recent life in some way resembles life of pre-Norman England, so that it is not surprising to find a Canadian poet of our time like Earle Birney, brought up in a pioneering society on the edge of wilderness, where existence was at times perilous and where the heroic view of life could still be sustained, being attracted to Old English poetry.

Not only has Birney freely parodied that poetry in a number of celebrated exercises like "Anglosaxon Street" and "Mappemounde," which look and sound as like the original as anything in Modern English possibly can. Not only does he like to call himself a scop and his poems makings, and insist on the importance of poetry being delivered orally and publicly as well as on the printed page, showing in these ways a desire to recreate the situation of earlier periods, when poetry did not seem, as it does now, an activity detached from the lives and preoccupations of common, active men. He also exemplifies in his life, and in the poetry that has emerged from the contemplation of his experiences, the theme of wandering that was so important to English bards at the crucial period when oral poetry first became wedded to writing. And wandering, in Birney's case, can be interpreted not merely as the driving desire to encounter strange landfalls and cultures, which has given us poems from four continents, but also as the equally driving urge to experiment in the forms of verse and the manipulation of language and even of nonlinguistic devices in the service of poetry. That the experiments have not been as productive as the travels does not diminish their relevance to the persona of Birney the Wanderer.

Perhaps no poem by Birney is more explicitly addressed to the pattern of wandering than "Mappemounde," which he wrote in 1945, returning by hospital ship from the wars. Evoking "the wanderer's pledges," it presents the sea as a great metaphor for Time, at whose bounds "the redeless . . . / topple in maelstrom   tread back never." Here the place that is wandered is given its actual as well as its figurative significance — "Adread in that mere we drift to

map's end" as Birney physically is doing across the map of the
Atlantic while he calls up the figures representing human destiny;
and so "Mappemounde" belongs to a group of poems in which the
focus is really on earth itself, on place considered not as static
setting but as dynamic environment alive with natural and cosmic
forces in which the wanderer becomes the observing peripatetic
philosopher rather than—as in most of Birney's best wandering
poems—the traveller intent on the meaningful human contact or
the episode potent with historic implication.

Perhaps the two most striking poems which exemplify this facet
of Birney's vision are his remarkable meditation in verse,
"November Walk near False Creek Mouth," which was written in
1961–63 and is his longest poem, and the late "Wind through St.
John's," written in 1977. Both are set in Canadian cities (cities of
the eastern and western extremities), and while, like all but the
most intimately erotic of Birney's verse, they are sensitive to the
sound of history, it is the history seen in the wider perspective
which comes when one is so deeply involved in a country's pattern
of existence that one can take particular destinies for granted and
look to the general condition, the macrocosm.

Very few of Birney's poems of foreign travel achieve that kind
of sweep. Perhaps "Machu Picchu" (1962) is the most notable
among them. In this poem about a Peruvian day Birney is removed from the temptation to particularize human situations
because he is in a city whose last human inhabitants died four
centuries and more ago, and he can see the Inca ruins on their
great mountain as a paradigm of the universals of inevitable death
and stubborn life, as of the Time that already in "Mappemounde"
had been seen as hemming "all hearts' landtrace."

> Upwards and bright with birds and orchids
> the undiscouraged forest reaches
> clawing over the great cliffs
> at the lowest rockstep
> and the tidied fruitless marketplace
>
> By grain   clod   stone
> the architrave crumbles   and the hill
> The corn terrace sifts to the Urubamba
> to the Amazon   joins the attrition
> of continents perishing into the sea

Stripped tomb and town of triumph
sooner or later you will finish dying
    like all of us
               Till then
   it is good and beautiful to see you stare
   out of your green humped cumulus
   of mountains and the human mist   you
   and Hiram Bingham and the high Incas
   obstinately into your Sun

In "November Walk near False Creek Mouth," Birney uses copiously the image — occurring in others of his British Columbian poems — of the Canadian west coast as the end of land, the extremity of wandering in the face of the great ocean which comes to symbolize something very close to Sartre's *néant*, to Hemingway's *nada,* the great luminous void into which all our thoughts and longings are absorbed. The poet walks at sunset, and the setting of a historic as well as a cosmic sun occupies his mind as it flashes back over the English of Saxon days, their rise to imperial power followed by their decline into faded impotence.

   I walk as the earth turns
   from its burning father
   here on this lowest edge of mortal city
   where windows flare on faded flats
   and the barren end of the ancient English
      who tippled mead in Alfred's hall
      and took tiffin in lost Lahore
   drink now their fouroclock chainstore tea
   sighing like old pines as the wind turns

But by the end of "November Walk" we have moved with the poet's eye through all the changing scene as he walks on the beaches among human beings on their small errands, observing the burning heavens and the descent of darkness over the earth, and realizes that all can be seen by man only through the darkling glass of the human condition.

   Higher than clouds and strata of jetstreams
   the air-roads wait the two-way traffic
   And beyond?   The desert planets
   What else?   a galaxy-full perhaps
   of suns and penthouses waiting

But still on the highest shelf of ever
washed by the curve of timeless returnings
lies the unreached unreachable nothing
whose winds wash down to the human shores
and slip   shoving

into each thought nudging my footsteps now
as I turn to my brief night's ledge

in the last of warmth
and the fading of brightness
on the sliding edge of the beating sea

"The Wind through St. John's" is a belated companion piece to "November Walk." A wind that has blown over every voyager since fishermen first came to the Banks off Newfoundland, and so suggests the slight importance of human history in the patterns of earthly time, becomes also a world-surrounding gale echoing the cosmic rhythms that make even earth's geography seem small.

Beyond Novaya Zembla
beyond the packice of the Leptev Sea
the wind will sweep
as it swept over Bering's bones on Wrangel
and skimmed the polar ice to Amundsen's Gulf
    polishing Hearne's name on a Coppermine rock
and come again declaiming through St. John's town
saying nothing

saying only that air and earth and sea will be one
and whirl in the Sun
within the reeling Circle

There is of course another aspect to poems like "November Walk" and "The Wind through St. John's" within the Birney canon. They punctuate the theme of wandering by inversion. Birney the traveller may have journeyed to St. John's, but in the poem it is the wind that journeys, and he, the observer, remains at the still point within "the reeling Circle."

In lesser degrees this kind of dialectical relationship between the land and the poet appears in many other of Birney's poems, but a more significant duality, I suggest, emerges in the constant interplay between Canada and abroad, which is clearly emphasized in the arrangement of *Collected Poems* (1975) on explicitly geographical lines. There are thirteen sections, covering various periods which, because of the sorting by place, often overlap. Four of the sections are entitled "Canada" and one "U.S.A"; there are sections for Europe, Asia, North Pacific, South Pacific, Mexico, South America and the Caribbean, and Australia and New Zealand. The thirteenth section is entitled "War" and dated 1938–1947; since it spans Canada and Europe and the seas between, it also can be regarded as defined by geography, as well as by history.

I think it was Bruce Nesbitt who once said that Canada has been Birney's Ithaca, and certainly it has been the fixed pole of his journeying, and also the setting of the first poems to show the sense of the subtle intermingling of place and person so characteristic of Birney at his best. John Sutherland remarked long ago, when *David and Other Poems* first appeared in 1942, that "of all our young modernist poets he is the only one who has made consistent use of a Canadian landscape," and if we are to take Birney's own datings, he was a landscapist from the start, since the earliest piece in *Collected Poems* is a revised version of a poem about a crow on a broken bull-pine, called "Kootenay Still-Life" and written in its first version when Birney was fifteen, and the next is a kind of genre-and-landscape piece written five years later and entitled "Old West Vancouver Ferry."

It was largely because he put the mountains of British Columbia into pictorial and effective verse in poems like "David" and "Conrad Kain" that Birney earned his first repute as a poet, with critics as various as Northrop Frye and A.G. Bailey remarking on the strength his metaphors seemed to have attained from the rugged land he described and on the skill with which, as E.J. Pratt pointed out, "the science of mountain climbing is . . . in detail and in principle made subject to the art of poetry." Of course, others of his Canadian poems were far wider in sweep, endeavouring with marked success, in, for example, "Transcontinental" and "North Star West," to express what Birney called, in the latter's final lines, "the welling and wildness of Canada, the fling of a nation."

Yet one turns to the mountain poems I have mentioned, and to others like "Climbers" and "Biography" and "Takkakaw Falls," to get Birney's sense of the real grit and grain of Canada and to understand the original impulses behind his wandering: the sense of mingled tragedy and achievement—so well exemplified in "David"—that he brought from his early mountain journeying, and of something perhaps even deeper that he took to it out of his foothills childhood, expressed best of all in a stanze of "Conrad Kain"; this poem, about an Austrian mountain guide transplanted to the Rockies, might with very little change be applied to the poet himself:

> At dawn he led them foot-torn and dazed
> over the last glimmering glacier
> through the lowest tumble of rocks
> to the blessed lake and the firm trail
> flattening to camp, to sleep   and to fame
> enduring in all who adventure in mountains
> —back from the first manning of Robson.
>
> Some think such victories are virtueless.
> As empty perhaps as Polar voyagings,
> or the wreaths of the runners in Pindar?
> He climbed, as another would read,
> because his mind was incurably curious,
> his body was clamped in the follies of boys
> and he was bred to the game.

The poet and the mountaineer—the affinity is clearly defined, when we are told that Kain climbed "as another would read." The poet's fame is as little in accordance with contemporary standards of achievement as that of mountaineers or "the runners in Pindar" (again a poetic link). And the poet's mind, as Birney's travels and his writings consistently manifest, has been "incurably curious." This particular poet certainly seems to have been "bred to the game," if one accepts that the earliest of his *Collected Poems* was first drafted when he was fifteen, while the line—"his body was clamped in the follies of boys"—takes on a strange premonitory significance when one reads it in conjunction with "Fall from Fury" (1977), the late poem in which Birney describes his fall from a beech tree when he was more than seventy which crippled him for the rest of his life. Indeed, it is the same kind of lifelong passion he attributed to Kain that Birney remembers as he clambers upward through the branches.

Each grasp tugged at the old zest
for a climb: the rock-fort a year ago
in Sri Lanka   and before   in my sixties
up the yellow spines of the Olgas. . .
at fifty-eight in cloud on the ribs
of Huayna Picchu. . . at thirty
inching down chalks on Lulworth cliffs
. . . twenty-one and over the icy necks
of the Garibaldis . . . and before that
the mountains of youth . . . Temple . . . Edith
all the climbings made in joy of the sport
and never with hurt
as now to the topmost vault
of the beechtree's leaves I rose
to the flooding memories of childhood
perched in my first treehouse
safe in its green womb

Poetically, Birney's world of journeying can be divided into three zones. There is Canada, loved physically and as the scene of the basic experiences of childhood and youth, yet — without being hated — always subject to scolding for its failure to live up to the demands of the poet's love.

At the other extreme there is the world of Asia, of Mexico and of South America, encountered between 1955 and 1963, which in the view of most astute readers produced the best of all Birney's poems and revealed for the first time the wideness of his sympathies and perceptions, justifying Milton Wilson's description of him as "a very local and a very global poet." These are the poems of dramatic meeting, in which Birney's encounters with a strange world and its inhabitants can be inverted into pungent comments on the wandering poet and the world from which he comes.

In between these two extreme zones of the familiar and the wholly exotic there are regions which have a deceptive semblance of familiarity, like the United States and Australia, and even the islands of the Caribbean, so that the poet is speaking the same language yet suddenly realizes how the varying ways in which it is used in fact reveal disconcerting differences of background and attitude. These are the poems in which Birney is most likely to turn to satire, and often, through attempting to get the sound of strange accents, he moves a long way in the direction of verbal experimentation.

Birney's first travels beyond Canada took him to the United States as a student and a young teacher in the 1930s, and to Europe as a soldier in the 1940s. These travels provided the basic material for his two works of prose fiction, *Turvey* (1949) and *Down the Long Table* (1955), each of which can be related to a cluster of his poems written at the time of which the novel refers. *Turvey* is a comic account of the absurdities of war, in much the vein of *The Good Soldier Schweik,* and *Down the Long Table* is a serious socio-historical novel in which Birney attempts to recreate the motives of political acts in the 1930s that lead his hero, Gordon Saunders, to stand in the 1950s before the table of a McCarthyite committee investigating subversives. But both are picaresque novels, constructed as a series of episodes linked by chains of space as well as time, and both, though their central characters are imagined, are based on the experiences of their wandering creator. Birney has never been a very inventive writer in a fictional way, and his novels depend as much as his poems on the transmutation of personal experiences and observations.

In my view — though not in Birney's — the transmutation has been more successful in the poetry than in the fiction. *Turvey* is the amusing *jeu d'esprit* of a poet, effectively satirical of the follies of men engaged in war, and essentially comic in its re-establishment of natural justice when Turvey, triumphant in the end, becomes the personification of Man victorious over the negative forces of modern society. *Turvey* is in many ways a very Canadian book, since it incorporates a great variety of Canadian types representing different regions and walks of life and talking in a hilarious mosaic of dialects; undoubtedly the cumbersome operation of the Canadian army as Birney portrays it can be taken as a criticism of the Canadian nation, which, as he indicates repeatedly in his poems, then seemed to him "dead-set in adolescence," lacking in a real will of its own to support its notions of independence. But there is another aspect to *Turvey,* for the action overflows into a world both geographically wider and historically deeper, as Turvey is taken to England, proceeds via various military misunderstandings to Belgium and Holland, becomes involved in a black-marketeering rings, and gets one brief and inactive glimpse of the front line, which quickly recedes as he is funnelled back to England and Canada and final defiant demobilization. It is a wandering novel, and, as in all picaresques, the constantly changing human relationships are shallowly sketched and there is no real development of character; Turvey does not grow mentally through experience; he merely becomes more knowing.

Down the Long Table is a less uniformly successful book than *Turvey*, perhaps because it makes too little use of Birney's considerable comic talents; perhaps it must be regarded as an essentially pathetic book, stressing the irony that long before reaching the investigator's table, Gordon was bitterly disillusioned with the left-wing activism which now returns to haunt him. The novel's main virtue lies in the vividness with which it tells of life among the warring Marxist sects of the 1930s. The real movement of *Down the Long Table* is — again — geographical wandering. It begins in a Utah college, continues in Toronto, takes Saunders bumming across Canada by freight train, immerses him in the varied and often very funny radical world of Vancouver, and sends him — all passion spent — full circle back to Utah, where he becomes a respectable academic, never anticipating that his past will one day explode into his present as old associates turn informers and denounce him to the witch-hunters. Until Birney publishes his autobiography we shall not know how closely Gordon's experiences in fact parallel his creator's, who himself taught in Utah and Toronto and was a Trotskyite organizer during the years of the Depression.

In the case of each of Birney's novels there is a group of poems which concerns the same area of experience. From the locales where Turvey endured the manifestations of military madness — a flamethrowing unit, a military hospital, a hospital ship — Birney wrote poems, but the most striking of all these links is that between chapter seventeen of *Turvey*, and the poem, "The Road to Nijmegen," written out of immediate experience four years before the novel gave its prose account of the journey to Nijmegen — one of the few occasions when the normally irrepressible Turvey "could not fall into gaiety." In this chapter, Turvey recedes uncharacteristically from the foreground, and it is Birney's own feelings that take over in the page or so of sober description of the Dutch people who have somehow survived the Nazi occupation. The novel describes the same perceptions as the poem, but they are differently contexted, since in *Turvey* they must be fitted in with the physical details of journeying, whereas in the poem they are framed by the poet's thoughts of his distant beloved, and human love is balanced against human misery in this most moving of all Birney's early poems. He describes with laconic starkness the graves with billy-tin epitaphs, the old men cutting chips from ruined stumps for firewood, the women riding like ships at sea on bare-rimmed bicycles,

> and the children
> groping in gravel for knobs of coal
> or clustered like winter flies
> at the back of messhuts
> their legs standing like dead stems out of their clogs

But then his mind turns, and

> Over the clank of the jeep
> your quick grave laughter
> outrising at last the rockets
> brought me what spells I repeat
> as I travel this road
> that arrives at no future
> and what creed I can bring
> to our daily crimes
> to this guilt
> in the griefs of the old
> and the graves of the young

"The Road to Nijmegen" operates a device that occurs time and again in the impressive Asian and Latin American poems of later years: the poet recording what he sees but also present in the poem, sometimes as the reflective observer, but equally often as an actor, or perhaps rather a person whose alien presence provokes action in others. "The Bear on the Delhi Road" is an example of the first, and "Bangkok Boy" and "Cartagena de Indias" are varying examples of the second.

"The Bear on the Delhi Road" is really a traveller's observation, an incident during a drive to Kashmir when the poet sees two men by the roadside training a bear they have captured in the Himalayas and are bringing down to Delhi as a dancing beast.

As Birney sees it, the task the men have set themselves is to break the trance of animal living (which is reality) and substitute for it the trance of human living (which is myth). And so in the poem the tamers appear not as cruel taskmasters, but as men who, in the process of ensuring their own living, transform without joy and with unpredictable consequences the natural order.

> It is no more joyous for them
> in this hot dust to prance
> out of reach of the praying claws
> sharpened to paw for ants
> in the shadows of deodars
> It is not easy to free
> myth from reality
> or rear this fellow up
> to lurch   lurch with them
> in the tranced dancing of men

It is almost a model poem of observation and statement, every word carefully picked, each line mosaically adding a particular fact, the feeling evident but controlled, the bear emerging as a kind of animal Samson, a figure at once of pity and pride, and all thrown into relief not by any extravagance of language, but by the power of the poet to render the strangeness (in terms of his own experience and his readers' experience) of what he is saying, and to use that strangeness to provoke a sense of universality.

"Bangkok Boy" concerns one of those countless minor encounters that make up the fabric of a wanderer's journeying, and yet which sometimes stand out with a preternatural vividness because in some sense or other they provide the clues that offer a meaning to the heterogenous chaos of most people's travel experiences.

The content of the poem is simple enough. Birney—the "towering strayed/tourist"—gives a bit of chocolate and a small coin to a naked little Thai boy, and the boy dances in uninhibited delight against the bizarre Bangkok backdrop of claw-roofed palaces and pagodas covered with broken china and shimmering in the sun, of ancient Ramayana frescoes and modern brothels. The staccato rhythm of the poem with its clipped—often one-syllable—lines beats out the sense of excitement in the child's dance.

> Scamper little Thai
> hot on those hot stones
> scat
> leap
> this is forever O for
> all gods' sakes

> beat out
> that first
> last
> cry of joy
> under the sun!

But that cry of joy rings out against the background of Asian misery in which the child, if he survives, will be submerged.

> before in the high world's
> clumpings
> you are caught
> slid lethewards
> on choleric canals
> to where the poles of klongs
> and rows of paddyfields
> are shaped to bend
> small leaping backs
> and the flat bellies
> of impets
> are rounded with beriberi

Joy is in the instant and must be thus experienced; time leads only to misery and death, life's inevitable ends. And the message is given its peculiar intensity by the vividness with which the strange physical setting of it all is delineated and also by a form that suggests we read the poem — aloud or in the mind's ear — at a rapid and percussive dance pace.

"Cartagena de Indias" is a much more complex — as well as much longer — poem than either "The Bear on the Delhi Road" or "Bangkok Boy." In a series of encounters the poet is pestered and tricked as he walks through the decaying old Spanish city, and he realizes how different a world is his from this poverty among the fragments of splendour, and how difficult that makes any contact on a level beyond the pettily commercial.

> Somewhere there must be another bridge
> from my stupid wish
> to their human acceptance
> but what can I offer —
> my tongue half-locked in the cell
> of its language — other than pesos
>   to these old crones of thirty
>   whose young sink in pellagra

> as I clump unmaimed
> in the bright shoes
> that keep me from hookworm
> lockjaw and snakebite

Quite unexpectedly he finds that missing bridge in one of those epiphanies which at times bring wanderers back to themselves and make the strange world comprehensible in terms of their own inner vision. He comes upon a grotesque monument — a massive concrete representation, ten feet long, of a pair of worn shoes, dedicated to a certain Luis Lopez. At the only bookseller's shop he learns that Lopez was the local poet who wrote a great sonnet about the "rancid disarray" of his city, in which he declared that he loved Cartagena and its people with the love "a man has/for his old shoes," and when he died the citizens remembered him with their bizarre monument. Here, as Birney recognizes, in this extraordinary relationship between a city and its poet, is the bridge that leads him into brotherhood:

> Descendants of pirates   grandees
> galleyslaves and cannibals
> I love the whole starved cheating
> poetry-reading lot of you   most of all
> for throwing me the shoes of deadman Luis
> to walk me back into your brotherhood

One of the features distinguishing "Cartagena de Indias" and other poems of the Asian and Latin American cycles is that Birney speaks in what one might call the tone of elevated conversation, varying its pace from poem to poem. The very strangeness of the encounters and their settings makes it almost necessary for the narrative to be direct, descriptive and reflective; it is notable that Birney rarely experiments technically in these poems — except to find the linear form most fitting to the particular occasion — or indulges in the tinkerings with language which characterize so much of his other verse. It is true that he will pick up, as in "Sinalóa," the way a westernized Mexican speaks English:

> Si sēnor, is halligators here, your guidebook say it,
> si, jaguar in the montañas, maybe helephants, quién
>   sabe?
> You like, dose palmas in the sunset? Certamente very
>   nice,

it happen each night in the guia tourista
But who de hell eat jaguar, halligator, you heat em?
Mira my fren, wat dis town need is muy big
   breakwater—
     I like take hax to dem jeezly palmas.

But the point here does not really lie in the manipulation of the language; Birney is really presenting what a traveller is likely to hear in Mexico, with humour but without undue exaggeration, getting his effect largely from the irony that he, the traveller with perfect English, is seeking a past which the Mexican himself rejects in favour of a culture whose language he can only imperfectly speak. Once again, there is a meeting which provides poetic comments on two worlds. Only the very occasional poem of these exotic lands is written in clearly experimental form; one is "Nayarít," where Birney unites the poetic with the pictorial by arranging the type on the page in such a way that as we read we seem to journey in sloping lines among the hills of this wild country, up and down the sides of its pyramids, beside the verticals of the *barrancas*.

Since they are well known to his readers, there is no need to discuss in detail the range of Birney's experiments in the sounds and looks of poems, which are often highly ingenious, but which should perhaps be classed as "entertainments" rather than "poems" to distinguish them from works of the calibre of "David," "November Walk" and "Cartagena de Indias," which have no need of whimsical adornment to wreak their profound effects. At the same time, when we accept the Wanderer as one of Birney's chief poetic personae, we have to recognize that the restlessness which has kept him journeying over the earth has also led him to an equally restless search for new forms.

This search has been sustained by Birney's professional concern with language, and by his interest in the linguistic experiments of others. At the beginning Birney already distinguished himself from the poets of his time by utilizing his academic readings in Old English and Middle English, and his adoptions of Anglo-Saxon alliterations and kennings were sometimes subtle and sometimes not, as in "War Winters" (1943).

    Sun
    proud Bessemer   peltwarmer beauty

these winters yoke us   We scan sky for you
The dun droppings blur   we drown in snow
Is this tarnished chimneyplug   in a tenantless room
this sucked wafer   white simpleton
you?

The wordplay of *Finnegan's Wake* was an almost equally early influence, if we are to accept Birney's claim that "Mammorial Stunzas for Aimee Simple McFarcin" was first drafted in 1931. The Surrealist collage finds its way rather belatedly into Birney's poetic practice in the 1960s, with patterns of found newspaper headings and snippets of news; he had already used the same device fictionally in *Down the Long Table,* though perhaps with a more documentary purpose, since the collages which have appeared more recently among his poems appear to be absurdist in intent, as indeed do most of Birney's "entertainments," such as the arrangements of type with their hints of remote connotations, and the elegant little line drawings, each making its tenuous and often sentimental poetic point.

In his most recent experiments Birney seems to have been running beside the poets who were young a decade ago, and who rediscovered for themselves a great deal that Dada and Surrealism had already developed forty years before. Perhaps the major irony has been to watch Birney, who missed the influence of such movements when he was young, falling under their revived influence in his sixties and seventies.

The most ambitious of Birney's experiments are really those poems about the mid-worlds of the United States and Australia, not strange enough to be exotic yet jarringly alien even in their familiarity. Poems about Americans of the 1950s and early 1960s, like "Appeal to a Lady with a Diaper" (written in 1956 and updated in 1971) and "Billboards Build Freedom of Choice," mingle the words used by advertisers with the substandard speech of the people to whom the advertisers appeal in a powerfully grotesque and satirical presentation of a mindless attitude to life that, by so representing it, Birney makes as alien as any exotic land: more alien, in fact, since here there is no bridge of brotherhood to link us.

Perhaps, indeed, it is because there is no resolution, either comic or tragic, that poems like "Appeal to a Lady" and "Billboards" succeed eminently in their immediate effect yet remain unmemorable. One is struck by the parodic truth of lines like:

```
yegotta choose fella yegotta
choose between
      AMERICA and UN—
between KEE-RISPIES and KEE-RUMPIES
between KEE-RYEST and KEE-ROOST-SHOVE
and brother if you doan pick
      RIGHT
you better
git this heap
tahelloffn
our
      FREEWAY
```

But this is not the language of reflection or emotion. We get the point, mentally, but we are not moved, except perhaps to a brief and formal anger. And the same, I think, applies to the poems of Australia, where Birney the wanderer was clearly driven into a frustration, which he transformed into contempt, by the impossibility of finding a bridge, because the differences between the two cultures were so ill-defined and the people he met seemed always to be retreating behind a screen of caricature familiarity. Hence Birney's trip to Australia produced little better than the heavy humour of "Strine Authors Meet":

```
A female macaw beckons me      the local Edith Sitwell?
   Yew the kin eyejin gander gisses a lecher?
   Jus gonna read pomes
Her bill falls with alarm
   Yer nat gander read peartree? Ow long yer gan an fer?
```

Do Australians really speak like this? Or is it a deliberately exaggerated linguistic pastiche? My experience of Australians leads me to conclude the latter.

It is evident that I find the overtly experimental poems the least interesting of Birney's works, though I accept them as products of the restlessness and curiosity that on another level made him the wanderer whose journeyings have inspired his best poems. But this does not mean that the "entertainments" have to be dismissed as irrelevant to Birney's progress as a poet. On the contrary, I think that it is his openness to the new and the unorthodox that has given Birney the freedom to find so felicitously, in his greater poems, the special voice and form appropriate to each situation. The ability to experience and to describe each place in its own individual terms is what distinguishes the good travel book, and

Birney has successfully transmuted that usually prose virtue into the inspiring element of an authentic wanderer's poetry as true to its place in history as that of Homer or of Byron or of the anonymous scop who wrote *The Seafarer*.

[1979]

Index

This book was financially assisted by the Government of British Columbia through the British Columbia Cultural Fund and the British Columbia Lottery Fund.